General Sterling Price and the Confederacy

By THOMAS C. REYNOLDS

Edited by ROBERT G. SCHULTZ

MISSOURI HISTORY MUSEUM

ST. LOUIS

DISTRIBUTED BY UNIVERSITY OF MISSOURI PRESS

Unfinished manuscript left by ex-governor Thomas C. Reynolds, deceased, and donated to the Missouri Historical Society by Hon. George Savage of Baltimore, MD.

This volume was presented to the Missouri Historical Society by Dr. C. A. Peterson, April 1904.

Library of Congress Cataloging-in-Publication Data

Reynolds, Thomas C. (Thomas Caute), 1821–1887.
   General Sterling Price and the Confederacy / by Thomas C. Reynolds ; edited by Robert G. Schultz.
       p. cm.
   Includes bibliographical references and index.
   ISBN 978-1-883982-68-3 (pbk. : alk. paper)
 1. Price, Sterling, 1809–1867. 2. Confederate States of America. Army--Biography.
3. Generals--United States--Biography. 4. Missouri--History--Civil War, 1861–1865. 5. Southwest, Old--History--Civil War, 1861–1865--Campaigns. I. Schultz, Robert G. II. Title.
   E467.1.P87R49 2009
   355.0092--dc22
   [B]
                                        2009027356

Distributed by University of Missouri Press
Cover designed by Renée Duenow
Cover background flag image ©iStockphoto.com/JordanFink
Printed and bound in the United States by Sheridan Books, Inc.

Table of Contents

Foreword   5

Editor's Introduction   7

Before the Civil War   11

December 1860 to June 1861   23

July 1861 to March 1862   39

April 1862 to January 1863   45

January 1863 to May 1863   51

May 1863, in the Trans-Mississippi Department   77

Helena, Arkansas, June 1863   85

Little Rock, Arkansas, August 1863   95

Spring and Summer 1864   111

C. A. Peterson's Additions   132

Appendix 1: Contemporaneous Material about the Price Expedition   153

Appendix 2: Background Material for Reynolds's Manuscript   219

Appendix 3: Members of the Confederate Congresses from Missouri   257

Notes   259

Bibliography   275

Index   277

*The editor dedicates this volume to the
St. Louis Civil War Round Table,
which celebrated its fiftieth anniversary in 2007.*

Foreword

History is a story, or, rather, it is multiple stories woven together from the fragments and remnants people have left behind. The historian's task, and the community's, is to preserve what remains and to disseminate the story of those who have gone before us.

Sometimes it's an exercise that seems to invite disappointment. Historian Simon Schama describes the potential frustration with an imaginative but appropriate metaphor: "Historians are left forever chasing shadows, painfully aware of their inability ever to reconstruct a dead world in its completeness however thorough or revealing their documentation. We are doomed to be forever hailing someone who has just gone around the corner and out of earshot."

General Sterling Price and the other people and events in Thomas Reynolds's 142-year-old manuscript have indeed gone around the corner. They may all be out of earshot, but we can still hear the echoes of the Civil War and even feel the remaining tremors of the deep divisions that wracked our country and alienated Missourians from family and former friends, often forever. As abolitionist Frederick Douglass stressed long after that war was over, "there are no bygones in the world, and the past is not dead and cannot die."

The past, all of the past, is alive in us. When we tell as much of the whole story as possible, its unhappy legacies as well as its beauties, we can attain a better share of the beauties that exist for all of us. We can often alleviate the burdens that have come down to us by compensating in the present and re-examining the problems with a stronger perspective. Perhaps we are blessed as well as doomed to be constantly seeking the past, for in retelling the old stories we can assimilate the elements of it that can assist us in preparing a better future.

This volume, from a fragile, handwritten manuscript in the collections of the Missouri History Museum, has multiple layers of its own, as editor Robert G. Schultz reveals in the introduction. The story, like so many stories, wound a somewhat circuitous way to our bookshelves. *General Sterling Price and the Confederacy* in this new form makes an interesting addition to the stories we tell each other about a part of our past, a piece of our history we can all share.

—Robert R. Archibald, Ph.D.

President, Missouri History Museum

Editor's Introduction

Sterling Price, in the eyes of Confederate Missourians, was an authentic heroic figure. A governor, a U.S. representative, and a Mexican–American War hero, he was handsome, well spoken, and popular. At the beginning of the secession crisis, he was a conditional Unionist, someone who was for the Union but not to the extent of suppressing the rights of individual states. Most Missourians agreed with this stand. In the November 1860 presidential election, more than 70 percent of the votes of Missouri went to Stephen A. Douglas and John Bell, the candidates advocating compromise. But Price's stand as a conditional Unionist rankled the secessionists in Missouri and elsewhere in the Southern states. Only after the Camp Jackson affair, in which Nathaniel Lyon and his mainly German American recruits surrounded and forced the surrender of the Missouri State Militia's "Camp of Instruction" on May 10, 1861, did Price's attitude change from conditional Unionism to secessionism. Similarly, many Missourians' attitude changed to secessionism.

Price was named major general and commander of the Missouri State Guard. But because of his previous conditional Unionism, he was not completely trusted by either Governor Claiborne Fox Jackson or Lieutenant Governor Thomas Caute Reynolds, both secessionists. Similarly, Jefferson Davis, president of the new Confederate States of America, trusted neither Price nor Jackson, the latter because of his temporizing actions during the secession crisis.

Once Price took command of the Missouri State Guard, he came into his own. He led by example, was fearless, inspired his men, and shared their hardships. They loved him and called him "Old Pap." They fought for him at Wilson's Creek and Lexington, Missouri, and at Pea Ridge, Arkansas. When, after Pea Ridge, Price and his men were transferred east of the Mississippi River, they again fought well but sought to return west of the river and fight for the liberation of their home state, Missouri.

Price's last hurrah was the expedition into Missouri in autumn of 1864. He had hoped that, upon his arrival in the state, Confederate sympathizers would flock to his banner. They didn't. Most of the sympathizers in Missouri realized that the Confederacy was failing, and they stayed away from his forces. The raid was a failure, and Reynolds, who traveled with the raid, was furious.

After the surrenders, many Missourians, including Reynolds, Price, and Brigadier General Joseph O. Shelby, fled to Mexico. (Jackson died in December 1862, and Reynolds became acting governor.) In Mexico, Price tried to establish a farming community but was unsuccessful and returned to St. Louis, racked with illnesses. Reynolds engaged in business in Mexico City. In 1867 in Mexico City, he began writing his version of events in a manuscript he titled "Gen. Sterling Price & the Confederacy." It was never completed, possibly because he had heard of Price's death. Reynolds also later returned to St. Louis.

After the Civil War, books and magazine articles about it began to appear. At first, many of these were Union memoirs. Only somewhat later did Confederate material begin to come out. Thomas L. Snead, who had served as Price's adjutant during the war, wrote his complimentary account of Price's campaigns, which appeared in volume 1 of the four-volume *Battles and Leaders of the Civil War* (New York: The Century Company, 1884) and as a separate book in 1886.

In 1898, the Reynolds manuscript was discovered among his papers and was donated to the Missouri Historical Society. For historians, the Reynolds manuscript has proved to be a proverbial gold mine of information. This is especially true since Price's personal papers were lost in a fire in the 1880s. Later historians, using a wide range of sources, including

The War of the Rebellion: A Compilation of the Official Records of the Union and Confederate Armies (abbreviated as Official Records, or OR;) and the Reynolds manuscript, have not been as kind to Sterling Price as Snead. No one has questioned his personal bravery, but his grasp of strategy and tactics has been questioned. Many accounts mention his personal vanity and his aggressive self-promotion as factors that limited his personal success. This being said, one must remember that Reynolds had a poor opinion of Price, and this opinion certainly pervades the manuscript.

Now for the first time, the entire manuscript is available in print. That this additional appraisal of Sterling Price is presented is important, but probably of equal importance are Reynolds's views of the inner workings of the Confederate government and in particular the challenges that faced the Trans-Mississippi Department of the Confederacy.

The original manuscript is still at the Missouri Historical Society in St. Louis. It was donated to the society by George Savage, the nephew of Thomas Reynolds. Savage found it among the papers left to him by Reynolds. This manuscript is handwritten on thin paper and is quite

Thomas C. Reynolds.
Photograph of a painting, no date. Missouri History Museum.

fragile. It was transcribed into typescript, apparently in 1904 by Cyrus A. Peterson, president of the society. There is a notation on the first page of the typescript volume: "This volume was presented to the Missouri Historical Society by Dr. C. A. Peterson, April 1904." Peterson was particularly interested in the battle at Pilot Knob, Missouri, during Price's expedition, and he published *Pilot Knob, the Thermopylae of the West* (Cyrus A. Peterson and Joseph Mills Hanson, New York: Neale Publishing Company, 1914), which draws on this manuscript. Throughout the typescript volume are a number of notes referring to specific *Official Records* pages along with some corrections of the typescript, all apparently in Peterson's hand. They appear in appendix 1.

This editor faced an initial question. Apparently, Reynolds loved long sentences and semicolons. There was a temptation to break up these sentences into more manageable chunks. However, this temptation was resisted and the manuscript was essentially left unchanged from the Peterson transcription, with the exception of the correction of a few spelling and typographic errors. The manuscript exists as one long document without any separations. The decision was made to add a few separation headings based on dates and specific events. Bracketed dashes ([———]) in the manuscript represent information that was not available to Reynolds in Mexico City; either his memory had failed or his notes were incomplete. This manuscript ends just before the Price expedition into Missouri in the fall of 1864. Peterson added some extracts from the Missouri Historical Society Archives and from the *Official Records* volumes as a way to indicate what the manuscript might have held if it had been finished. These additions appear at the end of the Reynolds manuscript. This editor has found some additional contemporary material relating to the Price expedition to augment that added by Peterson. It appears in appendix 1. In addition, other pertinent material relating to the manuscript, material dated before the conclusion of Reynolds's narrative, has been added as appendix 2. Finally, appendix 3 contains a table that lists the various members of the Confederate Congresses who were from Missouri.

Before the Civil War

City of Mexico, 10th March, 1867

I propose in this memoir to state, partly from memory, and partly from letters and memoranda, and with entire impartiality, the connection of Gen. Sterling Price[1] with military and civil affairs of the Confederate States and the State of Missouri, during the late civil war, in explanation of the course pursued towards him by their respective authorities, the true reasons for which had, to a great extent, to be kept as "secrets of state," during the continuance of the war itself.

Gen. Price first became known in national politics by his election, from Missouri, as a member of the first U.S. Congress in the presidency of Mr. Polk. Failing to acquire any position in it, he was not re-nominated by the Democratic Party (to which he had always belonged) and in disgust at that treatment (as I have understood from himself,) he resigned his place in Congress, in the spring of 1846, and being elected colonel of a Missouri volunteer regiment, took part in the Mexican war in New Mexico, etc. The American accounts of the war gave him credit for energy, activity and military ability; the Mexican accuse him of disobedience of orders, bad faith and useless bloodshed, in fighting a battle after he knew that a peace was concluded and hostilities had ceased. On Col. Jefferson Davis's declension of a brigadiership, it was given to Col. S. Price, who throughout the war was a special favorite and protégé of Senator Thomas H. Benton of Missouri, who kept up with him a frequent correspondence during his campaign in Mexico.[2]

⊷Sterling Price.⊶
Photograph, 1852–1856. Missouri History Museum.

Two incidents occurred in those campaigns to exercise an important influence on Gen. Price's character and future career. One was his quarrel with Mr. Francis P. Blair, Jr.[3] I have heard the statement of both in regard to it: from Mr. Blair at Jefferson City in January 1857, and from Gen. Price at Camden, Ark., in the summer of 1864. Mr. Blair considered his arrest as a piece of tyranny and an outrage on him by Gen. Price, then U.S. Military Governor of New Mexico, and attributed it to personal malice; even after the lapse of nearly ten years (in 1857), he spoke of it with great bitterness, and as fully justifying his violent philippic in the Missouri legislature, against Gen. Price, when Governor of the State. He justified his personal abuse of Gov. Price at the time when their respective official positions prevented the Governor from demanding "satisfaction," on the ground that he was retaliating for an outrage committed on him at the time when their respective positions in New Mexico prevented, and indeed precluded for all time, his seeking redress for it from Gen. Price; that as he had to pocket his outrage, he insulted Gov. Price in a speech at a time when the latter would have to pocket the insult in like manner. Mr. Blair added: "I consider him, however, a man of such courage that I believe he would have given his right hand to have been able, without violating his duty, to resign the governorship and challenge me." This feud with Mr. F. P. Blair Jr. and with his family, who shared his resentment, was considered to have influenced Gen. Price in his desertion of Col. [Thomas Hart] Benton in 1852, the period at which the latter, more publicly than he had previously done, entrusted the management of his political fortunes in Missouri to Mr. F. P. Blair Jr., Hon. Montgomery Blair, his brother, and Mr. B. Gratz Brown,[4] his cousin, all of St. Louis, MO., and allied himself more closely than ever with Mr. Francis P. Blair, Senior, at Washington City [Washington, DC]. But in General Price's own account of the matter to me in 1864, he treated the New Mexico incident as a petty quarrel between Mr. Blair and sum [sic] subaltern officer, with which he, as Governor of New Mexico, had really had very little to do, and in regard to which Mr. Blair's resentment had greatly surprised him; in general, his account treated the matter very lightly, and as of little importance in determining his subsequent political relations with the Blairs, against whom neither his manner nor his language evinced any personal ill-feeling.

The other incident was related to me by Gen. Price at Jefferson City, Mo., in January 1861, at my house, Gov. C. F. Jackson, Mr. Russell, Commissioner from Mississippi,[5] and Mr. McAfee, Speaker of the Missouri House of Representatives, being with us. While on a march with his command to attack some Mexican position, he received from his superior officer, an order (by letter) to return. He deliberately, but silently, determined to disregard the order, continued his march and gained an advantage over the Mexicans. By the first opportunity he stated the matter to Senator Benton at Washington City, and received soon in answer an approval of his course, and a promise to protect him against any censure. Accordingly, nothing came of the matter. I was struck at the time when Gen. Price related the above, by the light the incident shed on the state of discipline in the U.S. Army in the Mexican war, and also by his tone and manner in relating it, as above set forth. He evidently felt proud of it, and seemed utterly unconscious of any military impropriety in his disobeying orders and then seeking to shield himself by political influence at Washington City. The success on that occasion will aid in explaining his tendency, during the late civil war, to action independently of his official superiors, almost to the extent of insubordination; and also his singular unconsciousness of the unfavorable impression produced on those superior, by his frequent assertions to them that the troops he commanded were so devoted to him that they would mutiny or desert if separated from him.

After the Mexican war, Gen. Price's prominent reappearance in politics was on his nomination for the governorship of the state by the Democratic convention at Jefferson City in the spring of 1852. The history of his nomination was given me by Hon. John M. Krum at St. Louis in February 1861, in a conversation arising out of the general astonishment at his being a strong Union man in the Missouri convention, while but a short time before, on his visit to Jefferson City, his language had indicated that he was a secessionist.

The Benton and Anti-Benton Democrats had agreed upon a fusion in that convention of 1852, on the basis that the former being a majority of the party, the candidate for Governor should be a Benton man, that for Lieutenant Governor, an Anti-Benton, and so on alternately to the end of the ticket; but the fused convention as a whole was to select the candidates, and not each wing of the party select its share of the ticket. The Anti-Benton minority at once took measures to secure the fruits of this advantage. Gen. Thomas L. Price[6] was the choice of the great body of the Benton men, but especially distasteful to the Anti-Benton men. Accordingly in a caucus of some leaders of the latter, Judge Krum was selected to have an interview with Gen. Sterling Price, a Benton delegate to the convention, and conspicuous for the ardent support he had given Col. Benton not only before but since the division in 1849 in the Missouri Democracy on the subject of that senator. Judge K's report of the interview, concerning the policy which Gen. Sterling Price, if elected Governor, would pursue in regard to both the men and the measures of the Anti-Benton Democracy, being entirely satisfactory to the caucus, it was resolved to support him, in the convention, for the candidacy for the governorship. The solid vote of the Anti-Benton minority, added to a small portion of the Benton majority, secured him the nomination over General Thomas L. Price; and Dr. Brown, a zealous Anti-Benton man, was nominated for Lieutenant governor.

Col. Benton promptly denounced the ticket as a fraud, a bargain and sale, and "spit upon the platform"—all publicly in his speeches. Privately, he was reported to be especially severe on Gen. Sterling Price, whom he considered mainly indebted to him for both military and political position, and from whom he had expected unswerving fidelity. But the fusion was maintained; Gen. Price acted with consummate discretion, keeping very quiet and making no general canvass; and the entire fusion ticket was elected. Thenceforward, and as governor in 1853–57, Gen. Price vigorously opposed Col. Benton and sustained the Anti-Benton democracy. The election of 1856 completely demolished the Benton party in Missouri; of its remnants, some returned to the re-united or "National" democracy, the others joined the newly established "Republican Party."

In January 1857, the Missouri Legislature met, with an overwhelming democratic majority in each branch. Two senators were to be elected: one for the "short term" ending March 3rd 1861, and the other for six years commencing 4th March, 1857. For the short term, Gen. Price, whose gubernatorial term had just expired, Hon. James S. Green,[7] elected member of congress, and Hon. Willard P. Hall[8] were candidates for the nomination by the democratic caucus; the two latter had always been Anti-Benton democrats since the division in the party in 1849. Mr. Hall, however, being considered the least decided of the two in his states rights principles.

The selection of Gen. Price was urged by his friends mainly as a debt of gratitude to him on the part of the re-united democracy, on account of the admitted fact that by his opportune abandonment of Col. Benton, and his policy during his four years governorship, he had contributed more than any other one man in Missouri to that very triumph which placed two senatorships in the gift of the democracy; that he modestly asked the short term and had announced (as he did in a conversation with me), his determination, if elected senator, to ask no re-election; and that while his inferiority, in parliamentary talent, to either Mr. Green or Mr. Hall, was admitted it was urged that he had made a capable governor, that his messages showed ability and sound sense, and that his vetoes showed moral firmness and decision of character. The main objection to Mr. Green was that his election to the U.S. Senate would create a vacancy in his congressional district, and subject the democracy to the risk of losing it in a special election. It was known to but few at that time, though now no longer a secret, that Gen. Price's intellect was so limited that his messages were written for him by political friends; political (capital?) was therefore made for him by referring to those state papers. He himself carried on a quiet and dignified but active canvass for support with his usual skill, both at the gubernatorial mansion, and the lobby of the legislature.

In the vote in the democratic caucus, Mr. Hall received the largest vote, but not a majority. Mr. Green came next, and Gov. Price last, with a vote so small as to render his chance hopeless. He promptly withdrew, and his late supporters joined those of Mr. Green, who received the nomination over Mr. Hall, and was thereon elected U.S. Senator by the Legislature. For the long term, Gov. Trusten Polk[9] was elected senator over Mr. Phelps,[10] the latter being urged as was Gov. Price, on the ground of gratitude for the admittedly immense service in abandoning Col. Benton some few months after Gov. Price. But Gov. Polk, always an Anti–Benton man since 1849, prevailed in the face of the risk the democracy ran of losing the state in the special gubernatorial election made necessary by his election to the U.S. Senate.

It was very evident to me and many other observers of those two elections, that the same causes determined each. The friends of Col. Benton who were now re–united to the democracy after having stood by him until all hope of sustaining him was gone, could not be induced to reward the two great defections which were claimed and admitted to have sealed his political fate. The men who from the start in 1849 and at first in the meager minority, had opposed Col. Benton on principle, could see no difference between his position which Gov. Price and Mr. Phelps shared in 1849, and his position in 1853, when those two politicians abandoned him and joined his opponents when rendered nearly certain of ascendancy in Missouri through the support of the [Franklin] Pierce administration. These feelings were general, though not exclusively prevalent, in the respective classes mentioned; and both felt that it was safer to have the state represented in the U.S. Senate, in the troublous times then obviously coming, by men whose fidelity, in adversity, to their party and principles in the past, was a guarantee of fidelity to them in the future, rather than by men whose changes of party had indicated quite as much sagacity in joining the winning side, as repentance in abandoning the losing.

Events have shown the democracy of Missouri to have been correct in its appreciation of men on that occasion. Mr. Green and Mr. Polk remained true to the state and to their principles; the former in (poor?) health, remained in Missouri, and the latter, abandoning a senatorial seat and risking his large fortune, joined the Confederate Army. Mr. Hall and Mr. Phelps, after considerable trimming,[11] sided with the Federals, the former becoming the intrusive Lieutenant governor of Missouri under the rump convention, and the latter Federal military governor of Arkansas. After like trimming, Gen. Price was driven by the blundering arrogance of Lyon[12] into resistance to the U.S. government; to what extent his trimming continued afterwards, remained throughout the late civil war a matter of both doubt and anxiety to the Confederate government itself.

Gov. Price was visibly mortified and chagrined by his utter defeat in the canvass for the U.S. senatorship, and disdaining the suggestion of some of his friends that the democracy of his district would cheerfully send him to the U.S. house of representatives to fill the vacancy occasioned by Mr. Green's election to the senate, he returned to his home in Chariton county. He was generally regarded as completely shelved and dead, as a politician; though I remember to have heard a prediction by some who knew him well, that on Mr. Green's appearing for re-election to the U.S. Senate in 1861, Gov. Price would certainly be "on hand in full force," to pay him off for the defeat in 1857, for which Gov. Price had not forgiven him, though only the innocent cause. Mr. Green himself expressed to me in July 1860 the same opinion, and his belief that Gov. Price's retirement, in the well known secrecy of his habits, was merely to recover political strength to take some new position to that end.

His reappearance in politics took place at the democratic convention in the spring of 1860, at Jefferson City. He was a delegate from Chariton County, and considered to favor Mr. Stephen A. Douglas for the presidency of the United States. The friends of Mr. Douglas designed to make him president of the convention, but were out-maneuvered. When the contest for the nomination for the governorship became vexed, some thought of proposing Gov. Price as a compromise. I asked his view on the point, and he answered, I believe with entire sincerity, that he had no desire for the position, as he had once filled it, but would not decline it, should the convention voluntarily give him the nomination. My own nomination for the Lieutenant governorship had, as I knew, been so effectually prepared, even before the convention met, that I received it, by a motion for a unanimous nomination, before the first roll-call was over. I had, for various reasons, supposed that Gov. Price would feel bound to support some candidate from his own section of North Missouri, as the governorship was conceded to the "south of the river" (Missouri). About the time of the meeting of the convention, Mr. Geo. L. Pollard of St. Louis, informed me, however, that shortly before Gov. Price had declared himself in favor of myself, and expressed the intention to use his influence for me. I accordingly acted in concert with him on the subject, and asked him to place me in nomination in the convention, which he accordingly did. Not choosing to inquire, or even guess, whether his support, announced at so late a period and when the contest was virtually decided, was not merely an evidence of sagacity in choosing the winning side, and securing in advance a claim on the remembrance of the future president of the state senate, who in all probability would preside over (and might have a casting vote in), two elections for U.S. Senator: I determined on rendering him at once a fully equivalent service; besides, I had a strong personal liking for him. The nomination of Mr. C. F. Jackson for the governorship rendered almost certain his resignation of the best office in the state, the bank commissionership: Mr. J. M. Hughes and other gentlemen of eminence were known to desire it. Learning that Gov. Price was somewhat embarrassed in money matters, I inquired of his nephew, Mr. Thos. Price, who roomed with me, whether Gov. Price would not like to have that office; he at once answered that it would be the most acceptable favor imaginable to Gov. Price. As soon as I was nominated by the convention for the lieutenant governorship, I asked Gov. Stewart, as a favor to myself, that he should tender that office to Gov. Price. He did so, and it was well known at the time that to me, and to me alone, did Gov. Price owe an office which came just in time to save him from serious business and pecuniary embarrassment. When

◦Claiborne F. Jackson.◦
Photograph of a painting, mid-nineteenth century. Missouri History Museum.

I handed him Gov. Stewart's note offering him the position, he pressed my hand and thanked me most cordially. I mention these facts here mainly because on my controversy with him in 1865, the Alexandria (La.) newspaper, then edited by Mr. W. A. Seay, of St. Louis, charged that I was elected Lt. Gov. of Missouri through Price's patronage. The above is all the interchange of service between us up to that time of which I have any recollection; if there were any other, they were insignificant or mere courtesies.

After the convention Gov. Price remained very quiet. On the nomination of Douglas and Breckenridge as opposing Democratic candidates for the U.S. presidency, he quietly took sides for Douglas and advised

Gov. C. F. Jackson and myself to do so. During our canvass he remained perfectly quiet; I never heard of his doing anything to help our election, and his passiveness attracted my attention. I attributed it at the time to the ill-feeling believed to exist between Jackson and him, the (totally erroneous) current belief that Senator Green's support of Jackson and me was the result of some understanding at Chillicothe, that I would support Green for re-election in 1861, and to Gov. Price's inveterate habit of trimming, which led him to await the result of the State election before deciding on taking an active part in the contest between the Douglas and Breckinridge wings of the Democracy. Subsequently in 1861, Gov. C. F. Jackson in conversation with me, attributed Gov. Price's course to the remnant of old ill-feeling between them. I forgot its origin, but it was of sufficient strength to make Gov. Price express to me, on the offer to him by Gov. Stewart[13] of the bank commissionership, that Gov. Jackson would interpose difficulties, by delaying his resignation, or otherwise. An interview between them, however, removed those difficulties; but both Gov. Jackson and I were somewhat disappointed that Gov. Price, owing his appointment to me, and the facilitating his prompt reception of it to Gov. J., seemed to take no interest in securing our election in August 1860.

That election was decisive, Gov. Jackson receiving a plurality of about 7,500, and I one of about 15,000 votes. Soon after, Gov. Price became chairman of the State central committee of the Douglas democracy, and its success in the State in the presidential election of Nov. 1860 seemed again to place Gov. Price in a prominent political position.

December 1860 to
June 1861

But the general result in the nation was disastrous to the democracy, and especially to Mr. Douglas. The Missouri legislature met at the close of December, and the two sections of the democracy in it at once united. Soon thereafter Gov. Price, who had meanwhile kept perfectly quiet, came up to Jefferson City, his nomination for the Bank commissionership being pending or (more probably) about to be sent in to the senate for confirmation or rejection. Over two thirds of that body were "secessionists" or more properly speaking, "southern rights" men. There was a decided intimation, especially by Senators [R. L.Y.] Peyton, [Mosby M.] Parsons, and [Henry W.] Lyday, of an intention to oppose his confirmation, unless he should come out plainly and unequivocally as a southern rights man; it was even said that otherwise, Gov. Jackson would withhold his nomination. But Gov. Price soon removed all doubts. His conversation was decidedly secession and even warlike. I gave a dinner to Mr. Russell, commissioner from Mississippi, inviting Gov. Jackson, Gov. Price, and Mr. Speaker McAfee to meet him. There Gov. Price turned the conversation on his Mexican war experience, and was decidedly the most warlike of all of us. Among other remarks, he stated that he had already promised his neighbors to take command of them should a civil war break out, etc., etc. No one there had any doubt that Gov. Price was cordially with the most decided southern rights men, and his nomination for the bank commissionership was unanimously confirmed by the senate.

The bill calling for a state convention was passed; Gov. Price returned to his home in Chariton County, and almost immediately became a union candidate for the convention. Reports came of his making ultra union speeches; the amazement at Jefferson City, especially among the southern rights senators, may be imagined. The high officer, who alone had it in his power to exercise any control over the vast power of the banks in the state, had on the very battlefield, conspicuously gone over to the enemy. The "money power," now perfectly secure, was exercised against the southern rights party, the example of Gov. Price, considered most sagacious in discovering the winning side in Missouri politics, was followed by others; both causes contributed most powerfully towards the overwhelming triumph of the "conditional unionists" in the convention election. The convention met in February 1861, and Gov. Price was elected its President. In it, his votes were decidedly Unionist; the only exception being his voting with the minority toward the close of the first session of the convention, for a resolution to the effect that if the Union could not be preserved, Missouri should join the southern confederacy. When that resolution was presented, the reaction in Missouri, as well as in Virginia and Kentucky, against the first fit of unionism on the presentation of the "Crittenden compromise," had become perceptible; Gov. Price "trimmed" his political sails accordingly.

After the civil war began, the Missouri legislature met in special session May 1st, 1861. On Friday, 10th May, the Camp Jackson affair[14] took place. The tone of the press of Missouri and all accounts of the feeling throughout the state on account of that high handed move, place it beyond all doubt, that for the moment, fully four fifths of the population were ready to take up arms against the United States. On the afternoon of Saturday, May 11th or Sunday, May 12th, I visited Gov. Jackson at his office adjoining that of the Secretary of State in the capitol, and to my surprise and gratification, met Gov. Price in conference with him. Gov. Price had been in St. Louis on May 10th, and had just arrived from there in the train of that morning. An interchange of a few words between us intimated that he had determined to come back to the southern rights party. I at once advised Gov. Jackson to give him supreme military command, especially as armed volunteers were pouring into Jefferson City, and a commander of experience and reputation was indispensable. Gov. Jackson was evidently reluctant, and urged that the military bill[15] giving him power to organize the militia and appoint general officers, had not yet become a law. I answered that the "rebellion act"[16] which I had drafted and which had been passed on May 10th immediately after receipt of news of the Camp Jackson affair gave him discretionary powers; that under it he could commission Gov. Price merely to command troops, and on the passage of the military bill, give him definite rank under it; that I would agree to be "military secretary" under Gov. Price and aid him to the extent of my ability. After some further persuasion, I pointed out the advantage of having Gov. Price publicly and irrevocably side with us, the prestige of his position as president of the State convention, his reputation in the Mexican War, etc., Governor Jackson (who had said nothing in objection to these considerations), authorized me to draw up a commission in accordance with my views, and that he would sign it. I accordingly at once drew up a commission, under the "rebellion act" appointing Gov. Price to command in chief, all the forces to be called out to suppress the rebellion begun by Lyon and Blair at St. Louis, and authorizing him to appoint a military secretary. I also drew up a paper appointing me his "military secretary." After getting these ready, I had considerable difficulty and lost an hour or two, in hunting up the secretary of state to put the great seal to the commission, and in finding Gov. Jackson, who had left the capitol and gone into the town, but not to his house. It was one of his habits thus to get rid of importunity, and as he had plainly yielded more to my urgency than to his own judgment, I attributed his course to a desire to gain time for further consideration of so important a step. However, with the same air of hesitation as in our conference about making the appointment he signed the commission, either at his house or at some place where I had found him in the town.

I had arranged with Gov. Price to meet me at the office of the Secretary of State, and I immediately proceeded thither. Ascending the steps of the capitol, I encountered Gen. Robert Wilson, state senator from Andrew County, a member of the state convention, and a public man of deservedly great weight in Missouri. I told him about the commission and asked him to accompany me to present it to Gov. Price. He promptly consented and remarked: "I am glad Price is to take command; if those hot headed boys who are now commanding are left to themselves, they will carry us all to the devil." He alluded to Parsons, Peyton, Colton Green,[17] etc., who were taking charge of the volunteers arriving. We entered the secretary of state's office and found Gov. Price there; the great seal was attached to the commission (by, I think, Mr. Massey, Jr., deputy secretary of state), and on behalf of Gov. Jackson, I tendered it to Gov. Price. As he had previously promised me to accept, I was somewhat taken back by his remaining silent and seeming to be in a deep study. I thereupon stated to him that as his personal and political friend, and as Lieutenant Governor of Missouri, I urged his acceptance of the commission; and turning to Gen. Wilson, I requested him, as a senator and member of the convention, and a leading public man, to express his opinion. Gen. Wilson, in a few words, said that he considered it Gov. Price's duty to the state to accept the commission. After a pause of a few moments, Gov. Price said, in a tone as if he had come to a sudden decision, "Well gentlemen, I accept it, and rely on your support in the performance of my duties to the best of my ability." Gen. Wilson and I each responded, "You can count on our support." Gov. Price then signed my appointment as "Military Secretary," and leaving Gen. Wilson, we went into the town to the building which had been occupied as quasi headquarters by Gov. Jackson's adjutant-general. There we commenced consulting about the orders to be issued when Capt. Little[18] of the United States Army came in, and offered his services. I at once advised and Gen. Price promptly assented, to Capt. Little's taking my place and drafting the necessary orders, Gen. Price himself to sign them until provisions could be made by law for a staff. At once orders were issued for the drilling of the raw volunteers flocking to the town, and Gen. Price instructed me to find Capt. Colton Greene of St. Louis, and direct him to report for that duty. I soon found Greene at the Governor's mansion, and gave him the order; he was evidently surprised and dryly answered, "I don't know that Gov. Price has any authority to give me orders." I explained the authority just conferred, and Capt. Greene, though evidently not much pleased, at once went and reported for duty.

On Monday, May 13th 1861,★ I carried to Gov. Jackson, at his office in the capitol, a draft he had requested me to prepare of an address to the people of Missouri,[19] as his manifold occupations at the crisis left him no time to do so.

This address raised no question of secession, but enlarged on the U.S. Constitution in the attack on Camp Jackson, and called on the entire people of the state to form military organizations and arm themselves, but then merely to await the further orders of the state government. Gen. Price was with the Governor, and I read it to them both; I explained that its policy was to improve the universal indignation about the Camp Jackson outrage, and have every neighborhood commit itself, to sustain by arms the state government; that the universal ferment we could reasonably expect, would probably confine Lyon (who could not count on over eight thousand men), to St. Louis, and counterbalance the unionist excitement in central Illinois, as well as encourage the southern proclivities of southern Illinois; that if Lyon should venture to leave St. Louis to advance on Jefferson City, we could make the country swarm in insurrection around him, until, if he ventured too far, he would be lost,

---

★ Without access to my memoranda of those dates I am not very certain about this and some others of that time. The Camp Jackson affair took place Friday 10th May; I am inclined to think, from some minor circumstances I recollect, that all the previously related circumstances occurred on one and the same day, Sunday, 12th and that early the next morning Gov. Jackson asked me to prepare his proclamation.

and that we could also make St. Louis rise in his rear; that if compelled to leave Jefferson City, we should retreat along the valley of the Osage, drawing him towards the southwest and setting the populous secession counties on the upper Missouri to rise in his rear; that on the extent of the response to the call in the proclamation, our future course should depend; that if as general as everything indicated it would be, we could hold nearly the entire state and perhaps even St. Louis, call together the convention and have the state secede. Gen. Price cordially approved the address, suggested in one sentence an alteration which I at once adopted, as a clear improvement. Gov. Jackson also, in general terms, approved it, and left in my mind the impression (if indeed he did not specifically say), that he would at once issue it. Nothing specially was said about the reasons I gave for it, as above set forth. An additional reason, omitted above, was that if we should at once begin war, I did not believe Lyon had troops enough to do us harm, and that one certain result at least would be to produce a most powerful diversion to gain time for the defense of Virginia, and possibly determine Kentucky to abandon her "neutrality." In a subsequent conversation, Gen. Price agreed with these reason, even down to the detail of the retreat on the line of the Osage.

Busy with my duties in the legislature, I did not see Gen. Price or Gov. Jackson, except for a moment or two at a time, until after the adjournment of the legislature on Wednesday, May 15th 1861. The military bill had been passed and also one creating the office of major general. It was understood that the Governor had desired to appoint Gen. Price senior brigadier under the military bill (this would give him rank, but not necessarily actual command, as the bill provided for the governor's appointing any brigadier to command an "army corps"); but that Gen. Price refused to accept that rank, or his friends intimating that he would refuse, the office of major general was created by the legislature with a view to his appointment to it. On that afternoon, 15th May, I met Gen. Price in the street and commenced a conversation; I told him I was surprised that the Governor had not issued any address; he expressed surprise also and neither of us could conjecture why.[20] He had not received his commission of Major General, and doubted its being offered to him. I told him I considered my own appointment as "military secretary" to be no longer of any use, and I handed him back the commission. That day, or the next, Gen. Price received his commission as Major General. An examination of the bill shows that it made him virtually governor of the state.

Towards the end of that week, I had a conference with Gen. Price. I stated my apprehension that Gov. Jackson was inclined to temporize and gain time, or even adopt the neutrality system of his native state, Kentucky; that I considered delay fatal, and leading to transactions and compromises which would end in giving the Federals possession of the state; that for that reason, I intended to proceed at once to the Confederate States, and, treating the governor as morally under duress, ask as Lt. Gov. from Mr. [Jefferson] Davis, the entry of Confederate troops into Missouri to protect its government. I asked Gen. Price to give me written authority to make a like request for him as president of the state convention, he having told Gov. Jackson and myself that a majority of the recess committee of that body would call it together whenever he, as president would request it, and that a secession ordinance would readily pass the convention, if deliberating in safety. Gen. Price at once consented, and concurred with me in the opinion about the governor's policy. He stated at the same time that since Lyon had been superceded by Gen. Harney, there had been some telegraphing going on between Mr. Paschall, editor of the <u>Republican</u>,[21] at St. Louis, and a gentleman (whom I forget), in reference to some pacific arrangement; that the governor was inclined to it, and that he, Gen. Price, did not object to it, as it gave him time to increase and organize the troops continually arriving at Jefferson City.

I accordingly prepared a letter which he signed, addressed to me, that as Lieutenant Governor of Missouri, I designed applying in person to the President of the Confederate States for an army to enter Missouri in order to protect the legislature in its adjourned meeting in the following

September, he, as President of the convention authorized and requested me to make a like application in his behalf for troops to protect that body in a meeting which he believed it desired to hold in order to pass an ordinance of secession. My recollection is that the above were almost the precise words of the letter. It was plain and distinct about applying for an army. Soon after he had signed it, the news coming of disturbances (reported) at Springfield, Mo., and I intended to go through that town, a union stronghold, we consulted over the expediency of my taking with me so explicit a letter which, in the event of my arrest by those unionists, might prematurely disclose our plans. We finally concluded to destroy it, and substitute another addressed to me officially as Lt. Gov., and which he signed officially as President of the convention, in nearly precisely the following words:

> Understanding that you design to take certain measures to secure protection to the General Assembly of Missouri at its adjourned session in September next, I request and authorize you to take like measure for the protection of the State convention, likely also to hold a session soon.

We determined solely for the sake of absolute secrecy, to tell no one, not even Gov. Jackson, of the application to be made. I however, informed him of my intention to go to the Confederate States and offered him my service. He said he had already sent (or was about to send, I forget which), a commission to the Confederacy; but he was decidedly uncommunicative, and did not even mention the name of the commissioner. I thereon stated to Gen. Price my need of funds, and asked him to give, as Major General, some ostensible mission to me, on which he could advance me funds. He stated that the governor kept all the military funds under his direct control, and exhibited some little jealousy of interference with his authority, even by suggestions; that therefore he (Gen. Price) preferred not to ask him for funds for my journey. The day before Gen. Price left for St. Louis, my wife came up to see me, and to avoid observation, instead of her going to my lodgings at Jefferson City, we went to a small village, further west on the Pacific Railroad, and returned the next day, she continued on to St. Louis with Gen. Price, while I remained in Jefferson City until the afternoon train for the west came in. On it I proceeded on (I think) May 19th (or it may have been the 20th) on my journey to the Confederate States, my wife having brought me funds for that purpose. I could exchange only a few words with Gen. Price before he got into the cars. He stated that he had consented to a conference with Gen. Harney[22] at St. Louis; he had no time to be very explicit about its object, but I clearly understood his object to be to gain time and meanwhile organize the state forces; and he urged me to hurry on to Mr. Davis and effect our joint object. I feel pretty sure, from memory, that he said, "Get him to send in Confederate troops as soon as possible."

I have never had, either directly or indirectly any conversation with Gen. Price about his conference and agreement with Gen. Harney,[23] or his conference with Gen. Lyon;[24] the matter seemed too delicate for him and me to discuss. The hesitation of Gov. Jackson to appoint him to command, and the distrust evinced in what Gen. Price called his "jealousy of his authority," appeared to me at the time, entirely inexplicable. But in the winter of 1864–5, Mr. Lyday, of the Missouri Senate of 1861, and an intimate of Gov. Jackson, told me that he (L.) had an interview with the Governor, just about the time of Gen. Price's appointment to the major generalship, and with a view to oppose it, on the ground of his strong unionism and sudden junction with the Secessionists after Camp Jackson. The Governor told Mr. Lyday, that he had doubts of Gen. Price's being heartily with the South; but that he had had a conversation with him in which he (Gen. P.) fully pledged himself for secession; and that to gain the prestige of his military name, and his position as President of the State Convention, he had appointed him major general. Shortly before his death in Dec. 1862, Gov. Jackson said to Col. R. H. Musser of Mo. (who repeated it to me in Dec. 1864), that the "greatest mistake of his life was the appointment of Gen. Price to command the Missouri

State Guard; but that he discovered his error too late to remedy it." Col. Musser did not state whether Gov. Jackson assigned any special reason for considering it a mistake.

I also, from motives of delicacy, never asked Gov. Jackson to converse with me about the Price-Harney treaty. But I have heard his friends say that he gave Gen. Price full powers and unlimited discretion in the negotiation (as would appear from the treaty itself), and approved the result on account of Gen. Price's opinion that the state force was too weak to justify any rejection of Harney's demands. I never heard of any attempt by Gen. Price or his friends to shift from him the responsibility of that treaty. The most charitable explanation may be drawn from his subsequent military career of confident predictions of success, bold advances, bewilderment when real danger of failure appeared, and precipitate disorderly retreat from it. When he talked war to me at Jefferson City, his mind was in the first stage; he boldly advanced to negotiate in the second state; the sight of the Federal preparation, and the timid counsel of his convention colleagues at St. Louis, put him into the third; and the fourth, he signed the fatal treaty.

On May [——] 1861, I left Jefferson City for Fort Smith, Arkansas, via Springfield, Mo. At [——], Arkansas, I obtained from the telegraph office, my first intelligence of the agreement between Price and Harney, and it was so astonishing, that I doubted the accuracy of the telegram; but it proved correct. At Fort Smith I met Gen. Ben McCulloch,[25] commanding the confederate forces in Arkansas. I explained to him confidentially the object of my journey and the perfect check-mate it had received by the Price-Harney agreement, which I took to be in good faith a triumph of the "neutrality" policy. We conversed over plans of campaigns, and his suggestion, which I fully approved, was to push a confederate force into Kansas, if possible, as far as Leavenworth, with a view to enter North Missouri, should the development of events in Missouri call for, or justify it. But at the moment he had, practically, neither troops, arms nor supplies, and numberless difficulties to contend with.

At Little Rock I met Mr. [Aaron H.] Conrow (subsequently C. S. member of Congress from Missouri). He had been sent by Gov. Jackson as a secret agent to the Governor of Arkansas to procure arms and concert action. He was as much paralyzed and puzzled as myself by the Price-Harney treaty. He attributed it to Gen. Price and the influence he of course had over the governor in a military question, and neither of us could reconcile it with Gen. Price's declarations and authority to me. I told Mr. Conrow that it was my determination, in case that treaty should take definitively the shape of "neutrality," to enter the state by White River, issue a proclamation assuming the government of the state on the ground that (the?) governor was under duress and virtually a prisoner in the capitol, and calling on the people to rally to me to relieve the governor and free the state; and I asked him whether he thought the secessionists of the state would rally to the call and recognize my authority. He decidedly said they would, and he fully approved my determination. I told him that I would take no action before reaching Memphis, Tenn., where by communication with St. Louis I could ascertain whether the Price-Harney treaty was a definite adoption of the neutrality policy, or merely a trick, though a reprehensible one, to gain time for arrangements with the confederacy; or a combination of Price and Harney to disarm the secessionists, the unionists remaining armed and organized, which the good sense of Gov. Jackson would soon put an end to.

I arrived at Memphis on [——], and met there several secessionist refugees from St. Louis. Their report was that the secessionists regarded the Price-Harney treaty as a return of Gen. Price to unionism, and a betrayal of the cause; but that the removal of Gen. Harney from command, and the reinstatement of Gen. Lyon, having placed Mr. F. P. Blair Jr. again in control of Federal policy in Missouri, the well known hostility of Mr. Blair to Gen. Price would soon force him back to our cause, and the restless arrogance of Gen. Lyon would soon so nullify the treaty as to justify Gov. Jackson in treating it as a dead letter. At the same time the St. Louis newspapers brought accounts of Lyon's violation of that treaty in the Potosi affair and at St. Louis.[26] Considering it as virtually at an end, I wrote on June 3rd at Memphis, as the Lieutenant Gov. of Missouri, a letter to the President of the Confederate States, a like letter on behalf of Gen. Price as President of the State Convention (enclosing with it his written authority to me), and a private letter to Mr. Davis.[27] These I sent on immediately, by Mr. Geo. L. Pollard of St. Louis, Mo., to President Davis at Richmond. My copies of these letters were in a package of my papers placed in Gen. Polk's headquarters office, for safe keeping, whilst I was with Gen. Pillow's army at New Madrid in August 1861. In February 1862, Major L. C. Cabell inquired for me about them at Memphis at Confederate headquarters, but they could not be found. I therefore give the contents of those letters from memory.

My official letter to the Confederate President set forth that I was by the constitution of Missouri, the presiding officer of the general assembly, and by law the guardian of its security and the freedom of its deliberations; that it had adjourned to meet in the following September at Jefferson City; that the presence and menaces of a federal force in the state left no doubt that that body could not hold that session in that perfect safety, essential to its dignity and freedom of its deliberations; that the governor of the state, tied to the capital by his civil duties, was not able to take the necessary measures; that for all these reasons I designed reentering the state, and calling the people to arms, for the purpose of freeing it from federal control, and securing the capital for the meeting of the legislature; that as indispensable to the success of such a movement, I asked him to send with me a sufficient number of Confederate troops; that he could find in history many examples to justify that interference, it being no unusual step for one power to send troops into the territory of another, at the call of a high official of state of another, to protect him in the exercise of his authority and that the state of Missouri as a sister southern State, oppressed by a common enemy, had the very strongest claim on the Confederate States for such protection.

The official letter on behalf of Gen. Price was much shorter, being simply a formal demand for confederate troops, to protect the State Convention in meeting to decide the question of secession.

The private letter stated affairs as they stood at my departure from Jefferson City, and alluded very slightly, if at all, to the opposite and puzzling occurrence since. It stated that Gen. Price and myself were in favor of a proclamation by the governor, calling the entire state to arms, with a view to drive the Federal forces out of it, and by that formidable flank movement on the North Western states, aid the Confederates in Virginia; and thereon to call a meeting to the state convention which Gen. Price was entirely confident contained a majority in favor of secession; that after assenting to this policy, Gov. Jackson, from a failure in the moral audacity necessary for so bold a step, had determined on a temporizing and pacific policy; that thereon Gen. Price and I had resolved on the step taken in my accompanying letters, I to go to the Confederate States, to wait the decision, while Gen. Price would remain in command of the Missouri State Guard to aid the movement; that an overwhelming majority of the people of Missouri were in favor of her joining the Confederacy, but that the armed aid of the latter, at this particular juncture, was indispensable to the attainment of that result. In this letter, or in my official, I requested a prompt answer under cover to the Governor of Tennessee at Nashville.

As I did not understand, I did not attempt to explain the object of the Price-Harney treaty, seemingly so opposed to the object aimed at in Gen. Price's application for troops; I left it to be inferred, to make that treaty consistent with the application, that the former was either in fact the act of Gov. Jackson, or a trick of Gen. Price to gain time for arming.

After a trip to Louisville to meet my wife and conduct her to Nashville, I returned to the latter city, where on June [———], 1861 I saw Gov. Jackson's proclamation announcing the breaking out of hostilities between the United States authorities and those of the state of Missouri.[28]

Soon after, Major E. C. Cabell[29] telegraphed me from Richmond to come there at once, I arrived there on [——] and from Major Cabell's reports and my own conversation with Mr. [Robert] Toombs, Secretary of State, Mr. [Judah] Benjamin, Attorney General, and Mr. [Charles] Memminger, secretary of the Treasury, of the Confederate States, discovered a marked indisposition to grant the aid asked by the authorities of Missouri, although in addition to the application of Gen. Price and myself, one had been made for troops, by the governor through Major Cabell, his commissioner to the Confederate States with full power under the great seal of the state and by authority of the "Rebellion Act."

Finally President Davis gave an audience on [——], to Major Cabell and myself. Mr. Toombs and Mr. Walker, Confederate Secretary of War, being the only other persons present. After hearing the reasons urged by Major Cabell and myself in favor of intervention of the Confederacy in Missouri, and combating them by arguments drawn from the armory of straight laced state sovereignty doctrines (as in the subsequent official answer to our applications), he finally, with the air of a man conscious of the weakness of those arguments, and suddenly resolving to give his ruling reasons at whatever risk of offending, drew himself up in his chair, and compressing his lips, said to us,

> I find gentlemen, by your Governor's proclamation of June 12th, which I have in my hand, that in the conference between Gen. Price and himself and Gen. Lyon at St. Louis, he offered to use his state troops to drive out of Missouri, any Confederate troops entering it and (turning to me),

> Now at the very moment when he made this offer, you, Mr. Cabell, were here with a commission from him to me, and presenting his request for those Confederate troops to be sent into Missouri, to that had I assented to the request, those troops, even though with your Lieutenant Governor at the head of them, might have had to fight against, instead of with, Gen. Price's army. Now I think Gen. Lyon acted very

unwisely in not accepting Gov. Jackson's proposals, and Mr. Lincoln may send him orders to accept them. Gov. Jackson in his proclamation makes a merit of having proposed them; now, if I agree to send Confederate troops into Missouri at your request, can you give me any guarantee that Mr. Lincoln may not propose and Gov. Jackson assent to the agreement rejected by General Lyon, and compel these troops to retire before their joint forces?

Of course, no answer could be made to this, especially as the President's whole tone and manner showed both a fixed resolution and great disgust at what he evidently considered double-dealing and an insult to his dignity in setting a trap for Confederate troops to be used or opposed, according as the Missouri authorities might succeed or fail in making terms with the United States. Major Cabell and I remained silent, or at best contented ourselves with arguing feebly that whatever the previous vacillation, Gov. Jackson and Gen. Price had taken the final leap into the secession camp and could be trusted accordingly. But President Davis' mind was evidently made up, and the audience soon ended. A day or two afterwards, Major Cabell and I received the official answer to our respective applications, rejection [of] them on the mere technicality (and an erroneous one), that only a convention representing the sovereignty of the states, could legally be treated with by the Confederate States.

At that time, Gov. Jackson was very conspicuous before the public, and General Price regarded, especially in the South, as wholly secondary to him; indeed the treaty with Harney, Gen. Price's absence from the battle of Boonville, and his subsequent disastrous retreat to S. W. Missouri, had for the time being, completely obscured his military reputation.[30] At the time of the interview above mentioned with President Davis, I suppose that the prejudice in his mind on account of the facts disclosed in Gov. Jackson's proclamation was confined mainly, if not solely, to Gov. Jackson. I afterwards, however, was convinced that it extended to all who had a share in the conference with Lyon; to Gen.

Price and to Major Thomas L. Snead, who was at the conference, and who drafted the proclamation. The nice sense of Mr. Davis could not be wholly reconciled, by any explanation, to the policy which led to that offer to Lyon, or the publication of it, as a merit, to the world afterwards. He evidently regarded all three as sanctioning it in the one shape or the other; and none of them ever afterwards enjoyed his full confidence. In the fall of 1862 at Richmond, I asked from Major Snead a history of the transaction. He said that the proposition was suddenly started in the conference by Gov. Jackson, and that Gen. Price made a silent objection by pushing his knee gently against the governor's. But this version of a disapproval, is scarcely reconcilable with the manner in which the offer is mentioned in the proclamation of Gov. Jackson, prepared by Major Snead and, as he stated, approved by Gen. Price before its publication. Major S. also stated that Gov. Jackson made the offer in the expectation of a rejection, and with a view to make capital out of that rejection, in arousing the people of Missouri. I told Major S. that all three had better have hushed it up; for that Mr. Davis did not at all appreciate any such diplomacy in the face of a solemn invitation to him to send Confederate troops into Missouri.

July 1861 to March 1862

The prejudice above mentioned was so strong that it interfered seriously with the establishment of a cordial understanding with the Confederate government. In July 1861, after the battle of Manassas, Major Cabell induced Mr. Vice-President [Alexander H.] Stephens to visit President Davis with a view to induce him to recede from his resolution not to negotiate with Gov. Jackson. After the visit Mr. Stephens told Major Cabell, in strict confidence, that the real difficulty lay in the President's unwillingness to negotiate with Gov. Jackson personally; and Mr. S. added, "There is another man in your State with whom the President is willing to make arrangements." Major Cabell much surprised, asked, "Who is he?" Mr. Stephens answered, "Your Lieutenant Governor." Thereon Major C. at once telegraphed to me to come to Richmond, that it was of the utmost importance for me to come at once. The telegram reached me while on my way to Memphis to go to South East Missouri; at the same time Gov. Jackson, taking a different railroad, had passed me on his way with Gen. David R. Atchison[31] to Richmond, Va. I therefore telegraphed to Major Cabell declining to come, and asking "cannot the matter be attended to by Gov. Jackson?" I at the same time wrote to him that I was somewhat disgusted with the lukewarmness which the Richmond authorities seemed to feel towards Missouri, and was not inclined to be running backwards and forwards from and to Richmond to confer with them; that I had full confidence in his ability to manage our state affairs there; that the Governor of Missouri would soon be there in person; that the small amount of money that I had on hand had to be used with great economy, without unnecessary travel; and that I thought my presence needed in Missouri. I asked him to explain why he had called me back to Richmond. In his answer, he recounted the above conversation with Mr. Stephens. I therefore wrote him that I would not have become a party to any move even to induce Gov. Jackson to resign in my favor, and much less to any attempt to displace him; that he was now irrevocably with the South, and it was very necessary for our party in Missouri to be united, and Gov. Jackson's compulsory resignation would disgust his friends and injure us. In conversation with Major Cabell at Columbus, Ky., in the following September, he told me that through the influence and assurance of Gen. Atchison, Mr. Davis' distrust of Gov. Jackson was partially, though not wholly removed; that the bill of which Major Cabell by his untiring exertions, procured the passage through the Confederate Congress, authorizing the President to make a treaty with Gov. Jackson's government, and supply it with a million of dollars had been opposed by Mr. Davis; and Major Cabell stated to me his belief that had I been at Richmond, it could have readily been arranged that Gov. Jackson should resign in my favor, and thereon everything in the relations between Missouri and the Confederacy would have gone on smoothly and swimmingly. I still differ from him as to the expediency of such a change, and also assured him that Gov. Jackson would have bluntly declined any arrangement to remove him, either by resignation or otherwise. He was then at the height of his popularity in the South, the newspapers and crowds at the railroad stations making a hero of him, and even Mr. Davis' influence could not have induced him to forego the honors of his station; that besides Gov. Jackson had a high sense of duty, and would feel himself bound to perform that of executive of Missouri at such a crisis. His resignation would seem like shrinking from it.

Shortly after receiving Major Cabell's letter recounting the conversation with Mr. Stephens, I wrote to Mr. Davis, advising him to have full confidence in Gov. Jackson's fidelity to the cause, and to cooperate with him. Towards the end of October 1861, I returned to Richmond, Va., meeting there Major Cabell and Major Snead, commissioners of Gov. Jackson to negotiate an alliance between the Confederate States and the State of Missouri, preparatory to the admission of the latter into the Confederacy. Gen. Price's popularity was then at its height, and the quarrel between him and Gen. McCulloch had also become violent and notorious. The two commissioners urged the President to put an end to it at once by making Gen. Price a Confederate Major General (McCulloch being only a brigadier), and giving him command of all forces in Arkansas and Missouri. I energetically seconded their efforts

Ben McCulloch.
Steel engraving by George E. Perine, ca. 1865. Missouri History Museum.

in interviews with Mr. Benjamin, Mr. Memminger, Mr. Mallory, and Mr. Hunter, of the Cabinet, and finally with the President himself. They all expressed an appreciation of Gen. Price's services; but the President showing me the statute, based his refusal on the legal ground that he had no power to appoint a major general prior to the acceptancy into the Confederate provisional army, of the division he should command. Major Snead however, obtained from the President a quasi promise that if a Missouri division should be formed for Confederate service, Gen. Price should be commissioned to command it. This afterwards took place.

About that period, two incidents excited in me slight suspicions that the condition of Gen. Price's troops was not altogether such as the newspapers and his partisans led the public to believe and that the Confederate government had grave doubts of his military adequacy to an important command. Mr. James M. Loughborough[32] had met me, either at Memphis or Columbus, Ky., during my visit to the West in the fall of 1861, and from the incidents he mentioned as occurring under his own observation in Price's army, it was very clear that discipline in it was at the lowest ebb. Mr. L. also expressed to me, as the result of his observation, the opinion that the plundering and general lawlessness of the troops, and the management of the quartermaster and commissary departments in taking supplies for "scrip," or loose certificates of indebtedness of the State of Missouri, was rapidly disgusting the people with the Southern cause, especially as the Federals paid for their supplies in money. The other incident was an inquiry made of me by Mr. Secretary Hunter, whether it was true that Gen. Price was so unwieldy or inert that he could not remain long on horseback, and had to move about in an ambulance. I was amazed at the statement, told Mr. Hunter I had never heard it before, and that it must be either a mistake or an exaggeration; I asked him his authority. He said the statement came from ex-Senator D. R. Atchison of Missouri on his visit to Richmond in August 1861. The authority being conclusive, I dropped the subject, nor did Mr. Hunter resume it.

About the beginning of December 1861, the newly elected Missouri delegation to the Confederate Provisional Congress arrived in Richmond, Va., bringing a letter from Gov. Jackson to President Davis, suggesting the union of the troops in Arkansas and Missouri under one commander, expressing a preference for Gen. Price for the position, in the event that the President should not appoint him, that Gen. Braxton Bragg should be assigned to the command.

Before I saw the delegates, or received Gov. Jackson's letter, they had had an interview with Mr. Davis, in which, according to their own accounts to me, they had with importunity amounting almost to overbearingness, demanded as a mark of proper respect to the popular wish, the assignment of Gen. Price to command of all the troops in Arkansas and Missouri. The President finally ended the conference by drawing himself up haughtily, and saying, "Gentlemen, I am not to be dictated to." They promptly declared they had no wish to dictate, but they soon left.

In this state of affairs, they called me in to advise and aid. The unwise course of Gen. Price's partisans had given his claims the aspect of a personal controversy between him and Mr. Davis, and the element of opposition, overt or covert, to the President or to the Confederacy itself, in the press and elsewhere, were taking advantage of it to sow dissension and fan the flames of discontent. The delegates also, especially Gen. John B. Clarke,[33] promptly and plainly gave me to understand that, in accordance with old Washington usage, they alone were the authoritative exponents of the wishes of Missouri, and they evidently viewed with jealousy everything resembling interference on my part by way of influencing any action of the Confederate government. Indeed, their call to me to aid in procuring the appointment of Gen. Price to command arose, evidently, solely from the fact of Gov. Jackson's writing to me, and from their failure with the President. I concurred in their opinion and wish in favor of Gen. Price's appointment, and weighing all the circumstances above mentioned, I determined, on consultation with Gen. Clarke, to send to the President a copy of Gov. Jackson's letter to me, with an endorsement of my full concurrence in its sentiments; it should be noticed that Gov. Jackson's letter to me urged the assignment of Gen. Price to command, suggesting the alternative of Gen. Bragg. Gen. C. was entirely satisfied with this course, without my having any interview on the subject with Mr. Davis.

However, almost immediately thereafter, it became known that the President had resolved to promote Col. Heth to be a major general and send him to Arkansas; of this fact there is no doubt, as I got it from Col. Heth himself, who consulted me about the condition of affairs in Arkansas and Missouri; but I never knew for certain what command he was to have there, or what were the real reasons for his intended appointment. It was a tremendous blunder, without reference to Col. Heth's qualifications, to propose to give so young and undistinguished an officer two steps at once in rank, in order to set him not only ahead of McCulloch and Price, but every brigadier in the army. The opposition of Congress defeated the scheme, and Major General Van Dorn[34] was sent to command in Arkansas and Missouri. About the time it became apparent that the President would not give Gen. Price supreme command west of the Mississippi, I wrote him a friendly letter urging him to submit cordially and patriotically to what ever course the President might take. The appointment of Van Dorn seemed to entirely satisfy Price's friends. In the winter of 1861–2, Major Snead wrote to a friend at Richmond (I think, Major E. C. Cabell) to that effect, adding that Van Dorn had told him to tell Gen. Price that he (Van Dorn) would not allow a spade in his camp, alluding to the then prejudice of the southern soldiers against engineering and fortifications, a feeling of which Gen. Price, on account of his capture of Lexington, was the exponent.

After the arrival of the Missouri Congressmen at Richmond, I retired completely from public life, and going to South Carolina in April 1862, remained there until the death of Governor Jackson called me to the titular constitutional governorship of Missouri, and I returned to Richmond early in January 1863.

One of the first letters I received after my accession to the governorship (either in South Carolina or at Richmond) was one from Major E. C. Cabell, who in the preceding summer had become paymaster on Gen. Price's staff. It urged me to sustain Gen. Price, and Major Cabell had so far caught the unfortunate tone of most of Gen. Price's other friends, as to appeal to my fears by stating that any other course would lose me popularity in Missouri. I passed it by, assuring him, in my answer, of my friendly disposition towards Gen. Price. On my arrival at Richmond, I found both in the Missouri delegation and among others, a marked change of opinion and feeling in regard to Gen. Price, and I also was apprized [sic] of many facts previously unknown to me.

During the siege of Richmond by [Union general George B.] McClellan, Gen. Price had come on there with his staff, Major Snead[35] and others, and had not made a favorable impression. The object of his visit was to get himself assigned to command an expedition to Missouri, and on this being postponed rather than denied, his chief of staff, Major Snead, publicly in front of the Spottswood Hotel, made a great fuss over it, tore from his uniform the insignia of his Confederate rank, and declared that Gen. Price would go to Missouri any how, fight again under the "bear flag" (of Missouri). The accuracy of the statement was subsequently admitted to me by Major Snead, who regretted his excitement; but the notoriety of the occurrence, and Major Snead's remaining in his confidential position near Gen. Price, as well as the frequent intimations, by way of threats, by his friends, that Gen. Price would resign unless his demands should be complied with, occasioned the general to be regarded as tacitly approving that turbulent escapade of his chief of staff.

During the dark period of the siege of Richmond, a scheme was formed, though I do not know that it ever ripened into a regular plot, to displace Mr. Davis by a popular movement or pronunciamento and proclaim Gen. Price president or generalissimo. I had heard some whisperings of it when in Richmond the previous winter; but according to the accounts I received in January 1863, from Major Cabell and Mr. Vest,[36] congressman from Missouri, the movement had assumed formidable dimensions, and but for our success at the battle of Seven Pines, would probably have broken out. They described Senator [John B.] Clark [Sr.] of Missouri as one of the most forward in it, Major Cabell relating to me a conversation he had with that senator, to combat, though without success, his intention to join in so wild a project. Mr. Davis, in a conversation about it also in January 1863, spoke of Mr. Wm. M. Cooke,[37] congressman from Missouri, as one of the most active in it "going around in the streets and talking for it, while the enemy was in front of Richmond." Gen. Price, leaving his command in the west and coming to Richmond at the time when this project was on foot excited remark. Col. Wm. Preston Johnson, an aide of President Davis, also mentioned to me some turbulent remarks of Gen. Price in a speech to a crowd from a balcony of the Spottswood Hotel; but I forget the precise tenor of them, except like Gen. Price's speeches usually, that indicated a disposition to plan and act for himself, not very subordinate towards his official superiors, nor very respectful towards the President. It was also stated and generally believed that he had had a high quarrel with Mr. Davis at the latter's house, after their dining together.

Another incident had also excited much curiosity. Gen. Edwin Price, a son of Gen. Sterling Price, and a brigadier in the Missouri State Guard while under the latter's command, had been captured in the winter of 1861–2, under circumstances reported unfavorable to him.[38]

While his command was encamped on one side of a certain river in Missouri, he left it to sleep in a house on the other side, nearest to the pursuing U.S. forces. He was surprised in his bed by a detachment from them and captured. These were the circumstances reported, and some believed that his capture was intentional on his part, if not preconcerted. He was treated with great courtesy by the U.S. authorities and permitted to reside on parole at his own home. By special exertions of the Missouri delegation in the Confederate Congress, Mr. Davis was induced (or rather readily consented) to exchange him for a U.S. brigadier, prisoner to the Confederacy. The exchange made, Gen. E. Price (more generally known by his nick-name of Stump Price, from his low stature) visited his father in the Confederate army, and thereon tendering his resignation of his position in the Mo. State Guards, returned to his home, engaged in conducting, with great profit, the tobacco business formally carried on by his father, and at the same place. The Missouri press represented him as converted to Unionism, and the <u>St. Louis Republican</u> contained a remarkable leading editorial, treating the son's repentance of secessionism as indicative of the father's position and probable future course. None of these assertions had been, as far as I could learn, contradicted either directly or indirectly, either in Confederate or Union newspapers. It was reported however (I am pretty sure that Senator Clarke, in January 1863, stated to me, as coming to him from Sen. R. M. Smith, an intimate friend of Gen. S. Price), that the defection of the son had caused great anguish to the father, who had broken with him in consequence; and a moving story was circulated of some persons overhearing angry remonstrances and deep groans from the father as alone with the son, in his tent, he endeavored to persuade him from deserting the Confederate cause at a critical moment.

Another matter also had great effect on Gen. Sterling Price's position. In the preceding year (1862) began the so called "Copperhead" movement in Ohio, Indiana, and Illinois. Its precise object and extent was a mystery to the Confederate government, and people. It appeared sometimes as a "reconstruction" movement to restore the old Union, and at other times, as one looking to a "North West Confederacy," to *include Missouri*, and to remain independent and allied with, or to be united to, the Southern Confederacy. On one point, however, all reports agreed, viz., that Gen. Price had some connection with it,[39] and was to be its military leader.

The tone, if not direct statements, of Gen Price's organ, the Jackson, Mississippi <u>Argus and Crisis</u>, edited by his confidential friend, Mr. J. W. Tucker,[40] (sometimes called Deacon Tucker), of St. Louis, Mo., and some articles in it on that subject by a Methodist clergyman, Dr. B. T. Kavenaugh, also confidentially connected with Gen Price, tended to confirm those reports. But nothing was known from Gen. Price himself by the Confederate government on the subject.

A great change also had taken place in public opinion generally, and that of the Missouri congressmen, in regard to Gen. Price's military capacity. When I had left Richmond ten months previously, he was decidedly the "hero of the war." Senator Ballard Preston of Va., had told Major E. C. Cabell and me that the sensation created by the capture of Lexington was only second to that on the battle of Manassas; and that Vice President Stephens had remarked that "were he President, he would make Price Generalissimo." But since then the congressmen and the people had begun to learn what war is, and Price's failure at Iuka, the only battle at which he had commanded since his Missouri campaign, and his not particularly distinguishing himself at any battle in which he was subordinate, the knowledge spread of his lax discipline, and the increased respect of our soldiers for field works, had all combined to diminish his military standing, at least comparatively with other generals. One anecdote was very current to the effect that on his coming to Corinth, Gen.

[Pierre Gustave Toutant] Beauregard had courteously shown him over the field works and fortifications, on which Gen. Price remarked to Gen. B. with a contemptuous smile, that he had never seen but two fortifications, and those he had taken; a remark universally considered both silly in itself, and discourteous to Beauregard. President Davis also related to me, in explaining the quarrel between Price and [John] Pemberton,[41] that in the previous autumn on his visit to Vicksburg, Price accompanied Pemberton while showing Mr. Davis the various works he had erected; Pemberton was explaining a certain work in which he evidently took pride, and Price volunteered the remark, in a sneering tone, "I know nothing about fortifications," intimating by his tone and manner that he considered them not worth knowing; at which Pemberton's face colored up as if naturally insulted, but he made no retort.

In the Missouri delegation, Senator Peyton and [Missouri State Guard brigadier general Thomas A.] Harris, especially the latter, were open in their denial to Gen. Price of any military ability at all; the others were very moderate, almost non-committal, and all regarded as very unfortunate the position of quasi antagonism he and his friends had assumed toward the President. They had all become supporters, more or less decided, of the President, even Gen. Clarke and Judge Cooke had changed their sentiments.

January 1863 to May 1863

About the time of my own arrival at Richmond in January 1863, or very soon thereafter, Major E. C. Cabell of Gen. Price's staff came on there, and we had long and frequent conferences on Missouri affairs, the leading topics being Gen. Price's dissatisfaction with his position under Pemberton, his eagerness to command an expedition to Missouri, and the expediency of sending him there with an army. Major Cabell related to me that unless that eagerness was gratified, Gen. Price had said he would resign his Confederate commission, and if need be "bushwhack it" in Missouri; that on hearing of my succession to the governorship, he had talked thus to him, Major C, then added, "I believe Gov. Reynolds to be my friend, and that if I desire it, he will give me my old position in command of the Missouri State Guard." As such he proposed to re-enter Missouri, and believed he would soon have an army of 50,000 men. Such boasts were frequent with General Price, and I had heard of his using them in his proposal in 1862 to Mr. Davis. In answer to Major Cabell's inquiries about my action in regard to making Gen. Price again Major General of the Missouri State Guards, I merely said the question was a very delicate one, and that I should not decide it in advance of a necessity for doing so; and that the Confederate government might prevent that necessity by concluding to send him on a Missouri expedition.

Soon after my reaching Richmond in January 1863, Gen. Price telegraphed to me a request to await his arrival there, and I answered that I would do so. He soon came on, accompanied by Major Snead, and I had a very cordial meeting with both. I explained to Gen. Price in the course of our various conversations, my desire that the Confederate States should as soon as practicable send an army into Missouri, and that he should command it, but that there were many obstacles in the way including, as far as delicacy permitted my mentioning them to him, the matters heretofore mentioned as having impaired his influence.

With regard to the movement in 1862 for a pronunciamento against Mr. Davis, he assured me that he had not even heard of it, still less of any suggestion of himself the leader in whose favor the movement was begun. He expressed surprise at it, and condemnation of it, but remarked that it explained an incident which had somewhat surprised him, and which he then related. On Mr. Davis' visit to Mississippi in 1862, he, Gen. Price, had had a very agreeable interview with him, but in it, the President after remarking on the gigantic efforts of the United States, very pointedly inquired about as follows, "Under such circumstances, Gen. Price, would it not be folly for us to have divisions among ourselves?" Gen. Price answered, "Most assuredly, Mr. President," and thereon Mr. Davis with an air of relief, said markedly, "I am delighted to hear you say so." Gen. Price remarked to me that after learning from me the existence of the pronunciamento project, he understood what had puzzled him at the time in that conversation, and now thought it designed by the President to sound him as to that project. Soon afterwards I took occasion to assure Mr. Davis of Gen. Price's disclaimer, and related the above incident. Mr. Davis had forgotten it, but supposed he may have made, as he frequently did in his conversations on his visits to the country, some general remarks on the necessity of union and harmony. He smiled at General Price's imagining that he designed sounding him on his intentions of "pronouncing as a revolutionary President," indeed in all his remarks, which were not many about that movement, Mr. Davis spoke of it more as an insult and a silly attempt to create internal divisions in feeling, than as a serious project to displace him from authority. Yet such it really was.

In regard to his alleged quarrel with Mr. Davis at the latter's house in Richmond, Gen. Price explained to me as follows: After dinner, he stated at some length to Mr. Davis, his project of a campaign in Missouri, and his grounds for asking the command of the forces employed in it; mentioning among others, that he had fought forty battles and lost none of them, that he could raise an army of 50,000 men, etc., etc. The President listened very patiently, and at the conclusion of his remarks, instead of entering into the question of a Missouri campaign, abruptly asked Gen. Price, "Is it true, general, that in 1861, on some one's reporting to you that I intended to offer you a commission of Confederate brigadier, you said that you would trample it under your feet?" Gen. Price denied having made such a remark; but, continued he in his relation of the matter to me, "I had been gravely and earnestly giving him my reasons, which my experience in Missouri entitled me to consider not unworthy of the respectful consideration, for a campaign in that State; his contemptuously dismissing them in silence, and questioning me about a stale slander, thoroughly incensed me, and I then skinned him." I could not get from Gen Price the precise particulars of what he himself called his "skinning" Mr. Davis, further than that he gave very free vent to his feelings and opinions. Gen. Price added that during Mr. Davis' subsequent visit in 1862 to Mississippi, cordial relations were entirely restored between them.

But fearful that some ill feeling remained in Mr. Davis on account of this "skinning" of the commander in chief in his own parlor by a military subordinate, I cautiously sounded him on the subject, without giving Gen. Price's version, but only stating that he was said to have been rather discourteous on the occasion. The President who did not enter into particulars and evidently attached no importance to the incident, said he remembered nothing discourteous in Gen. Price's conversation or deportment; but that they made on him the impression that he was the "vainest man he had ever met."

In regard to the "North West" revolutionary scheme, I stated with great frankness to Gen. Price that the connection of his name as a leader with it had done him harm; that no executive, especially one leading a revolution, could look without jealousy on a military officer's connecting himself while in its service with another revolution to occur within the enemy's lines; that it was not only a species of military insubordination, but an interference with the foreign policy of the Confederate government; and that opinion at the South was much divided as to the real nature of the North West movement (whether for joining us, for separate independence, or for reconstruction of the union). As to the expediency of our encouraging it if disguised re-union, and even as to the extent to which we could trust to its good faith, many considering it a mere political maneuver designed solely to effect Northern elections. At the very opening of my conversation and before my presenting the foregoing considerations (in which he fully concurred), Gen. Price disclaimed any direct connection with the North West movement, and said, "I really know no more of it than what I learn from the newspapers and from common talk in the Confederacy." I alluded to the statement in the Richmond papers of those days that a lady had come through the Federal lines to his camp with communications for him from the North West revolutionists, and was at Richmond at the Spottswood, his hotel. He stated as an illustration of his proper respect to the Confederate government in the matter, that he had merely heard from that lady her statement on her coming to him in Mississippi in January 1863, and had merely referred her to the President, and facilitated her journey to Richmond. I decidedly applauded that course and advised his leaving that whole North West business to the President; he agreed with me in the propriety of that course.

As Major Snead was inclined to promote harmony between the President and Missourians generally, I did not bring up his escapade at the Spottswood in 1862, in my conversation with Gen. Price. But I pointed out to him the disturbing influence of Mr. J. W. Tucker in his journal, the

<u>Argus and Crisis</u>, published at Jackson, Miss., and universally regarded as an "organ" of Gen. Price; that its blind hostility to the President, and its interlarding that hostility with advocacy of the so-called "justice to Gen. Price," placed him in the seeming attitude of factious opposition to the President. Gen. Price warmly protested his disapproval of Mr. Tucker's tone, and said he had written to him, urging him to drop or change it; Mr. T. answered rather truculently, that he would edit his journal according to his own notions. Gen. Price disclaimed its being his organ.

In 1862, some of our members of congress (if I remember rightly it was Mr. Vest), wrote to Mr. Tucker remonstrating against the hostile tone of his journal towards Mr. Davis; I forget whether it was this, or a letter from some friend at Richmond, that led Gen. Price to write to Mr. Tucker.

After these very satisfactory conversations with Gen. Price, I proceeded with great earnestness, as the Governor of Missouri, to urge on the Confederate government his transfer to Arkansas, with a view to a campaign in Missouri. But so seemingly simple a matter encountered obstacles I had scarcely anticipated. Those most difficult to surmount proceeded from Gen. Price himself.

He vehemently insisted on the transfer not only of himself, but of all the Missouri troops in Confederate service, and at the same time with himself. In his conversation with me he urged this not only as feasible, despite the presence of Federal gun boats between Vicksburg and Port Hudson (which had either already passed the latter point or were expected to do so), and on account of the importance of having those disciplined and magnificent troops as an example to the newer troops in Arkansas; but also on grounds which were rather offensive and alarming, though he seemed entirely unconscious of their being so. He stated to me that their attachment to him was so absorbing, and their desire to go to Missouri so intense, that if he should be separated from them and be sent to Arkansas, he "feared they would behave badly." I inquired, "Do you mean that they would run in battle or join the enemy?" "No," he answered, "but they would leave their commands and go over to Arkansas to join me." I made no further comment or further inquiry of Gen. Price on the point; but Major Snead and Major Cabell confirmed Gen. Price's opinion. In his conversation either with Mr. Seddon or with the President (I think the former), Gen. Price stated that if his division should not be sent with him, its soldiers would "swim the Mississippi River to join him." This expression became generally circulated, and elicited various comment.

Major Snead gave me a copy of a general order recently issued by Gen. Price (and composed by Major Snead) which he said had been ne-cessitated by an actual mutiny of a portion of the Missouri troops, on ac-count of their desire to return to the State.[42] The order was remarkably unmilitary, in short, a stump speech, in which the troops were begged to keep quiet, assured that Gen. Price would never separate from them, and that the President had promised to send him and them to Missouri in the ensuing Spring. To my inquiry whether so considerable and efficient a body of troops (the same that afterwards at Port Gibson, checked alone, under Gen. Bowen,[43] the advance of Gen. Grant's army), could safely be taken from Pemberton's army, he answered that he had brought on with him a certificate of Gen. Rust[44] (I think) to a conversation be-tween him, Gen. Price and Gen. Pemberton, in which Pemberton had admitted he had answered some telegram of [General Joseph E.] John-ston or Bragg by a consent to spare a certain number (I think 5,000) of infantry to reinforce Bragg. This Gen. Price considered conclusive that Pemberton could safely let the Missouri division, about three thousand strong, go to Arkansas. Gen. Price seemed entirely unconscious that the only proper mode of bringing Gen. Pemberton's opinion to bear on the question, was by a letter from him directly about it; and that transferring troops permanently across the Mississippi to Arkansas was a totally different thing from detaching them from Mississippi to Tennes-see, whence they could be recalled by telegraph, and rapidly transferred back by railroad in a very few days. But, to avoid delicate ground, I made no observation to him on those points; the whole incident, however, weakened my confidence in Gen. Price's military capacity, and his power of preserving cordial relations with brother officers; for the certificate of Pemberton's remarks was given without apprising him of it. I strongly advised Gen. Price to make no allusion to it to either Mr. Seddon or Mr. Davis, especially the latter.

The consultations I had in reference to Gen. Price's transfer to Arkansas, were chiefly with Mr. Seddon, and a very little with the President. I urged it on the ground that whatever might be his deficiencies as a military man, and on which I could form no decided opinion, there seemed to be no doubt that in Arkansas and Missouri, and probably also in Texas, his name would attract large numbers of volunteers to the army. In regard to the transfer of his division with him, I told Mr. Seddon that I wholly discredited the soundness of Gen. Price's opinion that it would leave its colors to join him; that I claimed to know the people of Missouri, and that I could not believe a body of men composed, as was that division, of the best in the state, would disobey orders and leave the post of danger; that if there was any foundation for Gen. Price's opinion, so far from its influencing in favor of his request, it should be decisive against it; that if the alarming fact existed that a Confederate major general had three thousand of our best troops so under his control, that they would disregard their oaths of service to follow him, it should be tested and become palpable to the government without delay, as the danger might be infinitely less in meeting it now than at some future crisis in the war; and that if I believed in it at all, I should urge him to order Gen. Price at once to Arkansas and his division to Virginia; but the sole foundation of Gen. Price's opinion was probably a natural desire of the men to regain Missouri, but little connected with any personal devotion to him. I also urged that, independently of any wish of Gen. Price, I desired the transfer of his division to Arkansas on account of the influence so excellent a body of troops would exercise on the newer troops in that State; but that, that transfer should be decided on or denied solely on military considerations, especially in reverence to the security of Vicksburg.

Mr. Seddon promptly decided that the army at or near Vicksburg could not be reduced. His general plan of campaign was that for the present, the main object was to raise the siege of that place; expeditions into Maryland, Kentucky and Missouri, with such troops as could be spared for them should be organized in the spring, and he was fully aware of their importance as diversions to aid our defense of Vicksburg; that he hoped the siege of that place would be raised before midsummer; that on the event a simultaneous move would be made up each bank of the Mississippi River to recover Missouri and Kentucky, and perhaps bring about a peace; but that meanwhile to endanger Vicksburg by taking troops from its defense to be sent on expeditions northward, would be to subordinate the main consideration to those of less importance.

In a letter to Mr. Seddon of January 31st, 1863, I enclosed a copy of Gen. Price's general order (Special Order No. 82) stating to his command the President's *promise* to send him to Missouri in 1863.[45] In conversation with me, Mr. Seddon stated that he had not shown my letter or Gen. Price's order to the President, and he asked me not to allude to it in any conversation with Mr. Davis; that he, Mr. S. having inquired lately in conversation with Mr. Davis, about the promise alleged by Gen. Price, the President flatly denied it, and became excited about the matter, to the extent that Mr. S. had some difficulty in calming him and getting the subject dropped; that Mr. Davis was prone to regard such questions as questions not of recollections but of his veracity, especially in the case of Gen. Price since the insinuations against Mr. Davis on the occasion of his telegram to Col. W. A. Broadwell, in the winter of 1861–62, about "superceding" Gen. Price in Arkansas; and if the subject of that *promise* was not at once dropped by Gen. Price, there would be another quarrel preventing any arrangement to gratify his wishes. I said nothing on the subject to Gen. Price; but I think I got either Major Cabell or Major Snead to caution him on the subject, and the matter of Gen. Price's transfer being very soon decided, no danger arose from it. I remarked to Mr. Seddon that the whole trouble arose from Gen. Price's unmilitary habit of considering a superior's intimation to him of an intention (which that superior of course could change), as a promise to him as a leader in the war, and to be fulfilled at every sacrifice.

Immediately after this conversation and a long conference he had with Gen. Price alone, Mr. Seddon, taking the President's views, proposed, in a draft of a letter to Gen. Pemberton, a decision of the question of Gen. Price's transfer. It was that Gen. Price should go at once to Arkansas and report to Gen. Holmes; and that his division should be sent after him, as soon as it could be spared from the east side of the Mississippi, or an equivalent could be transferred in exchange of it, from the Trans-Mississippi Department. I at once approved it as all that could be asked under the circumstances at Vicksburg. It was submitted to Gen. Price and I urged him to express satisfaction with it, which he did, though with evident reluctance, and only because it was the best he could get. I said nothing about the ill-considered pledge in his late general order[46] (Special Order No. 82) that he could not separate from his division; the subject was a delicate one. But he made no allusion to that difficulty; the promise was probably a mere oratorical flourish of Major Snead in drawing up the order.

On receiving his orders, Gen. Price very soon left, via Lynchburg and Knoxville for Mississippi. Our understanding was that I should remain in Richmond to prevent any change in the orders (though I did not share his apprehension that any would be meditated), and that on his leaving Mississippi for Arkansas, he should telegraph me of the fact, in order that I might not be any longer detained in Virginia, but might at once commence my journey to join him in the Trans-Mississippi Department. We parted with entire cordiality, he promising me his support in my very difficult position of Governor of Missouri, and I feeling both that I had, through my personal influence with the President and Mr. Seddon, rescued him from the obscurity into which he had fallen and opened for him a pathway to new glory in the west; and that he both was aware of this, and felt under corresponding obligations to me, but several circumstances soon occurred to excite the suspicion that he was not entirely satisfied. Mr. Seddon, as an old personal friend, told me that Gen. Price had in his conference with him, exhibited marked "jealousy" of me. Mr. Seddon would not give me the details, excepting that on his referring to my opinion on some matter, Gen. Price made some disparaging remarks, indicating annoyance at the respect evinced for my opinion by Mr. Seddon. I told Mr. S. that it rather amused than annoyed me to find Gen. Price attempt to weaken my position with so old and intimate [a] friend as himself; but that the jealousy was pardonable, and far from exciting any ill feeling in me toward Gen. Price, would only lead me to endeavor to remove it by acts evincing my friendly disposition towards him; that for a man of his temper, it could not but be annoying to find himself affected, however slightly, by the influence, as Governor of Missouri, of a man twelve years his junior, and who ten years ago had been known to him as a new comer in the State while he, Gen. Price, was its Governor; and that his "jealousy" was merely the ordinary feeling of old public men towards their juniors, which the latter should take no offense at.

Two incidents occurred during Gen. Price's visit which also threw light on our then and subsequent relations. On one occasion when he, Major S., and I were returning in a carriage from some visit, Major S., expressing dissatisfaction and impatience at the delay in transferring Gen. Price to Arkansas, I said, "Don't be in too great a hurry, Major, let me manage the affair, and I think I will succeed in it." He answered in a very significant tone, but with entire cordiality, "I know you can succeed, if you are in earnest about it." I made no further remark; but it unpleasantly recalled to mind the general opinion that Gen. Price and his staff were less inclined to be grateful for services than to complain because those services did not obtain for him all he desired.

The other was that, soon after Gen. Price's arrival in Richmond, Major Cabell paid me a visit of two or three hours at my rooms and renewed the subject, incidentally broached by him previous to the General's arrival, of my appointing the latter to command the Missouri State Guard, in case he should resign his commission in the Confederate service. About the same time, Gen. Price had told me that his position under Gen. Pemberton was so disagreeable to him, that unless he could serve under some other commander, he would resign. Major Cabell's object evidently was to ascertain from me, without indelicately pressing the question, whether I would *promise* to appoint Gen. Price to that command on his resigning his Confederate commission. I presented to Major Cabell the great difficulties, legal and financial, in the way of re-organizing the Missouri State Guard, but told him I would not decide the question, as it was unnecessary to do so, until the President should decide that of Gen. Price's transfer to Arkansas.

That transfer was considerably facilitated by the support of it by the Arkansas delegation in Congress, and by a very decided letter written either to the President or the Secretary of War (or possibly to the Arkansas delegation; at least it was official), by Gov. [Harris] Flanagin of Arkansas, urging the removal of Gen. Holmes and the assignment of Gen. Price to command that military district. Since coming to Mexico, I heard, for the first time, that while at Richmond in 1863, Gen. Price aimed to procure the command of the entire Arkansas, Missouri and Indian Country forces. Major [Henry M.?] Clark of Arkansas told me that when he was at Richmond in Jan. 1863, Gen. Price, on very slight acquaintance, spoke to him about the wish of the people of that section that he should command there, that he could raise more troops than any one else, etc., and suggested, in very animated language, that the delegations from Missouri and Arkansas should call in a body on the President and insist on his appointment to that command. (Conversation of Major Clark with Capt. Richard Taylor and me at City of Mexico, 19th April, 1867). Major C. considered this a hint to him to get up such a cell, but was so disgusted with the vanity and egotism of Gen. Price on that occasion, that he never afterwards even called on him. Major C. confirmed my impression of the poor estimate of Gen. Price by Senator Peyton of Missouri; on General Price's arrival in Richmond, he asked Peyton if he intended to call on him; Peyton answered, "Why should I; I have had enough of that humbug." On Clark's speaking to Peyton about Price's desire to command in the West, that Senator not only declined to aid in the scheme, but intimated that Senator Clark would not favor it. In this he was mistaken.

Soon after it was settled that Gen. Price should be transferred to Arkansas (but perhaps not until after he had left Richmond), I received some information of an almost alarming character in reference to Gen. Price's position. In a conversation I had with Dr. Montrose A. Pallen[47] of St. Louis, Mo., we casually got upon the subject of Gen. Edwin Price's desertion in the preceding summer. Dr. P. was at the time of that occurrence, Medical Director of Gen. S. Price's headquarters, and the latter personally gave him the following account of the matter.

On Gen. E. Price's leaving Missouri to be exchanged and sent within the Confederate lines, he had an interview with Judge Gamble, the Union Governor of the State, resulting in a promise from the latter that, if Gen. E. Price, after being exchanged, should return to his home in Missouri and "keep quiet," he should not be molested, and should not be requested to take any oath of allegiance or other obligation to the United States or the Union State Government. On coming within the Confederate lines he consulted his father, who advised his accepting the offer; the reason given by Gen. S. Price to Dr. Pallen for this course were the following: The prominent or influential secessionists within the Federal lines in Missouri, were either in prison, or under bonds for neutrality, or cowed so that they feared to move. Gen. E. Price, under the protection of Gov. Gamble, could be very effective in keeping alive the Southern spirit, and preparing to join with a brigade his father on his expected campaign into the State in the spring of 1863. On the other hand, there was no position suitable to his rank and merits, open to him in the Confederacy, and if he remained in it, he would have to enter the army as a private soldier.

⇥Hamilton R. Gamble.⇤
Photograph by Scholten, 1860s. Missouri History Museum.

Governor Gamble was too intelligent a gentleman and too devoted to the Union cause for any one to believe that he could have granted so extraordinary a protection to Gen. E. Price, without some specific pledge that it would not be abused. By "keeping quiet" he and Gen. E. Price must have understood at least the most strict neutrality; if indeed the unprecedented favor that he should not be required to take the oath of allegiance to the Union government, did not indicate some agreement for secret service to it, in which his being allowed to pass for a secessionist would be a useful blind. The whole matter was very mysterious; yet one fact was very prominent in even Gen. S. Price's own version of it, viz., that in his and his son's code of morals it was permissible for them to requite Gov. Gamble's magnanimity and take advantage of it, by conspiring against his government within his lines. In none of his conversations, even the most confidential, and on the very subject of that Missouri campaign which Gen. E. Price was said to be secretly advancing, had Gen. Price given me, either as the Confederate Governor of Missouri, or as an old political associate and personal friend, the slightest hint of the matter; the silence of the President and Mr. Seddon and all others of his advisers, as well as the Missouri congressional delegation about the matter, in their conversations with me, was conclusive that, none of them knew his version of it. His communication of it to Dr. Pallen, as that gentleman stated to me, was in a moment of unrelaxed social conversation, unguarded and in answer to some very pressing inquiries of Dr. P. about the matter of placing him in the position of having either to denounce his son as a deserter (as he was generally considered), or disclose his alleged intentions in returning to Missouri. Under all these circumstances, even the dullest government could not but inquire: Was Gen. E. Price working in Missouri for some object hostile to the Union government or was he in collusion with it for some object hostile to the Confederacy?[48] Was General S. Price also in collusion with him? Were both working for some object concealed from both governments? In short, the fact being confessed by both that their code of morals permitted them to deal directly, and not merely through the ordinary, and despised agents of dirty military work, in cheating a government, was their real design to cheat Gov. Gamble, or the confederate government, or both?

Although Gen. Sterling Price had taken no pledge of confidence from Dr. Pallen in reference to the disclosure of his son's affairs, and Dr. Pallen had communicated it to me in like manner, and because he, as a Missourian, believed it his duty to acquaint the Governor of his State with so important an incident, I recommended Dr. P. to keep it to himself, and meanwhile carefully considered what course I myself should pursue in regard to it.

The principal reason for sending Gen. Price to Arkansas or on a campaign to Missouri, was his confident assertion, and the general belief that he would "draw" many more recruits to the Confederate army than any one else; I shared that belief. The great want of the Confederacy was men. To have compelled Gen. Price to resign on suspicion founded on his concealment of his share in his son's intrigue, would have deprived us of the advantage above mentioned; judging only from general principles, it was to be feared that, with his known facility for change, it might lead him even to join the Unionists on some pretext or other, or go back to Missouri to "keep quiet" with his son, or carry out his plan mentioned to Major Cabell, of going to the State to "bushwhack," in which event a stop to recruiting, or even desertion of Missourians from the Confederate army to join him might be apprehended, and he himself was quite capable of setting himself up in the State, as an independent leader, either as a revolutionary governor of the State, or on the "Northwest Confederacy" project, or any other that seemed to him most promising. To make his son's intrigue known as a cause for retiring the father, would have only created a big controversy, as many with too obtuse a moral sense to see that a government cannot safely trust in high and especially independent command, an officer capable of using his own son in treachery to a foe, or even to see any thing improper in such treachery itself, would have applauded it as Roman self sacrifice, and cried out against the new "injustice to Gen. Price." Besides, if Gen. E. Price really meant treachery to Gov. Gamble, it might be useful to the Confederacy, however much we might despise the traitor; and it would be ungenerous and impolite to expose him to any risk while in the power of the U.S. by a disclosure of his alleged intentions. Besides my own personal knowledge of Gen. Price up to that time, inclined me to attribute the affair solely to his obtuseness on the moral question, his restlessness in his desire to "keep himself before the public" by a new campaign in Missouri, his fretting in subordinate command and longing to be independent far off in Missouri where loose discipline could reign unchecked, and his habit, encouraged by the adulation of his partisans, of acting as if he were a co-equal of the government, a sort of independent chieftain or "power within the State," entitled to form and execute plans without reference to those legally his superiors. I did not consider him capable of any overt act of separation from the Confederate authority (except in his wild scheme to "bushwhack" in Missouri), much less of abandonment of the Confederate cause. In short, I proffered my own judgment of the man to the suspicion, or conclusion, which general principles of government, and the usual course of past history, would justify in the case of a discontented ambitious officer with the loose moral tone exhibited in the counsel he gave his son in regard to his course towards Gov. Gamble. Perhaps also gratifying his ambition by sending him, as a Confederate officer, in independent command to Missouri, would cure him of any desire, real or suspected of figuring independently of, or in opposition to, the regular Confederate authorities. Indeed from personal regard for him and old associations, I did not leave out of view the possibility of having him to lead, after his recovery of Missouri, a campaign in the North West, not as an independent movement by him, but as one authorized and controlled by Confederate authority, in aid of a "North West Confederation," or otherwise, as that authority might consider best.

But in taking this charitable view of Gen. Price's intentions, and adopting so kind a policy towards him, I of course felt bound in duty to the Confederate government, to take every reasonable precaution against the event of my being mistaken. Lest a knowledge of the Edwin Price affair might induce some hasty notion by the Confederate government, I concluded not to mention Dr. Pallen's statement to the President or any of his cabinet, or indeed to any one else. But the decided impression, very general, of the disposition of Gen. Price to be insubordinate, or even to be misled into some "pronunciamento," furnished a sufficient basis for arranging the precautions I proposed. The President, being too busy to have long conversations, I proposed to him, and he readily consented, that I should confer on Missouri and North West affairs, with Mr. Benjamin, Secretary of State. I did so, and both of us appreciating the dangers which might, especially at some critical moment, arise from the disposition above mentioned of Gen. Price, I suggested a generous policy towards him in the way of giving him commands affording legitimate spheres for a patriotic ambition, promoting him for any <u>real</u> success, but placing in command *under* him officers of such unquestionable fidelity and subordination, as well as capacity for controlling their troops, that should he ever attempt any insubordination or independent movement, he would find himself without support, and either quickly abandon it, or be easily crushed. I used the simile of comparing this course to constructing a wire fence around a pasture; it would be invisible to the animals quietly grazing within the enclosure, but should any one attempt to stray beyond it, he would find himself effectually checked by the wire fence which had previously escaped his notice. Mr. Benjamin at once accepted the suggestion as at once just and even generous to Gen. Price, at the same time securing the government and the cause against danger. Mr. B. earnestly and with evident sincerity declared that neither the President nor any of his advisers had the slightest prejudice against Gen. Price; that they had every inclination to afford him the amplest scope for patriotic ambition; but that unfortunately, his restlessness, the dictatorial tone of his friends in urging his advancement, their habit of threatening if their demands were not at once granted, and bringing congressional and newspaper "pressure" to bear in his favor; as also his propensity to get into quarrels with both his superior officers, his associates and subordinates, had done him great injury; and the connection of his name with the proposed pronunciamento against the President in the spring of 1862, and with the suspicious "North West" move, coupled with the other facts before stated, and the doubts of military men concerning his military capacity, made it the duty of the government to look carefully to eventualities in assigning him to a sphere of action. He said the perfect confidence the President had in me from our long personal friendship induced him to apprehend little or no danger from Gen. Price's restless ambition, where I, with the combined weight of the Authority of a Governor of Missouri, and of old and cordial personal relations with Gen. Price himself, should be constantly near him.

As a result of this conversation, and others subsequently with the President and Secretary of War, an understanding was had that I should carry letters (unofficial) from the President to Gen. E. Kirby Smith commanding the Trans-Mississippi Dept. and Gen. Holmes, commanding the District of Arkansas (and also to Gen. Pemberton), placing me on a confidential footing with them, in fact, almost constituting me a kind of unofficial adviser of the two former.[49]

It was also understood (in fact asked, and almost stipulated by me, but cordially granted as part of the "support" the President had promised me in our first interview after my reaching Richmond), that no appointment or promotion of a general officer in the Missouri Confederate troops should be made without first hearing me on the question; in point of fact, none was afterwards made except on my recommendation.

The only other incidents which occurred during my stay at Richmond in 1863, of any interest in connection with Gen. Price, were the following: On my consulting him about making Col. John Polk (later one of his "volunteer aides"),[50] my principal aide-de-camp, he made a profuse eulogy of his son, Capt. Celsus Price,[51] and stated that he would be just the kind of aide I would require; "but," added he, "I cannot spare him to you." As the subject of Capt. Price was thrust into the conversation, without any connection with Col. Polk, I considered it a feeler towards having me ask, as a special favor, that he should be "spared" to me: having no personal acquaintance then with Capt. Price, I of course turned the conversation. The conversation of Gen. Price and his confidential officers with him at Richmond, evincing considerable ill feeling towards Mr. Davis, I deemed it prudent before appointing Col. Polk to inquire of him, frankly but confidentially, his views and feelings in those directions; I asked him, in conclusion, "Should Gen. Price be misled into any position of active hostility to the President, would you sustain Gen. Price?" His answers were manly and patriotic; while he had a warm regard for Gen. P. and would aid in advancing his legitimate ambition, he would neither sustain nor tolerate any factious opposition to the President.

Col. Polk, desiring to rejoin his family at Jackson, Mississippi, left Richmond soon after Gen. Price; he was instructed by me to ascertain and communicate to me on my arrival there, the precise effect on the Missouri troops, of Gen. Price's separation from them. Gen. Price himself neglected to fulfill his engagement to telegraph to me about his departure for Arkansas; on meeting him afterwards I alluded to the omission, as delaying me at Richmond; his explanation was so frivolous that I forget its precise terms; I think it was that in the hurry of departure he forgot it. But I ascertained by telegraphing to Col. Polk, and as soon thereafter as I could conclude my business pending at Richmond, I left for Mississippi.

At Jackson, Col. Polk reported that Gen. Price's separation from his command had occasioned no particular emotion or sensation, either among the troops or with the public; the comparative indifference shown was in fact such as to excite surprise. He told me however, that he thought it his duty, as my aide-de-camp, to apprize me of the incidents which had occurred there. Gen. Price, with some of his staff, paying a farewell visit to Mrs. Polk, the General asked her when she expected to go to Arkansas; she answered that she and her husband, Col. Polk, were awaiting my arrival at Jackson in order to accompany me to Little Rock. Gen. Price then said to her, before all present, "You had better come with me, if you wait until Gov. Reynolds crosses the Mississippi, you will have to wait a long time; he has an office at Richmond (alluding to my being a commissioner under the Sequestration Act, a position I had not resigned) which he much prefers to campaigning and would rather be in Richmond than in Arkansas; I don't expect to see him again until after I have taken Jefferson City and then he will come after me to be inaugurated." Mrs. Polk replied that she was certain I would come; and there the subject was dropped.

Mrs. Polk confirmed the statement and both she and her husband expressed to me the opinion that Gen. Price had no good feeling towards me. I told them I would not let such ebullitions influence me, that Gen. Price, like many other Missourians, had perhaps been prejudiced against me by my not remaining with the army, as they could not appreciate that my position as Lt. Governor prevented my doing so; and that with him, as with others, I would trust to remove their prejudices by my conduct. Internally, however, I could not but feel that the general had intended to give the key note to his staff to commence the same game against me that his partisans had played on Gov. Jackson, viz., representing him as avoiding danger and keeping from the front when ever his duties called him, however, indispensably, to the rear or to Richmond. It also showed little recognition of my sincere and successful effort to have him transferred to Arkansas with a view to enable him to "take Jefferson City," that he should thus endeavor behind my back to undermine my authority by making me "unpopular" as a shirk. I especially asked both Col. and Mrs. Polk if Gen. Price made those remarks jocosely; they both said that on the contrary his tone and manner were that of serious advice; that had the remarks been jocose, they would either have not referred to them again, or would have reported them as such.

Another incident related to me by Col. Polk occurred at an evening party where several persons were present, among whom were Col. and Mrs. Polk and Mr. [E. T.] Cooper, editor of the <u>Mississippian</u>; it may have been at Mr. Cooper's house, but I am not certain. Gen. Price was enlarging in his usual boasting style, on his plans of campaign on reaching Arkansas; some one suggested that probably Gen. Holmes would not let him carry them out, and asked him what he would do in that event. Gen. Price answered with bitter emphasis, "If Gen. Holmes attempts to prevent me, or to degrade me, I'll put him in chains, and send him on to his master, Jeff. Davis."

All of Gen. Price's staff had left with him, except Capt. [——], who called on me on the night of my arrival in Jackson. Mrs. Polk soon afterwards told me he had requested her to inquire of me whether I would appoint him one of my aides, and that he had waited at Jackson to ascertain his chances of success. I told her to tell him that Col. Polk being already my aide for the St. Louis district, and Capt. [——] being also from St. Louis, the place was no longer vacant.

While I was at Jackson, Capt. [——], an officer under Major [Isaac] Brinker, Gen. Price's quartermaster asked for my influence with Gen. Pemberton to facilitate his obtaining transportation across the Mississippi for a complete set of cavalry equipments for about seven hundred men; Major B. had left them in his charge, and stated that Gen. P. had promised them to Gates' regiment to remount it when sent to Arkansas, and in any event wished them sent over at once, that he might have them at hand. In my conversation with Capt. [——], who was very frank in the matter, it came out that these equipments, of splendid quality and manufactured by Grimsley of St. Louis, were the property of the State of Missouri; on the passage in Arkansas of Gen. Price and his staff from Missouri State Service to the Confederate, these equipments were retained by Major B., by order, as Capt. [——] stated, of Gen. Price's had actually been brought across the Mississippi and kept boxed up and stored away for some possible contingency of their being needed by Gen. Price: and this while all that time, nothing was more needed in the Confederate service than such articles!

I at once had them taken possession of by one of the Missouri State officers, Capt. John Donaldson, and Grierson's raid into Mississippi occurring just then, and Gen. Pemberton needing those equipments pressingly, I sold them to the Confederate States, the proceeds of sale going into the military fund of the State of Missouri.

I had already, from conversations with Gen. Stith, quartermaster general of Missouri under Gov. Jackson,[52] learned so much of the utter confusion, attending the passage of Gen. Price's division from State to

Confederate service, in regard both to the retention of the State property by that division, and the neglect or inefficiency of the State officers in securing certificates, or other evidence, of the property transferred; and I was so convinced of the hopeless imbecility of the Confederate government in punishing delinquencies of its officers; that I contented myself with recovering the property. Had a Louvois[53] or a Stanton been at the head of Confederate military administration, I should have asked an investigation and the punishment of whoever should prove to be responsible for this bold appropriation, and dog-in-the-manger retention, of Missouri State property.

⇒*Major General John Bowen, CSA.*⇐
Photographed in uniform of Missouri state troops, ca. 1860. Missouri History Museum.

Before going to Arkansas, I visited the Missouri Division at Grand Gulf on the Mississippi River. On Gen. Price's departure, the command had devolved on Brig. Gen. Bowen, one of the brigades being commanded by Brig. Gen. Green,[54] and the other by Col. Cockrell.[55] I found in the conversations neither of the officers nor of any one else there, any evidence of a desire to go to the Trans-Mississippi Dept., or of any discontent at the departure of Gen. Price. In a conversation with Gen. Green, who was entirely impartial and had always been on friendly terms with Gen. Price, I stated to him what the latter and his staff had asserted at Richmond; and I asked him to give me frankly his views on the matter, for, as governor of Missouri, I considered myself entitled to them.

Gen. Green stated that the mutiny which had occasioned Gen. Price's general order [Special Order No. 82] was confined to about one hundred men, was not at all serious, and had been at once and easily suppressed; that it had nothing whatever to do with a desire to go to Missouri, or with any devotion to Gen. Price personally; that its sole cause was an opinion which some demagogue had put into the heads of those men, twelve months volunteers of 1861, and they were no longer legally in service in their then organizations, and could choose others or retire altogether; that convinced of their error, they had all returned to duty and were now serving as good soldiers.

He said that the fever about going to Missouri, and the cry about "injustice to Gen. Price," existed only at that officer's headquarters, and were mainly manufactured; that the troops by long service under good regimental officers, had become well disciplined, and almost considered their camps their homes; that they were favorites of the people of Mississippi, and were at Grand Gulf in one of the richest and most hospitable portions of that State, while on the contrary, Arkansas was remembered by them mainly for privations suffered there, inhospitality of the northern (Unionist) portion of the State, and squabbles with other Confederate troops serving there; that whatever might be their desire, and even that was a very quiet one, to take part in a campaign to recover Missouri, they would *prefer* serving in Mississippi to that in Arkansas, except some few, not exceeding one hundred out to the whole three thousand; that, that one hundred, consisted of the bad or discontented element, men who saw in a transfer to Arkansas an opportunity to desert and reach their Missouri homes by land more easily than they could with the Mississippi River between them, or desert and bushwhack, or get rid of the strict discipline of the Mississippi army and indulge their indolence or love of plunder under the loose discipline believed to exist in Arkansas; that the fever of Gen. Price to go to Arkansas and eventually to Missouri, originated to a great extent, in his impatience of a subordinate position, and his unpleasant relations with Gen. Pemberton; that his staff helped to keep it up from their own desire to go there, where they would be "bigger men" (as Gen. Green expressed himself), and in a Missouri campaign under Gen. Price, would figure more largely and be less under control; that for that reason, conscious, or unconscious to themselves, and from their habit of trying to please him by flattery, they encouraged his notion about the blind devotion of his troops to him, and perverted or exaggerated every incident (as that of the mutiny), to give color to that notion; that the troops were attached to Gen. Price as a "fatherly" kind of commander, calling him generally "old Pap," but their belief in his military ability had been considerably weakened; that the notion that any of them would desert to follow Gen. Price was wholly imaginary; and that he and other officers, and he believed, the command generally had a feeling of positive relief at being left to their purely military duties under a purely military man like Bowen, and being rid of the ceaseless political and military ferment and agitation of which Gen. Price's headquarters were the center. In giving this candid statement, Gen. Green declared that he had a most friendly feeling towards Gen. Price and great respect for him; that he blamed his staff, especially Major Snead, rather than Gen. Price himself for the state of things; and that he should not have expressed himself so freely to me, had he not considered it his duty

⇌Martin E. Green.⇌
Photograph, 1861–1863. Missouri History Museum.

to me, as the Governor of Missouri, to give me full and accurate intelligence as to the real condition of the command.

This conversation occurred the night before I addressed the troops.
In that address, I alluded to their proposed transfer to Arkansas; stated
that should I have the good luck to re-enter the capital of Missouri, I
desired that they should be with me; that the road to that capital lay less
through Arkansas than over the wrecks of the Federal gunboats in sight
of their fortifications; that until the time came for their return to their
own homes, they should cheerfully serve wherever needed; that if I had
wish in the matter, it would be that they should go to Virginia and show

even Lee's army what Missourians could do; and that in any event I had no wish to force them to exchange their present comfortable quarters for "that earthly paradise, Boston Mountains of Arkansas."

At that remark, many voices from among the soldiers, exclaimed: "We don't want to go there." That was the sole exhibition of any feeling by them during that portion of my remarks. My allusion to Virginia was intended to test fully their willingness to go wherever ordered; Gen. Green, the night before, on my inquiring how the command would like a transfer to the Tennessee army, said he thought it would prefer being sent to Virginia, to join Lee's army.

After my visit to the Missouri division, I wrote to Col. Wm. Preston Johnston[56] my letter of [——], to be shown to Mr. Davis. Gen. Green's statements in reference to that division were fully sustained by its subsequent conduct up to the close of the war.

May 1863, in the Trans-Mississippi Department

Crossing the Mississippi, I went to Shreveport, and in a conference with Gen. E. Kirby Smith,[57] commander of the Trans-Mississippi Department, had with him substantially the same understanding that I had had with the Richmond authorities in regard to Gen. Price and Missouri affairs generally. Thence proceeding to Camden, Arkansas, I soon learned of attempts, for the moment successful, to create feeling against me among the Missourians, similar to those practiced against Gov. Jackson, i.e., exciting the State creditors and others to expect impossibilities from the Governor, and then raising a cry against the incumbent because he did not perform those impossibilities.[58] These attempts proceeded from Gen. Price's headquarters as a center. Several friends, including Col. Polk of my staff, who were at Little Rock while I was at Camden, gave me either at the time, or on my own arrival at Little Rock, accounts of them. Col. Polk related to me a conversation in which he participated at Gen. Price's headquarters, the particulars of which I forget, but in which Major Snead and Capt. [——] were so violent in their abuse of me that Gen. Price, who was present, finally checked them. I determined to at once put a stop to this species of warfare. My correspondence with Gen. Price, Major Cabell and Major Snead in May and June 1863 gives the particulars of the controversy.[59]

Before writing my letter of [——] to Major Cabell, designed to bring matters to a head, I showed it to Col. J. T. Thornton[60] of my staff, as even on our short acquaintance, I had considerable confidence in his judgments, and he had but lately been at Little Rock; he entirely approved it as calculated to produce harmony by warning Gen. Price of what might result from a continuance of his staff's attack on me. To my own staff, especially to Cols. Polk and [W. H.] Cundiffe, and afterwards to Gen. Kimmel, I stated that I wished all my officers to avoid criticism of either the President or Gen. Price, as the best means of letting their dissentions die out; and that I also did not wish my staff to become, like Gen. Price's, any propaganda of popularity seeking for its chief (myself).

The old leaven of desire to seek controversy with the President and raise a cry of injustice and bad faith to Gen. Price was seen to work in Major Snead's letter of [———], charging a failure to perform a promise to send the Missouri Division to join him in Arkansas. My answer of [———] nipped the attempt in the bud by denying and disproving the allegation itself on which Major Snead's letter was based.[61]

In traveling from Shreveport to Washington, Ark., and thence to Camden and Little Rock, I was unaccompanied even by an acquaintance, and entirely unknown, thanks to the remarkable habit of the people of that section (and of Texas) in evincing no curiosity about travelers. This gave me an opportunity to quietly listen to the general conversation at the places where the stage stopped. I already began to evidence weariness of the war: there was no enthusiasm about Gen. Price's arrival, or if any had existed it had died away. The only allusion I heard made to him was in the remark of an innkeeper on the road from Shreveport to Washington, that now Price had come over he hoped our army would soon move into Missouri, because in that way Arkansas would be freed from both the Federal and Confederate armies. At Washington, I made myself known to several of the leading gentlemen, as also at Camden; in neither place did I discover the slightest trace of that popularity of Gen. Price which his friends claimed to be so marked in Arkansas. After reaching Little Rock, I inquired into the actual increase of the army by volunteering or by diminished resistance to the conscription since the winter, compared with former periods; no such increase was perceptible. I thereon frankly stated to the chief conscription officer my disappointment, as I had really expected that Gen. Price's popularity would greatly stimulate volunteering. That officer candidly said that the resistance (usually passive) to the conscription had its pretexts and excuses, varying with circumstances; that in the preceding winter, a not uncommon, but still by no means general pretext was that the conscribable men would volunteer to serve under Gen. Price, but did not like to serve under any other, or be drafted—Gen. Price's return to Arkansas being then considered next to impossible—but that since his arrival in Arkansas, though that particular pretext had died out, volunteering had not increased and the only change had been that other pretexts for opposing or evading conscription were in vogue.

Gen. Price had left Little Rock for Jacksonport [Arkansas] before I reached the former place. Major Snead, detained there by sickness, came to see me soon after my arrival. He introduced the subject of the recent controversy by remarking that, from the tone of my letters to him and that he knew of my letter to Major Cabell of [——] he feared that I considered him my enemy, but that he sincerely assured me that he had the most friendly disposition towards me; that he had merely expressed his decided dissent to my general order providing for a provisional government in the event of my death. I frankly told him that his deduction from those letters was perfectly correct, but that I was very happy to hear him disclaim any hostility. A long and very free conversation then ensued, the most important parts of which were the following:

Major Snead impressed upon me the overwhelming influence of Gen. Price, and used the expression that even with the limited opportunities I had as yet had of learning the feeling among Missourians, I must have seen that "in fact, Gen. Price is the State of Missouri," that I should support his advancement, cultivate his friendship, etc., etc. To my inquiry how he proposed to continue the State government in the event of my death, he said the remedy was very simple; Gen. Price would order or invite an election for Provisional Governor by the Missourians within the Confederate lines. To my inquiry how the government would be represented in the interim before the result of that election should be known, he gave no direct answer. My allusion to the advantage of having the provisional government emanate from that elected by the whole people of Missouri rather than from the small remnant within the Confederate lines, he broadly stated that these latter constituted the true constituency, and asked me by way of argument, and with an air of indignation, if on our recovery of the State, I would permit the Unionists, citizens under our old constitution, to vote in reconstituting the government? I answered that it would be time enough to decide that question after we had recovered the State, and that even then its solution, consistently with our constitution, would perhaps have to be sought in the inherent right of the surviving branch of the old government, to determine whom it would *recognize* as the coordinate branches, and as incident thereto, define the constituency it (in this case the executive) would recognize as entitled to elect those branches; and that, that inherent right had been considerably strengthened by the "Rebellion Act."

In the course of that conversation, I with frankness and courtesy stated to Major Snead that I was disposed to aid in obtaining for Gen. Price full scope for his legitimate and patriotic abilities; that, without admitting him to be "in fact, the State of Missouri," I appreciated his popularity and weight; that I had expected from him and his staff, some reciprocation of my successful effort at Richmond to have him transferred to Arkansas with a distinct view of his leading an army into Missouri; but that on the contrary, I had met factious opposition from his staff, and, to say the least, indifference, or tacit acquiescence in it, from the General himself; that I had not the slightest objection to any reasoning criticism of my official acts, but that exciting factious clamour or underhanded intrigues was a different thing, and in time of war could not be submitted to; that I had both the power and the will to war upon it; that I had come to the Trans-Mississippi Department with the express pledge of the President to support my legitimate authority as Governor of Missouri; that he, Major Snead, and Gen. Price's staff generally, had always been the focus of opposition to the authorities above them; that I would be sure to find out any attempt of theirs to weaken my legitimate official authority and influence; "and the moment I find it out," I added, "you may rest assured that I can and will crush it like an eggshell in a hand of iron." The major protested against the energy of my expression, and assured me that the staff had no such factious disposition. I remarked that I was glad to hear it, but it was well for them and me to understand each other, and he was at liberty to let them understand that I was not of a temperament to exhibit towards them the moderation shown by Gov. Jackson and President Davis under similar circumstances.

The conversation was thoroughly good humored on both sides; my remarks were made, and I believe Major Snead received them, not as in a menacing spirit, but simply as a candid warning of the consequence of a rupture. But the remark about "crushing" got somewhat generally known, and excited the ire of some of Gen. Price's staff. On an inquiry of some friends of what I meant by it, I said that if Gen. Price's staff should begin any cabal against my legitimate authority, I should on his failing to stop it, ask Gen. Smith to order the offending officers to the Cis-Mississippi country, or assign them to duty on the Rio Grande.

I accompanied Gen. Holmes[62] to Jacksonport, meeting there Gen. Price and Major Cabell and making acquaintance of Major McLean, Capt. Celsus Price, "old Capt. Price," Major John Taylor and others of Gen. Price's staff,[63] of Col. James Mitchell, Capt. [Alonzo W.] Slayback and others; and also meeting Gen. [William Henry] Parsons, Major John F. Howes, Col. Clay Taylor and many others, the principal part of the Missouri troops being collected about Jacksonport. The morning of my arrival I called on Gen. Price at his office; in the night he sent his band to serenade me; the next or the same day he called on me at my lodgings, and in a day or two afterwards I called on him at his; on this last courtesy Major Cabell said to me he was very glad I had shown it, as it contributed greatly to restore good feeling in Gen. Price towards me. In conversation Major C. further said that on his showing Gen. Price my letter of [——], he had expressed great surprise and regret, and had remarked that he had not thought me so "touchous."

Altogether my coming up to the army, my personal moderation combined with the declared intention neither to avoid nor to seek quarrel with Gen. Price and his partisans, and my marked courtesy to Gen. Price himself, had smoothed over all past discord and I anticipated harmonious action between them and myself in the future.[64]

Some incidents however, occurred there to produce on me unpleasant impressions as to the state of feeling and discipline at Gen. Price's headquarters. Some subaltern Confederate officer in his journey to Jacksonport recently had, without the slightest authority and contrary to law, "impressed" an elegant private carriage and horses of a secessionist gentleman and after using it had sent it back in a damaged condition. Gen. Price himself related to me the incident in a conversation we had on the lawlessness in the army; and he added, with the tone of a man who felt he had exhibited very great energy, "I determined to make an example of him, and I immediately ordered him to refund the gentleman what it had cost him to repair the carriage." I made no remark, but thought to myself that if that was "making an example" what would leniency be?

While visiting some of Gen. Price's officers at his wagon camp, the conversation turned on the Unionists of Missouri: "Old Capt. Price," a very worthy relative of Gen. Price, and a complete echo of his talk, being constantly near him, was present, and also Col. Clay Taylor; I forget who were the others. They were both very savage in expressing their intentions of personal vengeance on some they respectively named as having done them wrongs. Without entering into any discussion, I suggested to them that the treatment of the Unionists was a most grave and delicate question which the Confederate and State governments alone could decide; and that I believed even they, Col. Taylor and Capt. Price, would be in such excellent humor on being restored to their homes, that they would forgive even their worst enemies; I may also have added (though I am not positive), that at any rate, I trusted they were too good citizens to disturb any one the Governor of the State might pardon. But Capt. Price declared there was one man whom he would avenge himself on anyhow; and Col. Taylor said there was another whom he also would take personal vengeance on in any event. I did not continue the discussion, but it led me to use, in my address to Parson's division on the following Sunday, June [——], very energetic language in regard to the respect due the executive pardoning power, and the free use I was willing to make of it in bringing the Unionists to our support. In conversation about that period I also remarked our true policy was conciliation, and that if even Gen. Frank Blair should join us, I should be for giving him a military command.

A third incident was this: I visited the hospital at Jacksonport and finding the bread very bad, spoke very freely about it to the physician in charge. This visit becoming known, some of Gen. Price's staff made sport of it, as an absurd and undignified occupation for a Governor to be busying himself with. On inquiry, I learned that Gen. Price never visited his hospitals.

Helena, Arkansas, June 1863

Gen. Price agreeing with me that it was unnecessary for me to accompany the army to the attack on Helena,[65] I returned to Little Rock. That ill judged, ill planned, and ill conducted campaign originated with Gen. Price. Major Cabell told me that it was that of which he (Major C.) wrote in his letter to me of [——]. Gen. Holmes vacillated as to its propriety and did not finally decide on it until he came to Jacksonport, and held a consultation with Generals Price and [John Sappington] Marmaduke, who both advised it. Soon after the consultation, Gen. Price related to me that at its close, Gen. Holmes said to him in substance, "Gen. Price, I determine on this expedition with some fear of an unsuccessful result; you have great weight and popularity, and if the expedition fails, I rely on you to sustain the action taken in ordering it." Gen. Price assured him he would do so.[66]

After my return to Little Rock, the news of our failure at Helena, and of the fall of Vicksburg, began to reach that city about the same time. The first detailed intelligence came in a letter (or verbal report, I forget which), from Gov. Flanagin of Arkansas, who had accompanied Gen. Holmes; his account was published in a Little Rock paper, and because it rather indirectly hinted at a failure on the part of Gen. Price, the more noisy (chiefly "bomb proofs") among the Missourians immediately set about raising the stereotype cry of "injustice to Gen. Price;" but as the alleged "injustice" simply consisted in doing justice to Gen. Fagan[67], an officer very popular with both Missourians and Arkansans, the attempt was rather a failure. Soon after came a letter from Major Snead, in which

⇥ M. Jeff Thompson. ⇤
Photograph, 1861–1865. Missouri History Museum.

he gave his version of the affair, remarking that "as usual, Gen. Price took the fortification assigned to him to take." This key note was diligently repeated by Gen. Price's partisans, but it also failed to have any material effect in sustaining him against the pretty generally circulated charge that his failure to attack in time had occasioned the defeat. This revived the accusation that Beauregard, Van Dorn, and others under or with whom he had served, had found fault with him for slowness in executing orders. As I never heard this before, and on the contrary had supposed Gen. Price to be a very pushing commander, I endeavored to inform myself on the subject. The only positive information I got was from Gen. M. J. Thompson, who gave me a circumstantial account of what passed under his own observation on some occasion, I forget precisely which, when Beauregard at Corinth had planned a decisive movement, and the inertness, indifference, and slowness of Gen. Price and his staff rendered it abortive. Gen. Thompson stated that his disgust on that occasion was the main cause of his leaving Price's army and returning to Arkansas in 1862.

I took no part in the controversy about Helena, beyond advising in general conversation when the topic was introduced, that the crimination and recrimination should cease. I gathered the nature and scope of the controversy from such conversation as I heard, or from statements of my officers and others as to what was the "general talk." Whatever the real merit of the controversy, it was very evident that Gen. Price's "popularity" had no great strength when it ran counter to the "popularity" of some other officers, as, in this case, that of Gen. Fagan.

But in the deep anxiety for the future after the fall of Vicksburg, and the expectation raised by the announcement that Gen. E. K. Smith was about to come to Little Rock, the controversy about Helena seemed entirely to die out. Gen. Holmes and Gen. Price had returned to Little Rock, and the former falling sick, the command of the District devolved on the latter. But Gen. Smith, soon after his arrival, somewhat surprised me by communicating to me that Gen. Holmes and Gen. Price themselves were on the eve of a most dangerous quarrel, and that he had advised Gen. H. to seek counsel from me, as an impartial person, friendly both to himself and Gen. P., having the special confidence of the President and also of him, Gen. Smith. In this, Gen. H. had promptly assented and through Gen. S. requested me to visit him in his sick chamber; I at first hesitated to accept the invitation to intervene in the quarrel, but Gen. S. expressing great confidence in my reputed skill in "harmonizing" discordant element, and appealing to my sense of public duty, I consented to see Gen. Holmes.

Gen. Holmes gave me his account of the attack on Helena and read me his proposed official report.[68] It censured, though not acrimoniously, Gen. Price for not commencing the attack in time to sustain Fagan, and rather by inference than direct assertion laid on Gen. Price the responsibility for the failure to take Helena. His report concluded with the statement that he "ought to have taken Helena," but was prevented from doing so by his orders not being strictly carried out. In his oral statement he blamed Price for lukewarmness and for neglect of duty in being too far behind his division in the attack; he stated that when he, Gen. Holmes, rode into the fort captured by that division, Gen. Price was neither with it nor in sight. He also charged cowardice on Gen. McRae[69] of Arkansas, and complained that though Gen. Price had himself originated the charge, he had omitted it in his report of the operations of his division at Helena, and was now endeavoring to screen Gen. McRae from censure.[70] Gen. Holmes was moderate in his language in reference to Gen. Price, though he expressed a total want of confidence in his military ability, and spoke of Major Snead, as "the brains of the entire Price concern."

I declined to give Gen. Holmes any counsel until after I had carefully examined the reports of his division commanders and his own; he gave them to me for that purpose. Fagan's[71] showed that he commenced his attack at daybreak, as ordered, but failed because exposed to the fire of the fort which Price should have attacked at the same time, but which he did not engage until about an hour afterwards. Gen. Marmaduke's report[72] was somewhat confused, but clearly showed that his failure was accelerated, if not caused, by some mismanagement or misunderstanding on the part of Gen. McRae. It seemed to be rather a misunderstanding than anything else. Gen. Price's report[73] was in Major Snead's best and most adroit style of quiet but effective puffing. While a careful comparison of parts of it showed, yet a more general perusal of it concealed, the fact that though ordered to attack at dawn, Gen. Price did not do so until nearly an hour afterwards. Contrary to what I had understood to be Gen. Price's regular habit, the report was profusely complimentary to many officers, including all of his staff, by name, and in that respect most suspiciously resembled an effort to get up a "mutual admiration" society in support of an "agreed case" report of the campaign; for most of the officers named had evidently simply performed their routine duty, without any extra distinction.

While examining those reports, I had before me a St. Louis Democrat containing the detailed narrative of the affair sent in by an eyewitness at Helena. It conclusively showed the folly of ever having attacked the place, and that Price was an hour behind Fagan in the attack; it also gave details which both Price's report and Holmes' concealed, of the terrible blunder by which Col. [Levin M.] Lewis and hundreds of others of Parson's command were either slaughtered or made prisoners.

On my walk back from my first conversation with Gen. Holmes above related, at night, Gen. Price stopped me as I passed by his lodgings, and asked to converse with me. He had been informed that Gen. Holmes accused him of cowardice in not being with his division as it entered the fort at Helena, and was naturally incensed. I told him to disbelieve the report, and that his character for personal courage was so well established that he could afford to disregard it. In order to have his unbiased statement, I did not on our first conversation mention to him that Gen. Holmes had had a conversation with me about Helena; but as soon as (a day or two afterwards) I had formed an opinion on the Helena business, I let both him and Gen. Holmes know that they had both consulted me. Then also I told Gen. Price that I did not understand Gen. Holmes, in his conversation with me, as even insinuating any want of courage, but merely slowness in not being with his troops in the assault. In my subsequent conversations with Gen. Holmes, I did not ask him whether he meant to make any such charge; I considered it preposterous and not worth inquiring about.

In the same conversation with Gen. Price, he gave me his version of the Helena affair, and explained in the following, to me perfectly satisfactory way, his not entering the fort with his division. While his division was attacking, he and his staff remained concealed in a ravine separated by a ridge from a view of the fort, his officers observing on the ridge and keeping him apprised of the progress of his troops in the assault. He did not consider it his duty to expose himself unnecessarily, but as soon as the capture of the fort was reported to him, he mounted his horse and was proceeding towards the fort when, on reaching the crest of the ridge, he saw Gen. Holmes galloping towards the fort. He was about to do the same when one of his staff (I think it was Major John Tyler) suggested to him that he should, from delicacy, allow Gen. Holmes to have the éclat of being the first general officer to enter the captured works. Without any close reflection, he accepted the suggestion, and Gen. H. entered the fort before Gen. Price and even before Gen. Parsons, who commanded the attacking force. But both of these latter generals entered it immediately after Gen. Holmes, and were constantly under fire during the remainder of the contest.

The alleged cowardice of Gen. McRae was thus explained by Gen. Price. He, Gen. Price, seeing Gen. McRae going towards the rear in the direction of some felled timber, and suspecting shirking, sent Major McLean[74] towards him with a verbal order relieving Gen. McRae from command of his troops. On getting near Gen. McRae, Major McLean saw that he was merely engaged in rallying some of his men who had sought that shelter from the enemy's shells, and was soon leading them back to their brigade. Major McLean thereon returned to Gen. Price and stated those facts as reasons for not delivering the order; the general seeing his own mistake, approved of his adjutant's course.

In this conversation, Gen. Price was very much excited against Gen. Holmes, and in the course of his remarks said to me, "If Gen. Holmes attempts to degrade me, I'll put him in chains and send him to his master Jeff Davis." I put my hand on his knee, and in the most friendly tone, said to him, "My dear General, Gen. Holmes has no wish to degrade you, and could not do so even if he wished; but you do yourself great injury by such remarks; they amount to little when uttered, as now, to an old friend like me, who knows your ways and understands that by that language you intend merely an energetic expression of a resentment to a supposed injury. But do you remember that at Jackson, Mississippi, last winter, and before you could know whether Holmes was your enemy or not, you made that same remark before a considerable company, in which was Mr. Cooper, who is a strong friend of Mr. Davis, and may have felt himself at liberty to communicate that remark to some other friend of Mr. Davis at Richmond?" Gen. Price was most markedly taken aback by my question, and said he had no recollection of the circumstance; but he acknowledged his remark to be hasty, and became more moderate in his expressions.

There were several conferences between Gen. Holmes and me, and between Gen. Price and me, with a view to compose matters between those two officers. After reading the reports of the Helena matter and receiving the accounts of them both, I advised Gen. Holmes to call Gen. Price's attention to the omission in his report to account for the hour's delay in his attack. Holmes said this was contrary to military usage; each officer made his report as he thought fit, and the superior, if he found anything wrong, could comment in his own report, or prefer charges, but not ask for an amended report. This principle of red tape circumlocution gave me a flood of light on the condition of the Confederate service; but Holmes said Gen. Price would make a supplemental report, or as a courtesy to him, he, Gen. Holmes, would embody in his own report whatever fact Gen. P. would furnish him in explanation of that disastrous delay. I stated to Gen. Holmes that Gen. Price had given as the main cause of the delay the desertion, through fright or treachery, of the guides who were to conduct his division.

After this (second) conversation with Gen. Holmes, I saw Gen. Price, and advised him to adopt one or the other of Holmes' suggestions, my own decided opinion being that he should make a supplemental report or, if admissible, withdraw that sent in and substitute another. Among the reasons I gave him for that advice was that he owed it both to himself and his division to explain their being an hour behind Fagan in commencing the attack. He took the advice under consideration, and the next day informed that he had concluded to make no change in his report. He gave no reason for this decision. I thereon apprised both him and Gen. Holmes that as I had to leave at once for the conference to which Gen. Smith had invited the Trans-Mississippi Governors, I could not continue my mediation in their dispute. I never ascertained how it ended.

Either during the period of my mediation above described, or just before it, Gen. Price paid a visit to Gen. Holmes, and in his elation of it to me stated that some remarks of Gen. Holmes had irritated him, and that he thereon "skinned him." Apprehensive of the injurious effect of it, I inquired of Gen. Holmes about the conversation; but he described it as perfectly courteous, with no incident of any irritating nature, as far as he knew, to either of them. It reminded me of Gen. Price's "skinning" President Davis; but I never could discover what kind of talk Gen. Price meant to describe by that expression. Whatever it was, Gen. Price never seemed conscious that to use it was both to boast and to confess to a discourtesy, in the case of two men, neither of whom would put up with one.

During this period of Gen. Price's command at Little Rock, an incident occurred to throw additional light on his notions of discipline. During one of my visits to him at his office, Col. Schnabel,[75] of Rolla, Missouri, was brought in under arrest. The officer having charge of him presented the papers relating to the arrest, but Gen. Price asked [for] an oral explanation in regard to it. From the statement(s) of both it appeared that Col. S. was endeavoring to raise a command for himself in Northern Arkansas, and had impressed supplies to feed his recruits. As he had no authority to do so, and it was against both general orders and an express act of Congress, the Confederate commander in the section where

Col. S. was recruiting, arrested him and sent him up to Little Rock for trial. Col. S. frankly admitted the impressments, and set up no authority to make them, but said he was unaware of the general orders or act of Congress. After reflecting a moment and examination of the papers, Gen. Price turned to Col. Schnabel, and with his most benevolent style of countenance, and affectionate tone, said to him, "I have known you a long time Colonel; you served under me in the Missouri State Guard; and I don't believe you would intentionally violate the law or do any-

E. Kirby Smith.
Photograph by E. and H. T. Anthony, 1861–1865. Missouri History Museum.

thing wrong; I therefore discharge you from arrest." Col. S. thanked the general for his decision and disclaimed all intention of doing anything wrong. The office in charge of Col. S. seemed utterly taken back by the decision, and with an air as if he feared he might have to change places with the prisoner, explained in an apologetic tone, that he had merely obeyed orders in bringing Col. S. to Little Rock, and was not to blame for his share of the transaction. Gen. Price reassured him and the two left the room. Gen. Price resumed the interrupted conversation with me, but I never learned whether any formal written order was ever made in the case, or whether any reparation or compensation was ever ordered to be made to the farmers whose property had thus been illegally taken. But of course no reform of the plunder system of the (generally self-constituted) recruiting officers in North Arkansas and South Missouri could be expected under such management at headquarters. The only palliation of Gen. Price's looseness in such matters was that, as far as I could learn, Gen. Holmes was no better, and Gen. Price was merely temporary commander of the district. But as Gen. Price was well known to follow only his own opinion in military management, that looseness was evidently a defect of his own, and not at all an act of deference to his commander.

Before leaving Little Rock I advised Gen. E. K. Smith that, on account of the severe illness of Gen. Holmes, Gen. Price should be left for some time in command of the district, and Gen. Holmes be urged to go to the Hot Springs for the rest of the summer to recruit [*sic*]. This advice was taken, and I accordingly apprised Gen. Price that he might consider himself as likely to have charge of affairs in Arkansas, and I advised him to prepare for the expected Federal expedition against Little Rock.[76]

Little Rock, Arkansas, August 1863

After the Marshall conference,[77] I remained several days at Shreveport with Gen. Smith, and during my stay, he received from Gen. Price the most encouraging dispatches and telegrams in reference to his ability, with the troops already at Little Rock, to defeat [Union major general Frederick] Steele's attempt to capture it. One of these telegrams I advised Gen. S. to give to the Shreveport newspapers, merely to relieve the public anxiety; and it was accordingly published. It proved afterwards very opportune in relieving Gen. S. from all responsibility for the loss of Little Rock, when some of Gen. Price's partisans got up partially a report that he had been left without the reinforcements he had demanded from Gen. Smith.[78]

While I was at Shreveport a report came that Gen. Holmes was about to return to Little Rock and resume command. I had lost all confidence in Holmes' military capacity, and on that account and the obvious impolicy of a change of commanders in the midst of a campaign, I urged Gen. Smith to give Holmes positive orders to remain retired until the Little Rock affair was over. Gen. Smith seemed reluctant to do so; but (whether from his orders or advice, or from his own sense of propriety, I never knew precisely) Gen. Holmes, though he returned to Little Rock, did not resume command; he however gave Gen. Price his advice in the operations.

On my journey back to Little Rock, I stopped at the camp my staff had retired to near Arkadelphia, and there met Gen. Kimmel and Col. Polk, lately from the former place. They both brought from Gen. Price's headquarters, most encouraging accounts, and were of the opinion that Steele would soon retire. I was therefore completely thunderstruck on learning, as I was proceeding to Little Rock, that it had been evacuated.[79] I met on the road Senator Robt. W. Johnson of Arkansas who, as volunteer aide of Gen. Price, had been with him throughout the short campaign. He was very bitter in his language about the loss of the city, and believed it could have been successfully defended. In the course of his remarks, he said that either Price or Kirby Smith were to blame for it, and that one of Price's staff (I think, Major Snead) had told him that Smith had not sent the reinforcements Price had asked for. I apprised Col. Johnson of the dispatches and telegrams received at Shreveport, and of the reports brought by my officers who met me at Arkadelphia. This satisfied him either that he had been misinformed or that Price had asked for the reinforcements too late for them to be sent.

While the army lay near Arkadelphia, the universal dissatisfaction of the Arkansans with Gen. Price, and his almost total loss of military prestige even among the Missourians became very apparent. It was currently reported that Gen. Holmes and *all* the general officers under Price, at Little Rock except Gen. [Daniel M.] Frost, considered the evacuation a blunder, and that Steele could have been beaten back with great disaster to him. At various times since, I ascertained from Holmes, Fagan, Marmaduke and Parsons that they did hold that opinion; the official report of the Federal officers almost conclusively shows that it was correct, or at least that the evacuation was precipitate and unnecessary at the time. A feeble attempt was made to shift the responsibility of Price's blunder on to Gen. Frost, by asserting that Gen. Price was unduly influenced by his military opinions; Frost himself being generally considered over cautious and inclined to retreats. I think Col. John W. Polk informed me of that defense; but it was soon abandoned as it evidently did Gen. Price more harm than good as it represented him as under tutelage to an officer of such little reputation as Gen. Frost. Gen. Price himself, tacitly almost admitted his blunder, explained it to me by stating that all the reports he

⊷General Daniel M. Frost, Missouri State Militia.⊶
Photograph by J. A. Scholten, ca. 1860. Missouri History Museum.

could get of Steele's forces represented them as greatly superior in numbers to his; I think they gave the number as eighteen thousand, while Price's force was about nine or ten thousand; and on my asking him if the scouts and spies who brought him those false reports were of his own choosing, or merely inherited from Holmes, he jumped at this additional defense, and said that they were the latter. But as the brigade and division commanders, and the army generally, seemed not to have over estimated Steele's forces; and as the statements of persons coming from Little Rock, and finally the authoritative report in the Federal newspapers, gradually convinced everybody, that the attacking army was very little superior, if indeed it was equal, in effective force, to that which, in some sort of moral panic, Price had ordered precipitately to evacuate the city; the blow to his military reputation was crushing.

The reaction on his popularity was equally marked. Major E. C. Cabell, in conversation with me about that time, on the renewed quarrel between Price and Holmes, remarked to me that to his great surprise and mortification the troops, even the Missourians, evidently were wholly indifferent about it, and that he feared Price was losing his popularity. Col. Colton Greene told me that his (Price's) hold on the confidence and affection of the troops was so feeble, that should his enemies think it worth while to take the trouble, it might be destroyed altogether. I remarked to each of those gentlemen, that no body had any interest in injuring Price, as the quarrel between him and Holmes about Helena and Little Rock was generally regarded as a mere personal squabble; but that Gen. Price had extraordinary recuperative skill, was an experienced popularity seeker, and would quietly but actively electioneer himself into a good part, if not all, of his old popularity with the troops. Conversing on the subject with my aide, Col. Cundiffe, he told me that on the retreat from Iuka, he noticed even stronger manifestations against Price than had occurred in reference to Helena and Little Rock, the murmurs and even curses being so loud, that Price seemed entirely played out; but he and his staff set to work, with their wonderful skill, and he became in two or three months, seemingly as popular as ever.

Retaining my opinion that that popularity should be cultivated within safe limits, as a means of drawing recruits in our ever contemplated expedition to Missouri, I did all I could to sustain him, without taking any part in his quarrel with Holmes. I increased both in public and private, my manifestations of respect and friendship. Visiting him one day, he took me aside and remarked with some feeling, "Governor, whenever I am in trouble, I feel like coming to you for advice." I said he could rely on my sincerity and friendship, and then he entered into a long detail of his controversy with Holmes. I gave him the advice, and he agreed to follow it (and did so) that he should bear with patience any annoyance he might feel at continuing to serve under Holmes; that for some time past I had been convinced of Holmes' unfitness for command in the West, and had been quietly but determinedly endeavoring to have him relieved, and either Gen. Price put in command or some officer sent there whom Gen. Price could pleasantly serve under; and that, without awaiting the result of my efforts at Richmond, I would at once make a strenuous effort to induce Gen. Smith, then expected to arrive at Arkadelphia, to take the responsibility of removing Holmes, and leaving Gen. Price in command, until the President could be heard from. Gen. Price seemed perfectly satisfied with this course.

On Gen. Smith's arrival very soon thereafter, I had a long conversation with him to the effect previously stated to Gen. Price. I offered to relieve him of responsibility in the matter, as far as I could, by making him an official communication, as Governor of Missouri, and even as chairman of the committee of Trans-Mississippi Governors asking him to relieve Gen. Holmes and giving my reasons therefore; and I offered to take with the President the whole responsibility of the transaction. My own observations to Gen. S. and his own more recent interview with Gen. Holmes had greatly shaken his confidence in the military capacity of that officer but he still retained enough to make him hesitate to take the bold step, especially with an executive as jealous of his prerogative as Mr. Davis, of removing a district commander enjoying the President's special confidence, in order to place the district under a general in whom the President was known to have no confidence at all. Besides, Gen. Smith doubted his authority to remove a district commander. But he consented to lay all the facts before the President and solicit authority to remove Gen. Holmes, and meanwhile he would assign Col. [J. F.] Belton to be Holmes' chief of staff, in the hope of his supplying some of the glaring defects in the administration of the district. I communicated at once to Gen. Price the substance of the conversation between Gen. Smith and myself, and though we were both disappointed with the result, he seemed disposed to follow my advice of keeping perfectly cool until the decision of the President could be had.

Soon thereafter, Gen. Price and his command were ordered southwards to the Little Missouri valley, and very soon thereafter I moved my own camp to the neighborhood of Washington, Arkansas. Just before leaving Arkadelphia, I heard of the death of Col. Peyton, Confederate Senator from Missouri, and on my visit to take leave of Gen. Holmes, I mentioned the fact, and inquired of him whom among the officers of the Missouri troops he thought would be the best person for me to appoint to the vacancy. He very soon answered, after considering a few moments, "There is your big man, Price, why do you not appoint him?" I remarked that he was needed in the army; and Gen. Holmes stating his reluctance, and in fact inability to advise me in a purely civil matter, the conversation changed to some other subject.

On my reaching my first camp near Washington (on the same or the next day), I rode into the town, and called on the Arkansas Senators, Johnson and Mitchell[80] who, as I have learned, had expressed an anxiety to see me; they informed me that it was to advise with me about the senatorial appointment, and I told them that I had come into town with the object of consulting them on that very subject. They both urged the appointment of Gen. Price. Their principal reasons were that it would relieve the district of the difficulty arising from the Price and Holmes quarrel; that Gen. Price would from his position and popularity, be a kind of representative of the wants of the whole Trans-Mississippi Department, and be able to enforce its claims; and especially, in reference to Missouri, that as they, especially Col. Johnson, felt confident of a recognition of the Confederacy very soon by France,[81] and consequently a treaty of peace with the U.S. The state should be represented in the Senate by a man of his great prestige in order to prevent a sacrifice of its interests in fixing the northern boundary line of the Confederacy. "If the treaty should propose to exclude Missouri from the Confederacy," said Col. Johnson, warming up, "imagine the effect of Gen. Price's rising up in the Senate and making a feeling appeal to it, talking of his sacrifices in leaving his home, his wounds and sufferings in the field, etc.!" I did not discuss these reasons, but told these gentlemen I would give them a careful consideration.

After deciding (that same day or the next), to appoint Col. Waldo P. Johnson[82] to the vacant senatorship, I sent for Dr. Mitchell to come and see me at my second camp near Washington, to which I had removed; Senator Johnson of Arkansas had meanwhile left for Red River. I told Dr. Mitchell of the appointment made, and gave him, to be communicated to his colleague, my reasons for not following his advice. They were mainly the following:

Gen. Price, whatever his military defects, was so connected in the public mind, especially among Missourians, with the idea of a campaign in Missouri, and so much was expected, in the way of recruiting there, from his popularity, that it was my fixed purpose to have him at least join in and if possible, command such an expedition which I fully expected would take place in the ensuing summer. For the same reason, the retirement of Gen. Price from the army, even to go to the Senate, would be regarded by many, especially as the fall of Little Rock seemed to bar an entrance into Missouri, as a proclamation of definitive abandonment of Missouri, as a State; any abandonment could not outweigh the force of that retirement; independently of that, Gen. Price had been so conspicuous in urging such an expedition, in season and out of season, that his resignation of a military position would be considered proof that he, himself, had given up all hope of such an expedition, and believed that the only chance for the recovery of the State to the Confederacy lay in diplomacy and the action of the Confederate senate. The effect of such conclusions in the public mind in Missouri itself, and even among Missourians in the Confederate army, might be very injurious. The relief Gen. Price's appointment to the vacant senatorship might give in the matter of the Holmes quarrel was not of much weight; that quarrel might be adjusted, did not effect the troops who were indifferent to it, and if persisted in, should be neutralized by the ordinary appliances of military discipline and control. Besides, I hoped Gen. Holmes himself would soon be transferred to some other field of duty, and the retirement of Gen. Price, instead of doing good in a military point of view, might do positive harm, by aiding to fasten Gen. H. on the district, in removing one of the reasons for transfer, viz., the difficulty of making him and Gen. Price act harmoniously. I told Dr. Mitchell that I knew this reason would not weigh with him, as he desired the continuance of Holmes in command in Arkansas; but that he must excuse my acting with reference to Missouri interests, convinced as I was, that the inclination of Gen. Holmes to a timid defensive policy and firm opinion against any campaign into Missouri, that as long as he commanded in Arkansas, we could not expect that bold policy which alone could retrieve our affairs in the Trans-Mississippi Department.

These military and political reasons, I stated to Dr. Mitchell far outweighed any which could be alleged in favor of Gen. Price's appointment to the vacant senatorship, and both he and Senator Johnson were wholly mistaken, from ignorance of Gen. Price's political career, as to the part he would be most likely to play in congress. As he was no debater, and with no aptitude for legislature, he would be a cipher in the Senate in these two respects. But he had considerable skill in intrigue, and a gift of popularity with the people. The natures of him and Mr. Davis were intensely different, both of them irascible and with old causes of difference; it was therefore almost certain that Gen. Price, as a Senator, would soon be led into a blind opposition to the President. At the next election of Missouri congressmen, he would exert his influence to have Major Snead and others of his partisans elected representatives, and under his guidance, aided by skill and activity of Major Snead, the Missouri delegation, instead of yielding, as now, a discriminating and independent support to the President, would become the focus of a most injurious agitation against him, under the shade and protection of Gen. Price's popularity. As Dr. Mitchell and Col. Johnson, as well as my self, believed that the best policy was to sustain the President, they would give full weight to those reasons.

To the argument of Col. Johnson in reference to a treaty of peace, I gave more weight than to those last mentioned, and had carefully considered it. The picture Col. J. had drawn of an appeal to the Senate by Gen. Price on account of his sacrifices, etc., was, however, wholly imaginative. It was very generally known to Missourians, and probably to others, among whom might be some senators, that instead of making sacrifices in the war, or losing property, Gen. Price and his family were better off than they would have been had the war never taken place. He had brought out to Texas all his slaves, had received in gold in 1862 his pay as a major general commanding the Mo. State Guard, and in the Confederate service the presents his popularity brought him had enabled him to live certainly on less than his pay; while his son, Gen. Edwin Price, was making a fortune in the tobacco business at his father's old establishment and none of the property of either in Missouri had been disturbed. Therefore, far from his producing any effect in the Senate by such an appeal, Gen. Price would only run the risk of being retorted on by Senators who had really sustained losses.

But on more general grounds, I recognized the force of Col. Johnson's suggestion, that in the adjustment of a boundary line advantage should be taken of Gen. Price's influence to obtain the best terms for Missouri. This could be done without sacrificing any of the advantages to result from his now remaining in the army; and a bird in the hand should not be given up for two in the bush. I had no faith whatever in a speedy peace, but should I be mistaken, and a treaty come before the Confederate Senate prior to Feby. 22nd, 1864, North Missouri, the principal bone of contention in such an event, was represented by Senator Clark, and had all its three congressional districts represented. Gen. Harris, one of its representatives being specially influential with the President; of the four districts of South Missouri, but two were represented, and one of them by Mr. Vest, also of influence with the President, and from his residence on the Missouri River, inclined to stand up for the retention of North Missouri within the Confederacy. Gen. Price could be appointed by me a commissioner to proceed to Richmond to advocate the interests of his section; and with him as an outsider, Messrs. W. H. Johnson and [John B.] Clark in the Senate would be even stronger than Clark and Price in the Senate and any one else as a commissioner; for while Johnson would acquire weight by being in the Senate, Gen. Price as commissioner of the State would have just as much influence as if he were a Senator, except as to having a vote on the treaty itself.

In this last mentioned respect, it was also my duty to give South Missouri its due weight. It comprised 4/7 of the population and nearly 2/3 of the territory of the State. It would be very possible that the question of peace or war might depend on our consenting to give up North Missouri in exchange for South Kansas, or even making the Osage the boundary. While I was not prepared to form in advance any opinion on such an alternative, I would be doing wrong in depriving South Missouri of an equal voice on that subject in the Senate; it should have its senator there to vote as he might judge best. To appoint Gen. Price would be to give North Missouri both senators, and in him moreover a politician vitally interested in having the boundary go north of the Missouri River; for by an unlucky wording of the Confederate constitution he would be for the next fourteen years, ineligible to the Presidency to which he aspired, unless the town of his residence in North Missouri should be included in the Confederate territory. I did not suppose that any treaty of peace Mr. Davis would sanction would fail to obtain the requisite majority in the Senate; but should a treaty sacrificing some territory in order to obtain peace and independence for the great body of the Confederacy be opposed in the Senate, it would not be just that it should be defeated by my giving North Missouri an additional Senator, personally and specially interested to reject it.

Should, however, such a treaty not come before the Senate until after Feb. 22, 1864, there would be another chance of following the counsel of Col. R. W. Johnson in regard to appointing Gen. Price. On that day, the seat of Senator Clark would become vacant, and as Congress would not meet, probably, until the succeeding fall, there would be ample time to see if the prospect of a treaty would justify me in appointing Gen. Price. I had not considered, much less decided, whether I would or would not reappoint Senator Clark; but I would certainly feel justified in either leaving the vacancy for a reasonable time unfilled, or in filling it with some gentleman who would be more likely than Gen. Clark, to consent to resign in order to let Gen. Price take his place when a treaty question should arise. In such a question also, any advantage of having Gen. Price in the Senate would not be diminished by North Missouri's having an undue representation; and the objections on account of his possible opposition to Mr. Davis would also fall away almost entirely. A treaty would be acted on without much, if any, reference to the views of senators on the policy of the President during the war, and an election of a Senator by the legislature of Missouri, included in the Confederacy, would ensue immediately after a peace and relieve me of all responsibility in the matter. Even without reference to that, the attainment of independence would give Mr. Davis such prestige in the territory, whether large or small, securing that blessing, that no regular or considerable opposition to him would exist.

Apart from the question of having Gen. Price in the Senate to vote on a treaty of peace, the reasons of the appointment of Col. Waldo P. Johnson were decisive. It was a fixed rule in Missouri politics to distribute the Senators territorially, and that no one congressional district should have both the governor and a senator. I therefore could not appoint a St. Louis man. The late senator, Col. Peyton, was from the same section as Col. Waldo P. Johnson, and this latter was the last person elected by the Mo. legislature to the U.S. Senate. He was eminently qualified and a warm supporter of the President. Besides he was a friend of strict discipline in the army, and my observation of the legislature of the Confederate Congress had convinced me that it lacked strength in that respect.

I added that while, as Dr. Mitchell could see, I had most carefully considered the reasons of himself and his colleague, my own opinion still was, as expressed in my first address as Governor to the people of Missouri, that the Senate of the United States and of the Confederacy would, if the war ended in our independence, have very little to do, in fact, in determining the boundary. The right of secession being triumphant, the several states, and even parts of the States, would determine for themselves which federation they would join. The greater probability was that the unity feeling in the North would even lead more states there to ask admission into the Confederacy than it would choose to receive, and the probable result, as Hon. W. W. Boyce said in a speech in the U.S. Congress a year or two before the war, would be that the boundary would run between the Ohio River and the Lakes.

Dr. Mitchell expressed himself entirely convinced by my reasons, and knowing Col. Waldo P. Johnson personally, thought I could not make a better selection; he believed such would also be the opinion of his colleague, Col. R. W. Johnson, and of the public. He expressed much surprise at the facts, previously unknown to him, about the state of Gen. Price's private fortune.

About the period of my conversation with Dr. Mitchell, Major E. C. Cabell visited me with a letter from Gen. Price of [———] asking an interview with me offering to come to my camp (which was about 40 miles from his) to see me; Major C. explained that it was about the vacant senatorship which he advised me to offer to Gen. Price. I asked him if the General desired it; he answered that he believed he did, though he was not authorized to say so. I gave Major C. the military reasons I had stated to Dr. Mitchell for Gen. Price's remaining in the army; and informed him that the appointment was already made though kept secret in order not to increase the risk of the new senator's crossing the Mississippi River; the enemy, if aware of his rank might make extra efforts to capture him and object to release him if captured. I therefore did not communicate to Major C. the name of the appointee.

A few days after Major Cabell's visit, I received one from Judge [George C.] Watkins, volunteer aide on Gen. Holmes' staff. He urged the appointment on political grounds similar to those given by Col. R. W. Johnson, but made no allusion to the relief it would give in the Holmes imbroglio. I expressed to Judge Watkins, as I had done to Messrs. Mitchell and Johnson, and to Major Cabell, my doubts whether Gen. Price would consent to go to the Senate, as it would virtually shelve him; but Judge Watkins told me that in a recent conversation with him, Gen. Price had expressed a wish to retire from the army, as he found that at his age the hardships of campaigning were beginning to tell upon his constitution, and he needed repose; that this conversation had led him (Judge W.) to seek the interview with me. I told him the appointment was already made, though kept secret. I gave him the same military reasons I had given Major Cabell for my not offering the appointment to Gen. Price. In addition, I stated, that even if Gen. Price desired the senatorship, it was only from transitory discontent at his present position, and that, viewing him as indispensable in a Missouri expedition, I would do wrong in gratifying that discontent by tempting him to quit the army for the Senate. I told Judge W. that a sense of public duty was my guide in this matter, even at the risk of displeasing Gen. Price and his friends. "Suppose," I said, "I appoint him senator and he accepts. If no expedition to Missouri ever takes place, I might justly be blamed for shelving in the Senate its most prominent advocate; if one is made and fails, everybody, and with some semblance of justice, will say that it might have been otherwise had Gen. Price commanded it; even should it succeed, many would be found who would say, I had taken advantage of a momentary discontent of Gen. Price to shelve him into the Senate, and deprive him of the glory of that success.[83] With my decided conviction that he ought to remain in the army, I cannot as executive of Missouri deprive her of the advantage of having him lead, or at least join in an expedition to the State; nor should I, as a public man, be expected, unless in a very clear case, to run the risk I have mentioned of having my judgment, and perhaps even my motives, severely criticized."

Judge Watkins seemed (and if I recollect rightly, expressed himself) satisfied with my reasons. The desire of Gen. Holmes' friends to settle the imbroglio, by getting rid of Gen. Price was very evident. Some coincidences of dates and movements, which I cannot recollect precisely now, made me inclined to believe (though I could not be certain) that Gen. Holmes himself had set the movement on foot by writing from Arkadelphia to Col. R. W. Johnson (his warm friend), at Washington, Ark., while I was journeying from the former place to the latter. Gen. Price subsequently (in his visit to my house at Marshall Texas the ensuing spring), [stated] that about the time Col. R. W. Johnson saw me at Washington, Ark., he had written to him (Gen. P.) expressing his desire to see him appointed senator. On the same occasion, Gen. Price told me he had not desired to fill that vacancy, or indeed to go to the Senate at all, as he was no debater.

Col. Waldo P. Johnson came to me at Shreveport on [——], 1863 to receive his commission as senator. As we both held the same opinion concerning the incompetency of Gen. Holmes, he readily consented to urge at Richmond the transfer of that officer. Col. J. had made, on his way to Shreveport a friendly visit to Gen. Price's camp. He related to me an incident which had occurred there, and which revived my attention to the Edwin Price matter, which I had heard very little of for some time past. On Col. J's recent visit to Gen. Price, Capt. Celsus Price had shown to him and others photographs of Gen. E. Price and his children which Gen. E. Price had recently sent to his father, through the enemy's lines (I believe through Memphis), Col. J. expressed his surprise that Gen. S. Price kept up any intercourse with his son whom Col. J. found in his recent visit to Missouri was universally regarded as having fully deserted to the Federals; and still more that Capt. Celsus Price should let the fact be known. He asked me if I knew anything which could throw light on the mystery, and I thereon related to him in secret what Dr. Pallen had told me, and I acquainted him, for his consideration in recommending promotions, or voting as a senator on nominations, with the line of policy agreed on in my conference with Mr. Benjamin the preceding spring. Col. J. substantially coincided with me in those views.

On [——], 1864, Gen. Price, on a journey back from a visit to his family in Texas, remained a day and night at my house in Marshall. Our conversation related mainly to the appointment of a successor to Senator Clark and the approaching summer campaign. The principal points are stated in my memorandum of those conversations.

I happened casually to be at Shreveport when Gen. Holmes sent to Gen. Smith an application to be relieved of the command of Arkansas. It was owing, as Gen. Smith told me, mainly to my arguments and pressing instances that he granted Holmes' request, and thus left Gen. Price to succeed him.

Major Howes, having reported to me that in addressing his troops on his return from Texas, Gen. Price had said to them that "if his counsels should be followed, he was confident they would pass next Christmas in St. Louis." I had with him a correspondence on the subject of his opinions concerning the coming campaign, and urged him to send his views to Gen. Smith. The latter showed me his letters (in the hand, and evidently the composition, of Major Snead), but I neglected to procure a copy of it. It, as well as Gen. Price's subsequent letter to me considerably impaired my confidence in Gen. Price's candor and military judgment. He asked for the recovery of Little Rock a force evidently greater than could be spared for the purpose, or even supported in the campaign; and it looked to me rather like a mere maneuver to enable him to say hereafter that Little Rock could have been retaken if his advice had been followed. His letter to me contained a flagrant misstatement of the facts of the Texas campaign, which he should have known as he was in that State at the time; and his theory of a future campaign was simply absurd and engendered a suspicion that he used military phrases he did not clearly comprehend. Still I had confidence that in an exclusively Missouri campaign his local knowledge would compensate for any deficiency in military capacity.

The spring campaign in Arkansas neither increased nor diminished in popular estimation, the military standing of Gen. Price, while it greatly added to the reputations of generals Marmaduke and Shelby, especially the latter. The escape of Steele from Camden and the battle of Jenkins' Ferry[84] excited considerable controversy in conversation; but the responsibility of those mishaps was so divided, at least in popular estimation, between Generals Smith, Price, and Fagan, that the general result of the campaign on Gen. Price's standing was as above stated. There was however, one indication that he had lost ground in it with the Arkansans. The *Washington [Telegraph]* (the sole Confederate newspaper in the State), in summing up the campaign, and giving merited praise to several officers by name made not even an allusion to Gen. Price. This brought out a complaining communication from some friend of his; and the editor only made the matter worse for Gen. Price by stating that he considered it unnecessary to name especially the district commander, as everyone would understand that he was entitled to the credit of the general result.

I had supposed that my standing by Gen. Price in his controversies with Holmes, and aiding him to get over the damage done to his reputation by the affairs of Helena and Little Rock, and my being almost the sole cause of his being left in command in Arkansas and thus having a chance to reinstate himself with military men and the public; that, in short, fifteen months steady and successful support of him from his arrival in Richmond to the end of the Arkansas campaign of the spring of

1864, had removed all the "jealousy" he had shown in the early part of 1863, and secured harmonious relations between us for the future, and indeed claims on his active support. But I was destined to find myself mistaken, as I had been a year before.

My refusal to reappoint Gen. Clark to the Confederate Senate had produced, even in advance of any suspicion even of who was the actual appointee, a determined effort on the part of Gen. C. and his friends, to administer to me what they called a "popular rebuke" by electing him to the house of representatives; of course everyone who had any grudge against me, or even against Mr. Davis or Gen. Smith whom I was known to maintain and be sustained by, joined in the effort, with a view to weaken me by having me appear "unpopular." The attempt signally failed, Gen. Clark being elected mainly by reports that all his opponents had withdrawn; but it led many unwarily to "show their hands."

In my consultation with Gen. Price in the preceding winter about Gen. Clark, he had freely admitted that Senator's defects, such as his fickleness, disregard of truth, and drinking habit, and also stated himself to be aware that at heart he was rather inimical than friendly to him, Gen. P. but he had advised me to reappoint him solely on the ground of mere expediency as regarded myself personally, to avoid making Gen. Clark an active enemy and having a political "fuss" on the subject. I had not asked him to take sides with me in the question of Gen. Clarke's successor, but I expected at least neutrality. But Col. J. W. Polk's letter to me of [———] showed that he was engaged, in his way, in giving fuel to the flame Gen. Clark was endeavoring to excite. I had learned during the preceding fifteen months to understand Gen. Price's peculiar tactics in such matters. Apparently neutral and retired, he would in fact exert a powerful influence by hints to his staff or "strikers," or remarks to persons likely to make them widely known. Col. Polk, at that time rather sore against me on account of my reduction of my staff, and his consequent resignation and a gentleman given to general and social conversation, was just the kind of a person Gen. Price would select for that purpose, on the supposition that that soreness would make him, though it did not, inclined to do me a disservice. I did not make any effort to learn whether Gen. Price had given his influence to Gen. Clark in any other way than by the remarks to Col. Polk. Indeed the announcement immediately after the election that I had appointed Col. Lewis turned the tide so completely, that the Clark fuss became a mere tempest in a teapot, and I lost all interest in tracing its ramifications. But the votes being all *viva voce*, the election returns showed that Clark obtained most support precisely in the quarters where Gen. Price had most influence and least support where he had least influence, as for instance in Parsons's division; and even in the brigade commanded by Gen. Clark's son, the father's vote was comparatively not as strong as in Gen. Price's body guard and other troops immediately near him. In remembering this general result I forget whether Gen. Price himself voted; my impression is that he voted for Clark, and voted early so as to set an example. From Col. Polk's account verbally to me afterwards, quite an excitement was got up in Gen. Price's immediate neighborhood about my "injustice to Gen. Clark;" Col. P. himself held tickets from him and electioneered for him at the polls.

This incident, and that disclosed in my correspondence with Major Cabell in relation to the report started by Dr. [——] one of Gen. Price's most confident officers, disclosed the continued existence of the old "jealousy" and of a disposition, at least on the part of Gen. Price's immediate surroundings, to be on the alert for what they would consider a chance to hit me a blow. But as these blows had always been fended off, I cared little for the covert hostility, and the overwhelming importance of the public interest made me entirely disregard it, and Gen. Price's "jealousy" in deciding on his share in future military operations.

Early in the preceding winter a letter came from Washington by flag of truce mail, to Richmond, addressed to Senator Clark of Missouri, by Hon. James S. Rollins[85], member from Missouri in the U.S. Congress, and covering a letter from Gen. Edwin Price to President Davis. In the letter to the President, Gen. E. Price stated that he desired to visit Texas to see his mother there and attend to some business; that President Lincoln had given his consent to the visit and the return of Gen. Price to Missouri; and he requested a safe conduct from Mr. Davis for the same purpose. The letter of Major Rollins to Senator Clark requested him to present Gen. E. Price's letter to Mr. Davis and use his influence to get the safe conduct requested in it. Major R. expressed continued regard for Gen. Clark, and advised him to abandon the Confederate cause, assuring him of a cordial reception should he return to his old home and friends in Missouri. These expressions Mr. Vest considered sarcastic, but I could not but regard them as sincere; for Major Rollins was entirely too polished a gentleman and too shrewd a man to request a favor and at the same time play off sarcasms on the person from whom he requested it.

The letter of Major Rollins came sealed, but was opened in the office for the exchange of prisoners (to which the letters by the flag of truce boat were always sent), and the letter to President Davis was at once forwarded to him. It was in the morning and, Congress being in session, the President sent to Mr. Vest at the House of Representatives, a message requesting to see him. He immediately walked over to the office of the President whom he found with some of his cabinet. He handed Mr. Vest the letter of Gen. E. Price to peruse, and after he had read it, said: "What do you advise me to do about it?" Mr. Vest after a moment's reflection, answered, "I decidedly advise you, Mr. President, not to grant the request." "Then," said Mr. Davis, "I have no further hesitation, I shall refuse it." This was all the conversation, but Mr. Vest said the President's manner was peculiar and expressive, as if the letter had seemed to him extraordinary and suspicious.

In the evening, and after that interview of the President with Mr. Vest, Senator Clark received the letter of Major Rollins, and mentioned it to a knot of the Missouri members, among whom was Mr. Vest, who thereon related what had passed between him and Mr. Davis. Thereon, Senator Clark stated (and, as Mr. Vest assured me, falsely) that Mr. Davis had consulted him before Mr. Vest, and he also had advised him to refuse the request of Gen. E. Price. Mr. Vest attributed this course of Gen. C. to his loose habit in that regard, and his impulse to counteract any impression that the President had more confidence in Mr. Vest than in him. Gen. Clark expressed also great indignation at the suggestion in Major R's letter. Mr. Vest thought this indignation arose from Gen. Clark's seeing that the suggestions were intended to be sarcastic. I thought differently, and feared that Major Rollins, an intimate political associate of Senator Clark in the old Whig party, understood him better than others, and had sincerely contemplated working on his well known turn for despondency, and opening the door for negotiating with him for a return to Federal allegiance.

Mr. Vest further related to me, that in his canvass for re-election to the Confederate Congress, he received a great number of letters to carry to the Trans-Mississippi Department, and among them one for Gen. S. Price from Major Thos. Price[86] at Selma; these without examining the address he placed with the others. On reaching the camp of Gen. Price's command, he proceeded to distribute them, and found one sealed without address. Presuming it to be to himself, he opened it, and commenced reading it, but soon discovered it to be a letter from Gen. Edwin Price to his father or Major Thos. Price (I forget which), and intended for perusal by the former; in it, Gen. E. Price was very severe on Mr. Vest for having, as he believed, prevented President Davis from giving him the safe conduct he had asked. Concluding that the letter was the one Major Price had given him for Gen. S. Price, he presented it to the latter and explained how he came to open it. Gen. Price expressed himself entirely satisfied with the explanation. "But," continued Mr. Vest in his narrative to me, "as I knew Gen. Price to be devoted to his sons, and rather vindictive, I thought it best to make an effort to counteract the effect of the letter on his mind." Therefore, Mr. Vest informed him that he had read the letter inadvertently as above stated, and he explained to him his action at Richmond on Gen. E. Price's application. On this, Gen. S. Price told him that he had acted rightly, and proceeded to explain the reasons and object of his son's return to Missouri, precisely as he had done at the time to Dr. Pallen, as related to me by the latter at Richmond in the winter of 1862–63. Gen. Price further told Mr. Vest that he had from considerations for his son's personal safety as well as to prevent the discovery of his plans, kept secret the fact that he had returned at the instance of his father; that although he, Gen. S. Price, knew that the circumstances had done them both great injury, he had patiently suffered the imputations against his son, and the suspicions of himself; that he felt that he could no longer do so; and that though he wished his explanation not to be generally circulated, lest it should become the subject of camp gossip among the soldiers or get into the newspapers, he did desire and authorized Mr. Vest to communicate it to President Davis, and such other persons as he, Mr. Vest, might think proper. Although I was not named as one, Mr. Vest considered that I should be made aware of all the facts.

Mr. Vest abstained from expressing to me any opinion of these facets and so did I to him. He stated, however, that all his information about Gen. E. Price's course in Missouri was to the effect that he had become a zealous Unionist, and was regarded as such universally by all parties in the State. I told Mr. Vest that such was also the uniform tenor of the information which I received. Mr. Vest was under the impression that Gen. S. Price had favored or at least had done nothing against his re-election to Congress. I told him that my own intelligence from Gen. Price's camp led me to believe that, on the contrary, he would have attempted to defeat him had there been any chance of doing so; but that from Gen. Price's habit of secrecy and of working through others, no certainty could be arrived at on the subject, though from his general habit of feeling, it might safely be presumed that he could not relish the re-election to Congress of so avowed and decided a friend of President Davis as Mr. Vest was.

This conversation with Mr. Vest occasioned me much anxious reflection. A comparison of the dates of Gen. S. Price's communication with his son in the fall of 1863, as discovered by Senator W. P. Johnson of his two months visit in Texas in January and February 1864, and of his son's application to President Davis in Dec. '63 or Jan. '64, pointed to the conclusion that they had arranged for a meeting in Texas that winter. On his way back from Texas, Gen. S. Price had remained a day at my house, and in our long, full, and confidential conversations in reference to the prospect of a campaign in Missouri, he had made not even the most distant allusion to his son. This, with his previous utter silence of that subject, indicted that their plans, whatever they were, were not such as they liked to communicate, even in secrecy, to the Confederate executive of Missouri. His authorization to Mr. Vest to explain the matter to the Confederate President showed that this high officer had also been kept in the dark on the subject. Gen. Edwin Price's asking permission to visit his mother, and not even hinting an expectation to meet his father, was also evidently a clumsy effort to conceal the design to confer with the latter. To complicate the matter still more, my secret intelligence from the North West, and the public action of the leaders of the Democratic Party there, conclusively established that the opposition to Mr. Lincoln's administration, and the conspirators against it (Knights of the Golden Circle, American Knights, etc.), aimed exclusively at the reconstruction of the old Union on a pro-slavery basis, and were as much opposed as Mr. Lincoln himself (if not more so) to acknowledge the independence of the Confederacy. While many public men expected and some desired at least a partial reconstruction of the old Union as a final result of the war, a premature movement, especially a military one, with that object could only have divided and weakened the Confederacy. As General Price was universally regarded, and even mentioned in the Southern Press, as the destined and perhaps already selected leader[87] of a military movement for a "North West" republic, united to or at least allied with, the Confederacy, the profound mystery of his operations through his son, without the sanction, or even knowledge of his military superiors, or the Confederate governments, State or general, demanded attention. The concealment from President Davis was the more remarkable as Gen.

Price in his interview with him in 1863 had been boastful of his means of doing great service in Missouri, and yet made no allusion to the aid he expected (as stated to Mr. Vest), from his son's undermining the State with a conspiracy to rise on his coming. It was also very evident that his explanation to Mr. Vest was only extorted by his danger of falling under grave suspicion, if he omitted it.

After careful reflection, I resolved to keep Mr. Vest's communication entirely secret although that gentleman, in the spirit of Gen. Price's authorization to him, had not placed any restriction on my discretion in extending it to others. To have taken any action on it, even unavowedly so, for instance, by giving Gen. Price some command distant from Missouri, would have produced a fuss on the part of himself and his partisans, and the public would have been left in the dark as to the real motive for the evident distrust of him. To have retained him in a command near Missouri, or placed him in a command in a Missouri campaign, but under some one else would have produce the same effect, and besides have irritated him at the very moment when it would be in his power to do mischief and perhaps even, from his "rule or ruin" disposition (which came out so clearly subsequently in his controversy with me, and his conspiracy to arrest Gen. E. Kirby Smith), have led him into some dangerous act of military insubordination. On the other hand, to trust him fully and sustain him, as long as the road of his ambition and that of the Confederate policy lay together; in other words, to continue him in chief command in Arkansas and get up an expedition for him to Missouri, but at the same time to surround him with subordinate generals exclusively devoted to the Confederacy, and not strictly subordinate (as the plan agreed upon between Mr. Benjamin and myself), would at the same time obtain for the common cause all the service he could render, gratify his ambition to every legitimate extent, avoid any "Price creation," so absurdly dreaded by the Richmond authorities, and provide reliable safeguards against any abuse by him, for purposes of more personal ambition of his opportunities in independent command. In short a *fide sed vide* policy seemed at once the most generous towards him, and the best for the common cause.

At the same time that I resolved on this policy of generosity and confidence, I wrote to Gen. Price himself, my letter of May 17, 1864.[88] Its objects were to exhibit my disposition to trust and oblige him, to elicit a frank explanation in return, and also by apprising him of the fact that his son was still an officer of the Missouri State Guard, attract his attention to the fact that any real adherence to the Federals might, in the event of our recovery of Missouri make his son amenable to my jurisdiction for the punishment of his desertion; though I had little hope of eliciting this last result in Gen. S. Price's mind, as his extreme confidence in his ability to control absolutely in Missouri affairs, would preclude his imagining even for a moment, that any executive of the State would ever dream of daring to send a son of his for trial before a Court Martial. The letter above mentioned was sent to Gen. Price by the regular military courier mail from Marshall; but I never received any answer.[89] As that mail at that time was extremely safe and regular, no letter by it to or from me having ever been miscarried, I have no doubt that my letter reached him, and that I would have received his answer had he sent one. Even after making allowance for his uncivil habit of not answering letters, I considered his silence an indication that there was much he wished to conceal in his relations with his son, Gen. Edwin Price.

The incident in relation to Dr. Wooten's[90] statement on the authority of Col. Norton (as receiving it from Gen. Price) to Major E. Cabell, of an (erroneously) alleged reflection by me on Major C; and the same physician's slander about my conversation with Gen. M. M. Parsons in relation to appointing him a Confederate Senator, appear from my correspondence on those subjects. Those incidents indicated a continuous covert and unscrupulous hostility towards me personally by Gen. Price's special partisans, and a disposition on his part (to judge at least by his acts), rather to shield them than to check it. In addition, I will mention the following particulars.

Gen. Price had not answered my letter to him in reference to the statement affecting Major Cabell, but on my reaching Camden, Ark. In August 1864, I determined, in justice to the friendly relations between Major C. and myself, that a thorough explanation should be had. I accordingly mentioned the matter to Gen. Price, who at once said that our conversations at Marshall in the preceding winter about my filling the vacant senatorship, Major Cabell's name had not even been mentioned. He even went so far as to say that he had no recollection of its being mentioned at all in any of our conversations on that occasion. In this he was mistaken, the facts being as stated in my letter to Major Cabell on the subject. This conversation (at Camden) took place in the porch of Gen. Price's house, only he and I being present. Soon afterwards, Major Cabell came in with others, and going with him into Gen. Price's room, I told him of Gen. Price's statement, and offered to call the General in to confirm it in person. Major C., though, stating himself to be extremely mystified in the matter, declined to have me do so, saying that he was perfectly satisfied. Had I then been aware of Gen. Price's recklessness in assertion or denial, I would have called him in and had him repeat to Major C. what he had just said to me. On one of the days immediately succeeding my arrival at Camden, Gen. Price and I were riding out together, and Dr. Wooten passing us saluted, but as I did not at once recognize him, I did not return the salute. Gen. Price, supposing that I intended deliberately to cut the doctor, began to palliate his conduct in the Cabell matter, stated that he was a very excellent man, meant no harm, etc., and would feel hurt by my cutting him; he (Gen. Price) asked me to be on courteous terms with Dr. Wooten. I explained to Gen. Price that I had not recognized Dr. W.; that though I considered him to have acted maliciously and falsely in the Cabell matter, I was naturally averse to quarrels, would forgive him, and as a mark of my deference to his (Gen. P.'s) wishes, would treat Dr. W. civilly. I accordingly did so in my subsequent visits to Dr. [William] McPheeters and Major Cabell, who both had quarters with Dr. W.

In June and July arose the question of a campaign to Missouri. Gen. Marmaduke paid me a visit at Marshall, and we discussed the subject fully, as well as the qualifications of Gen. Price and his position towards myself and others. Gen. Marmaduke, as the senior cavalry general from Missouri, desired to command a cavalry expedition into the State and that I should accompany him. He had a very low opinion of Gen. Price's military capacity, and believed him and his staff, so malignantly hostile to him, Gen. M., that if Gen. P. should command the expedition, he desired not to go with it. He expressed his belief that should he go,

John S. Marmaduke.
Photograph by Scholten, 1884–1886. Missouri History Museum.

a regular plan would be formed and carried out by them to ruin his military reputation, throw on him the blame of any disaster that might occur, and perhaps even have him killed or captured. I told him that I could not credit such unscrupulous hostility, but that should a grand expedition to Missouri take place, he would certainly have to accompany or command it; that I would go with it, and that I pledged myself to him that if any attempt should be made to do him injustice, I would officially take up his defense and see him righted.[91] He stated his firm conviction that Gen. Price cherished a bitter hostility to me; he did not give his facts or reasons, and I rather discouraged his doing so (it being a subject I desired to have no discussion about), stating that I could not allow the facts, even if correct, to influence my action as Gen. Smith's adviser; and that in determining whether to recommend Gen. Price for the command of the expedition (should one be resolved on), I would impartially weigh both the praises of him by his friends, and the almost universal opinion of regular military men that he had no military capacity whatever. The decided opinion of Gen. Marmaduke against Gen. Price's military capacity, the first time I had heard him express it, struck me the more forcibly as in answer to my inquiries about Fagan, Shelby, Clarke, Colton Green and other officers, he was loud in their praise, and exhibited a most marked absence of everything like personal sensitiveness or professional jealousy.

The evident reluctance of Gen. Marmaduke to serve under Gen. Price, and the civil consequences which might result from that circumstance; the difficulty of placing Gen. Marmaduke himself in command of all the cavalry in the Arkansas District, indispensably for the expedition, as to do so Gen. Fagan, an excellent officer and his senior in rank, would have to be relieved of his command of the Arkansas cavalry; the doubt of the expediency of placing Gen. Fagan himself in command of the expedition, as he had never been in Missouri, and his selection would excite the jealousy of the Missouri officers and troops, infested as they were with pestilent demagogues, whose stock in trade consisted greatly of appeals to State pride; and the doubt whether Gen. Price, even were his reputation gained in the command of infantry or of infantry and cavalry combined, a deserved one, was adapted to command a body composed exclusively of the latter; all induced me to think of some one else than the officers above named for the command of the contemplated expedition. To Gen. Shelby, otherwise perhaps the best officer in the Department for a rapid dashing expedition, a sort of a surprise campaign, want of rank was a bar, as he was the junior cavalry brigadier of the whole Trans-Mississippi Army. After the spring campaign of 1864 on the Red River, the reputation gained in it by Gen. Richard Taylor[92] had turned my attention to him, and I had even mentioned to him my hope to see him in a Missouri campaign. But meanwhile, politicians and local influence had got up a most uncalled for and injurious quarrel between him and Gen. E. K. Smith, resulting in his being ordered just about that time to the east of the Mississippi. Gen. [John B.] Magruder was considered indispensable in the southern portion of the Department, as second in rank in the Department, he should remain at a convenient proximity to the commander in chief, and not be sent on a distant expedition, and besides, an artillery officer in the old U.S. Army, he was not known to have any special qualifications for an exclusively cavalry command. My attention was therefore attracted towards Major General Buckner,[93] the fifth officer in rank in the Department, Gen. Smith, Lt. Gen. Taylor, and Major Generals Magruder and Price being his seniors.

As far back as July 1863, I had urged the Secretary of War (through Col. J. T. Thornton whom I sent on to Richmond about that time), to have General Buckner made a Lt. General, and sent to the Trans-Mississippi Department, Lt. General Holmes being recalled. On learning from me soon thereafter of the step I had taken, Gen. Smith urged the matter on the Richmond authorities. Our design was that Gen. Buckner, being second in rank to Gen. Smith, should practically assume the administration of the Trans-Mississippi Department, and leave the latter free to conduct operations in the field. With their customary slowness, the Richmond authorities delayed action on the matter for nearly a year, and then sent Gen. B. with only his old rank of Major General. A secondary reason of my own for asking for his transfer in 1863, was that in case any necessity should arise for displacing Gen. Price from command of the Missouri troops, or placing some one immediately over him in that command, Gen. B., popular with those troops and as a Kentuckian able to rely on the support of the large Kentucky element in them, would be specially fitted to neutralize any demagoguery Gen. P. or his partisans might attempt in such an event. The same reason now pointed him out for the command of the expedition, as in case it should not be given to Gen. Price, he and his friends would be sure to make a big fuss, and raise the cry of "injustice" to him.

Gen. Buckner being then on a visit to Marshall and not yet assigned to any command, I broached the subject to him, but he declined consenting for me to propose him to Gen. Smith for command of the Missouri expedition. He stated, with great modesty, that he distrusted his fitness for it; that his friends and himself considered him better adapted for organization of troops and administrative duties than for active campaigning, and that he preferred the original object for which he had been asked for by Gen. Smith, that of aiding in the administration of the Department.

Finally about the end of July 1864, Gen. Smith and I consulted in regard to the expedition, and the choice of a commander. Under all circumstances of the case I advised him to give Gen. Price the command, but to send with him the best division and brigade commanders and an unusually efficient staff.[94] Gen. Smith was reluctant to adopt this plan; speaking of Gen. Price's military ability, he said to me, "He is absolutely good for *nothing*," and in support of this opinion related to me several incidents of the campaign, under his own personal observation, against Steele about Camden in the preceding spring. He had instructed Gen. Price so to dispose his forces as to be able to check Steele in leaving Camden to effect a junction with [Nathaniel] Banks on the Red River, a movement known or suspected to be intended by Steele; and to guard the roads leading southwardly from Camden, in order that any movement of Steele in that direction might be promptly known. (It may be that Gen. Smith told me merely that he had apprized [sic] Gen. Price of the supposed or discovered plan of Gen. Steele, and expected from his common sense that he would take the precautions above stated.)

On Gen. Smith's going to Camden, he found those roads entirely unguarded, so that if Steele had left that town with the object of effecting a junction with Banks, he would have been undiscovered, or at least unchecked, until he could have secured a long start over Price; and of course Price's forces were sufficient for him to guard those roads without impairing the efficiency of his watch on the other outlets from Camden. On his arrival at the camp near Camden, Gen. Smith proceeded at once to Gen. Price's headquarters; he found him busy in being introduced, by a citizen, to the reinforcements Gen. Smith had sent him. Gen. Price stood on a slight elevation on the side of the road, and as each company of those troops marched by, the citizen pointing to the general, said to the company, "Gentlemen, this is General Price," on which the latter smiled and bowed, while the troops (strangers to Gen. P. and to the influence to which he owed his popularity, itself rather factitious than real) gave him a stare and passed silently on. Saluting him, Gen. S. passed on to his (Gen. P's) quarters, expecting him at once to follow; but after waiting awhile at his quarters, he sent for him, as he wished to learn from him at once the condition of military affairs around Camden. General S. was much disgusted by that most unmilitary exhibition of demagoguery in the midst of a vitally important campaign; of course the proper mode of a commander's making himself known to troops strangers to him is to review them. Other incidents, which I cannot more accurately remember, more related to me by Gen. Smith, all pointing to the conclusion, to which Gen. S. had come, that Gen. Price was not even a military man of some merit, greatly exaggerated by his partisans, but on the contrary entirely destitute of *every* military quality, except mere personal courage, a mere figurehead or puppet, operating by chance of following the suggestions of his subordinate commanders or others of some military ability around him, especially his then chief of staff, Major Thos. L. Snead.

Gen. Smith on the same occasion related to me an incident which occurred in the same campaign, as illustrative of the danger of giving Gen. Price an independent command, on account of his inclination to tyrannize over those to whom he felt hostility. Soon after Gen. S. arrived at the camp near Camden, Gen. Price accompanied by Major Snead, waited on him to complain of Gen. Marmaduke's management of the cavalry division under his command. Major Snead did all the talking, Gen. Price sitting by and occasionally nodding assent, and closed by asking of Gen. Smith the extreme measure of relieving Gen. Marmaduke of his command, in the very midst of the campaign! The objections made to Gen. Marmaduke seemed to Gen. Smith very frivolous, and indeed consisted almost wholly of an opinion of Gen. P. and Major Snead that Gen. M. had no military capacity and did not cordially sustain Gen. Price in his military operations. Gen. Smith, without much, if any, discussion of the objections, stated to Gen. Price and Major Snead, that he considered General Marmaduke one of the best and most rising officers of his age and rank in the Confederate service, and that he could not think for a moment, of so hastily putting on him the disgrace they requested. It was subsequently and plainly the general opinion of the public in Arkansas, as well as of the offices and troops engaged in that campaign, that whatever of success was in it, was due mainly, if not wholly, to the handling of the cavalry by its immediate commanders, including Gen. Marmaduke.

Gen. Smith and I had never previously conversed so fully and unreservedly in reference to Gen. Price's military qualifications or defects, but the importance of the contemplated campaign obliged us to do so. I mentioned the claim of Gen. Price and his friends, and the current belief, that he had the talent of surrounding himself with an unusually efficient staff; that my knowledge, from the condition in which he had left the staff affairs of the Missouri State Guard had occasioned me some doubts of that talent, but that he and his staff formed such a skillful "mutual admiration society," that it was difficult to get at the real facts on that point; that one of my objects in having urged the appointment of Gen. Price to the command of the District of Arkansas was to test his military administrative capacity, a talent which, as I supposed, lay chiefly in the selection, support, and control of an efficient staff.

Gen. Smith stated that as a district commander of Arkansas, Gen. Price had been a complete failure, a model of inefficiency. His chief quartermaster, Major Brinker, kept the best table in the army of the District, and was both zealous and efficient in providing for the comfort of headquarters, especially of General Price personally; that on account of his reputation, and Gen. Price's boasts of his superiority, as division quartermaster, Gen. Holmes had made him District quartermaster, and he had continued as such under Gen. Price; but that he had proven in that new sphere, an utter failure. The adjutant, Major Mclean, was an excellent bureau officer, keeping his books and papers in admirable order, but had little administrative talent. His chief surgeon, Dr. McPheeters, and chief paymaster, Major Cabell, were most excellent officers. His chief ordnance officer, Col. Clay Taylor, was inefficient, and had even among Gen. Price's friends, the reputation of being so. His aides, both regular and volunteer, were mere pleasure-seeking young men, of use only to carry orders. His chief engineer, Capt. [T. J.] Mackay, was a good officer, but unavoidably had had little chance of exhibiting his abilities. The above estimate of Gen. Price himself and of Major Brinker, came from Gen. Smith himself; that our comparison of opinions, and at this date I cannot remember whether the specific estimate of each officer originated with him or with me.

In deciding on a commander for the Missouri expedition, two considerations weighed, and necessarily so, which are remarkably illustrative of those defects in the Confederate people and government which perhaps more than any other two separate causes, contributed to the failure of their attempt to secure independence.

One was this: However disputed was General Price's military capacity, there could be none as to his skill as a politician and especially as a military demagogue. His curiously composite staff, with its ramifications and correspondents both inside and outside of the army, and a specific organ in Mr. Tucker's newspaper at Mobile, formed a powerful machinery for puffing Gen. Price himself, and unscrupulously and often falsely attacking everybody who stood in his way, or became the object, justly or not, of his or their jealousy or dislike. A species of terrorism was exercised or attempted over every one who could influence Gen. Price's fortunes, especially over the Missouri Congressmen and others con-

Earl C. Van Dorn.
Photograph by E. and H. T. Anthony, 1861–1865. Missouri History Museum.

nected with Missouri or Trans-Mississippi affairs. Generals McCulloch, Van Dorn, [Thomas C.] Hindman, and Holmes, successive commanders of the Arkansas District, Gen. Pemberton, commanding Gen. Price in Mississippi, Governor Jackson, Gen. Harris, members from Missouri of the Confederate Congress, and even President Davis had been successively the object against which it had been, with more or less success, employed. The favorite, almost exclusive mode adopted, most sillily, by Gen. Price and his friends for advancing his fortunes was attack and abuse of, and terrorism over, instead of efforts to gain over, conciliate or secure, those who could advance him. The sole exceptions to this rule of conduct were Senator Peyton, Gen. E. K. Smith, and myself, and even we only partially so. Senator Peyton was a decided "unfriend" of Gen. Price, but too formidable as a popular orator, and a favorite of the army, for Gen. Price's friends to attack him hastily. The disposition to bully me was checked in the manner heretofore related; that to assail Gen. Smith began to be exhibited in July 1863 in a conversation Major John Tyler, volunteer aide of Gen. Price, had with me at Little Rock: I closed the conversation by stating, with some vehemence, that as long as I sustained Gen. Smith, I should treat an attack on him, direct or indirect, precisely as I would an attack on myself. It was well understood, from my conversation with Major Snead, heretofore related, that I should meet any attempt at terrorism by an effective counter-terrorism directed against the officers themselves engaged in it. I heard nothing more of attacks on Gen. Smith until after the Missouri campaign; then the Price faction endeavored to make up for lost time. But the terrorism above mentioned had produced one effect clearly; however it may have diminished the number of Gen. Price's friends, it had made most men, especially military officers, indisposed to expose themselves to the public abuse and both public and secret attacks sure to be directed against any one supposed, whether correctly or incorrectly, to stand in the way of Gen. Price.

A constant piece of tactics of Gen. Price's partisans was, in his success to claim all the credit for him, in his failures to lay all the blame on somebody else, and in any failure of his superiors to claim that there would have been no failure had he commanded. He ostentatiously claimed a preference over every body else in commanding an expedition to Missouri. Inevitably therefore, any other commander of it, if successful, would be treated as having stolen his thunder, and be persecuted therefore, or if unsuccessful, be doubly damned for having failed where Gen. Price would certainly have succeeded. Any commander placed over him in such an expedition, would have to suffer the same attacks which had been directed against McCulloch, Van Dorn, and Pemberton. I have the decided impression that this state of things had much to do with Gen. Buckner's disinclination to command such an expedition; but I cannot now remember whether I gathered it from his language or heard it from others.

The other irregular consideration which had to be duly weighed was the dread by the Richmond government of political dissention and the interference there of mere politicians in purely military matters.

President Davis himself had been both by nature and education, not at all subject to any such dread, and inclined rather to underestimate than exaggerate the weight due to political considerations in determining on military measures. But the constant trouble the "Price imbroglio" had given him, the project to depose him in 1862, and the plan of Gov. [Henry] Rector of Arkansas and others, in that year, of making the Trans-Mississippi Department independent of the Confederacy, had, as both Gen. Smith and I believed, produced in him a continuous fear of so fatal an event, and consequently a great desire for calm and harmony among the restless politicians and turbulent elements of that section. Better informed on the ground itself, Gen. Smith and I had no such fear. But we shared the President's desire for a calm and harmony, and felt that sound policy demanded every reasonable effort to prevent the discouraging and demoralizing effect on the Richmond government of any dissentions or popular excitement in the Trans-Mississippi Department.

Now it so happened, as our ill luck would have it, that harmony and an exultant feeling of confidence in our military leaders had but just been produced by the retirement of Gen. Holmes, and the repulse of the Federals in Texas, Louisiana and Arkansas, when the controversy of Gen. Taylor, and the Louisiana politicians, with Gen. Smith, and that of Gov. Murrah of Texas, backed generally by the politicians of that State, with Gen. Magruder, arose to disturb us.[95] To add to these elements of discord, a controversy with so violent a man as Gen. Price, especially, as I considered (though as the fact was unknown to Gen. Smith, he could not be influenced by it) in view of the Edwin Price connection, was to be avoided if possible. This was especially the case as Col. [Guy M.] Bryan, of Gen. Smith's staff, had recently returned from Richmond, and stated that the administration there was evidently "afraid of Gen. Price," i.e. desirous of avoiding all controversy or trouble with him. That administration, unlike Mr. Stanton, President Lincoln's War Secretary, had not seen that no risk is too great to secure *absolute* subordination among the military.

Under all these difficult circumstances, and from these mixed political and military considerations, I gave it to Gen. Smith as my opinion, that the command of the expedition should be given to Gen. Price; that the best and most reliable division and brigade commanders should be furnished him; and that the most efficient staff officers should be furnished him. I told Gen. Smith that while giving him this opinion, I must not be considered as urging it on him; that he should decide solely on his own judgment and responsibility; but that whatever his decision, I should sustain him, both with the President and the public, in adopting whatever the difficult and delicate circumstances might suggest to him.

During the last day or two of this conference, Gen. Price who had been sent for by Gen. Smith and came from Camden, Ark., was in Shreveport. Suffering from illness (chills and fevers, I think he said it was), he was attended by his physician, Dr. McPheeters. I had little conversation with him about the proposed campaign.

Baltimore, Md., June 30, 1898

I found this unfinished statement among the papers left to me by my uncle, Thomas C. Reynolds, and I send it to the Missouri Historical Society for Preservation.

Geo. Savage.

Note from C. A. Peterson

It is to be regretted that Governor Reynolds never completed the preceding manuscript, as his narrative had just reached the most interesting feature of the difficulties between himself and General Price, at the point where his narrative stops in 1864.

The following pages are taken from the correspondence of Governor Reynolds, within the period concerning which he has omitted to write, and may serve to supply the matter upon which he would certainly have treated had he continued his manuscript.

[Editor's note: The above note was apparently added by Dr. C. A. Peterson about 1904. The original manuscript—handwritten—is in the possession of the Missouri History Museum, St. Louis, as is a typewritten copy, also apparently done by Peterson. The following items were included by Peterson as part of the typescript.]

OR, ser. 1, vol. 41, pt. 3, p. 1000

Camp near Boonville, Mo., October 10, 1864.

Maj. General S. PRICE,

Commanding, &c.:

General:

On your verbal assurance at Camden that your chief quartermaster would provide shoes for the horses and mules used by me in the present campaign I omitted to bring any along with me. Repeated applications by my quartermaster to that officer during my stay near your headquarters, and to General Shelby's quartermaster during my stay with him, have failed to produce anything but studied neglect of my necessities in this respect. One horse and two mules of those used by me or my attendants have had (and the others will soon have) to be abandoned as worn out for want of shoes. Every blacksmith shop on the line of march being seized for the use of the Confederate Army, my quartermaster can procure no horseshoes from citizens, and the wholesale pillage of horses and mules, as of goods generally in the vicinity of the army, has made it impossible for him to obtain anything by purchase. In fact, in an expedition designed to re-establish the rightful government of Missouri the Governor of the State cannot even purchase a horse or a blanket, while stragglers and camp followers are enriching themselves by plundering the defenseless families of our own soldiers in Confederate service. To-day my quartermaster reports to me that for want of shoes the four mules of my ambulance are so nearly worn out that they cannot travel longer than a day or two more. They belong to the Confederate States, having been assigned for my use on this expedition through the courtesy of General E. K. Smith.

As the ambulance is the only conveyance I have for the baggage of myself and all my attendants I respectfully request that you direct the proper officer to have them exchanged at once for others belonging to the Confederacy and likely to stand the fatigues of travel.

I am, General, very respectfully, your obedient servant,

Thos. C. Reynolds

Gov. of Mo.

Manuscript in Missouri History Museum files

Head Quarters Marmaduke's Divn.

Dec. 8, 1864

Gov. T. C. Reynolds,

Dear Sir:

Lt. Fackler of Gen. Marmaduke's staff has informed me that you intend publishing a letter denying the statement which has been made that Gen. Marmaduke was intoxicated on the day of his capture, and that you desire to know whether such a course would be deemed appropriate by his staff.

As the Chief officer on gen. Marmaduke's staff, and at the request of the other officers of his staff, I have the honor to signify our thanks to you for the active interest you take in the reputation of our chief and so brave and true an officer, and to say that we believe no better course could be adopted than the one you suggest to destroy the slander and the slanderer.

I am very Respy. Gov.

Yours, etc.

Henry Ewing, Maj. & Adj.

Received, Marshall, Texas, Dec. 14th, 1864

Answered, Dec. 21st, 1864.

Generals Price, Marmaduke, and Cabell in the Missouri Campaign. Letter published in the *Marshall (Texas) Republican,* **December 23, 1864, and reprinted in John Newman Edwards,** *Shelby and His Men: or, The War in the West* **(Cincinnati: Miami Printing and Publishing Co., 1867; reprint, Waverly, MO: General Joseph Shelby Memorial Fund, 1993)**

To the Public.

Marshall, Texas, Dec. 17, 1864

Hearing of reports industriously circulated, charging Generals Marmaduke and Cabell with drunkenness in the battles last October, near Independence and the Osage River, and putting on them the responsibility for disgraces and disasters which the almost unanimous opinion of the army at the time justly attributed to the glaring mismanagement and distressing mental and physical military incapacity of Major General Sterling Price, I deem it merely my duty, as executive of the State to which those captive officers have rendered important services, and of which the first named is a native, publicly and officially to brand those charges as base and baseless.

From my own observation of General Marmaduke at Independence, and the statement of several gentlemen who were with him or General Cabell in the actions referred to, I can confidently assert that in both they were perfectly sober and fully sustained their high reputation for ability and chivalric courage. Having had in the late expedition to Missouri frequent continuous intercourse with them, on the march, in camp, and in the field, I owe it to them to declare that I have never seen, or heard of, any deviation by either from the strictest sobriety throughout the campaign, and that they are generally and justly regarded as ornaments to their profession, enjoying the unbounded confidence of their commands.

The affair at Independence was thus explained to me by General Cabell the day after it occurred: As General Marmaduke was ably and successfully checking the enemy in our rear, a body of Federal cavalry, coming unobserved on a by-road on our flank, dashed into that town. The numerous camp-followers, dead-heads and stragglers there, loitering, carousing or plundering, incontinently fled and suddenly burst, in wild panic with shouts of terror, on the two brave and disciplined Arkansas regiments, which, marching in soldier-like regularity, composed the rear of Cabell's brigade. Unprepared for this furious charge of our own friends on their rear, those regiments were unavoidably thrown into confusion, and in the disorder the Federals captured Cabell's cannon. The enemy being checked by the prompt and skillful dispositions of General Fagan, our scattered troops soon rallying, rejoined the main body with little loss in men or arms. Thus the license occasioned by the neglect of General Price to control his army, was the direct and palpable cause of that day's misfortune, which powerfully contributed to demoralize the troops.

Of the disgrace and disaster which befell our arms near the Osage, the facts are too well known, both in the Federal army and in our own, to make concealment of them a matter of policy. A determined foe to all whitewashing, and having long believed that our cause has suffered not only from failures to encourage meritorious young officers, but also from concealments and even imprudent denial of misconduct of generals and troops, I consider our true public interest to demand a pitiless disclosure of the real causes of that defeat.

Despite the brilliant results obtained by General Price's juniors, when sent on expeditions away from the main body, his immediate command had produced not one indisputable success, and numerous incidents which necessarily became more or less generally known to the officers and troops at large, had produced a widespread, and scarcely concealed distrust of his leadership. He chose a circuitous route by Dardanelle to the Missouri frontier, when the direct road east of Pine Bluff was open to him; took twenty-three days to get over only three hundred and eighty miles between Camden and the border, and with all this slow progress his army was marched, camped and led so unskillfully that teams and cavalry horses were nearly broken down and his train much damaged. His want of proper acquaintance with the district he had so lately commanded was remarkable. He took the wrong road on the first day out from Camden, and lost nearly two days by going first down one bank and then up the other of the Fourche La Fave; he was ignorant that the enemy had a telegraph line along the Arkansas river, and apprized [*sic*] of there being three hundred pounds of telegraph wire at Dardanelle, he left it there uninjured; designing to cross the Arkansas river where it abounds in fords, he encumbered himself with pontoons, which were never used; and in approaching White river he greatly damaged his train by leading it over several miles of rocky precipices, miscalled a road, while Fagan's division, pursuing the usual route, suffered no inconvenience. He lost several hundred of his best soldiers in the repulsed attempt to storm the well ditched fort at Pilot Knob, which the Federal commander abandoned, as the St. Louis papers previously stated he would have to do as soon as our artillery could command it from the neighboring mountain. The garrison, unobserved, evacuated the place by night, carrying off its field artillery, and no less important a personage than Colonel [Thomas C.] Fletcher, then Lincoln candidate, and since chosen for the position of Federal governor of Missouri, well known to be there with his regiment. General Price refused to order immediate pursuit; Shelby left for eighteen hours to await orders at Potosi, reached Caledonia only two or three hours after that force had passed through; the brigades tardily sent after it were wisely withheld, when worn out by a forced night march, from attacking it in the entrenched position it had found time to construct; and it thus effected a complete escape to Jefferson City, in time to reinforce the garrison there before our army reached it. The dilatory march from Pilot Knob to Jefferson City; the failure to destroy any portion of the North Missouri or Hannibal and St. Joseph railroads, almost unguarded, though that section swarmed with guerrillas glad to obey an order to do that work; and the consequent reinforcement of that garrison by troops sent rapidly over those roads, all diminished our chances of securing the capital. The confused operations before it may be judged by the facts that our ammunition train came near being led into the Federal lines, and when the army encamped at night, neither of the two officers next in rank to General Price, Fagan and Marmaduke, was informed, or could learn the location of any division but his own, or of General Price's own headquarters. The city could have been taken the day he neared it; it was then defended mainly by raw militia, most of whom our friends said were anxious to surrender or even to join us. The State House, with its lofty dome, lay that day in full view of a gallant army confident of victory; next morning, whether wisely on correct information that large reinforcements had reached the enemy in the night, or unwisely from hesitating generalship or mistaken policy, General Price suddenly ordered a retreat, on the road to Springfield.

The considerations which had led the executive of the State to suggest, and the sagacious commander of this department to sanction so seemingly hazardous but in reality perfectly practicable a campaign, had proven more than well founded. The enemy was wholly unprepared. The State had been stripped of troops to sustain Grant and Sherman: to put down even petty bands of bushwhackers, official appeals had been in vain made to the inhabitants to organize military companies. The Unionist militia had become demoralized and partially disbanded; everywhere it had offered only a feeble and reluctant resistance. The Federal troops in the North were more than fully occupied with the enforcement of the draft, and Missouri itself was intensely agitated by that measure and an exciting political canvass. The audacity of the expedition made both people and authorities incredulous of its reality. General [William] Rosecrans was meditating a pleasure trip to the Hermann fair on the 15th of September, when he received news that General Price was "about to invade the State with five thousand cavalry." The only reinforcements on which General Rosecrans relied to meet them was A. J. Smith's corps, about four thousand strong, which Marmaduke's old brigade alone, under Colton Greene, had whipped last summer on the Mississippi, and which was yet to come from Tennessee, thoroughly demoralized in repeated thrashings by [Nathan Bedford] Forrest. On the 23rd of September, our advance, under Shelby, had entered Fredericktown, within three days' quick march of St. Louis; and it was not until the 26th that Rosecrans, doubtless discovering the inadequacy of his forces, and avowing fears of the mines "secret conspirators" were about to explode under his feet, sank pride in wisdom and issued his general order number one hundred and seventy-six, piteously imploring "every citizen" to "bring arms if he had any, horses if he could, and ride and fight as scouts." He cried, "The case admits of no delay." Discharged and furloughed soldiers he "appealed to in this crisis." Business was suspended in St. Louis; guerrillas were reported to have entered the County itself; cautious men were sending away their families and effects. There were symptoms of lukewarmness and discord. Citizens in forming a company published a resolution that they would not march beyond the city limits; the Germans refused to serve under General Blair, and Rosecrans had to yield by placing them under Colonel Brown. The McClellan men suspended political meetings for fear of being suspected of rebellion. [William "Bloody Bill"] Anderson's butchery of two hundred Federal soldiers in North Missouri a few days before had spread a black flag panic among the citizen soldiery. On the 27th, eighteen hundred men, chiefly Iowa troops, said to be of A. J. Smith's corps, evacuated Mineral Point, about fifty miles from St. Louis, on the approach of less than two hundred of Shelby's men. Opinions were freely given in our army, and by officers of calm judgment, that in the panic, mutual distrust and confusion of the Federals in that great city, either Marmaduke or Shelby, with a division of their old troops, could have dashed in and taken it, liberating its thousands of Southern sympathizers, and opening a door to the four hundred thousand "rebels," an official report to Mr. Lincoln asserts to be secretly organizing in the Northwest. At this juncture, when active boldness would have been consummate prudence, our army remained at Fredericktown till the 26th, blundered at Pilot Knob till the 28th, and then took the road to Jefferson City. And now that even the capital was to be left without a serious effort to occupy it, the disappointment of the army was marked.

Turning off from the Springfield road it was headed toward the Missouri river. It suffered a surprise at California, when the prompt sagacity of Marmaduke and a daring charge of [Solomon George] Kitchen, with his regiment of new recruits, saved it from a dangerous attack in flank. It was again surprised at Boonville, where a force, estimated by those who fought against it at only fifteen hundred cavalry, came unobserved on to the very edge of the town, near enough to have shelled General Price's own headquarters; and when his generals proposed to go out and disperse or crush it, his timid policy permitted its undisturbed retreat. That night he removed his ammunition from the fair grounds, whereby the question naturally suggested itself to everyone whether the wisdom thus shown evinced any in having placed it there, within convenient shelling distance of the opposite bank of the

Missouri river. These and many other incidents of equal importance
had confirmed the distrust previously felt.

Other facts less generally known or noticed had a tendency to increase it among those whose confidence if gained, might have impart-
ed itself to all. Before his entrance into Missouri, he refused the offer
of an accomplished officer to form the dismounted men into Infantry
as the nucleus of a larger organization of that arm of service, indispensable in effecting his avowed purpose of holding the State; nor did he
at any time attempt such an organization, though it was asserted that
many of the troops would have readily entered into it. Captured bayonets were thrown away, and after his attention had been called to this
abuse, it remained uncorrected, so that for want of them infantry could
not have been formed later in the campaign, had he at last ordered it.
While his highest general officers rarely knew his plans, the enemy
often discovered them; when he talked at Independence of consulting
his division commanders about attacking Leavenworth, St. Louis papers
several days old contained a dispatch from Rosecrans to [Union major
general Samuel R.] Curtis, coolly informing him of that design as one
declared by General Price himself. In consequence of this and previous similar information, the militia of Kansas were already gathering
in mass and making forced marches to meet him at their frontier. How
he found his way in a country or got his ideas of its topography was an
enigma, for he sneered at maps and declared he never looked at them.
He availed himself little, if at all, of engineering or reconnaissances, and
even neglected the simplest pioneering. Supplied with numerous staff
officers of high repute for efficiency, he neither guided, sustained nor
controlled them, so as to derive from their talents the greatest benefit
to the army. He could not know the strength of his own forces, for returns were neither made nor insisted on, and the new recruits were not
even mustered in until after he had returned to Arkansas. His indecisive
policy so paralyzed everything that, even with a chief commissary of
great energy, his private soldiers were kept on half rations of bread and

meat in the Missouri River valley, teeming with supplies, and at Pilot Knob he left behind shoes enough for his whole army. Even his well known claim that his name would draw recruits, proved a delusion. It soon became manifest that the ten thousand new soldiers who in about three weeks had rushed to our aid, and the still greater number of others who, in that heroic uprising of the noble Missouri people, were preparing to join us, were impelled solely by love of liberty and devotion to the great Confederate cause: while his leadership was a positive drawback among men whose past sufferings made them keep vividly in mind the fact that twice before in this war, he had headed on the Missouri river an enthusiastic, martial people, and whatever the causes or excuses, had as often been driven away from it.

Nor were his military habits, conspicuous to every one, calculated to inspire confidence. His regular course was to sit in his ambulance at the head of his train on the march, rarely mounting his horse; to sip his copious toddy immediately after·going into camp, and in view of the soldiers passing by, and soon after generally to take a nap—a mode of life entirely virtuous, but not precisely in accordance with established conceptions of the kind of hero needed to free an oppressed people. His somnolency was marked; although his practice was to make no halts for rest in the day's march, yet one day on the road from Camden to Dardanelle, he stopped the whole command for about half an hour and took a nap on a carpet spread out under a tree. On the whole campaign, as far as I observed or could learn, he never reviewed or personally inspected even in a cursory manner, any portion of his army, its camps, or even its sick and wounded, or its hospitals. On the field of battle his movements and countenance unmistakably indicated, not the activity or fire of genius, or even the calm of routine generalship, but only puzzled bewildered anxiety. His outfit was on a scale that even Federal generals dare not adopt. Three vehicles with fourteen mules carried him and the personal effects and camp equipage of his mess. Of course his staff imitated, though to a far less extent, this ill-timed luxury; and that bold and hardy cavalry, accustomed to leaders who sleep in storms under trees, and cook their simple, scanty rations on sticks and boards, gazed with unconcealed amazement on a pomp and circumstance which to their shrewd minds foreboded anything but glorious war.

The disorder in his army was terrific, and the main cause of it palpable; he could not enforce laws, regulations or orders, because he conspicuously violated them himself, or permitted his immediate officers and attendants to do so. Even his camps had no sentinels or efficient police, if any. But perhaps nothing contributed more to throw everything into confusion and harass and fatigue his troops than his singular order of march, sometimes called the tail foremost or topsy-turvy system of moving an army. The regulations permitting the order of regiments in brigades and of brigades in divisions to be changed "for important reasons," he not only made this exceptional course the rule, but applied it to the order of divisions in his immense cavalry force. On the day's march the division which had marched and camped in the rear the day before, passed to the front, the other troops halting till it had done so. When the hour for march was dawn, the rear division of the day often could not move until midday, and as often got into camp near midnight; and some ingenious mathematician is said to have ascertained, by patient calculation, that with two more divisions this system would bring the whole army to a permanent dead halt, unless the rear division should begin its day's march on the day after—an expedient actually adopted by Shelby's division in the first (afternoon) march from Boonville. In this Virginia reel of regiments, brigades and divisions, bewildered stragglers and new recruits got completely lost, until at last, a common sense cutting the Gordian knot of military blundering, they gradually ceased attempting to find their companies, and adopted the regular practice of bivouacking to themselves in what was well known as the "stragglers' camp." The origin of this system of marching is obscure; but a gentleman who witnessed its effects in the Missouri State troops under General Price in 1861, has hazarded the plausible conjecture, based on the similarity of operations and results, that it is merely an enlarged application of the mode in which that renowned warrior, Baron Munchausen, killed the lion by thrusting his arm down the animal's throat, and turning him wrong side out by pulling his tail through his mouth.

Under such management of an army, of course outrages and crimes could not be repressed. I cheerfully testify to the strenuous efforts of the commanders of divisions and brigades, and the officers generally to preserve discipline and order. Nor should any one judge harshly of private soldiers yielding to the combined temptations of a rich country and an almost total withdrawal of restraint. It must also be remembered that the chief reason why many of the soldiers themselves finally joined in the universal pillage was their consciousness that under a weak and suspected administration of the army, thieves following it were appropriating the very goods which the Government desired lawfully to procure for the legitimate use of those troops or the comrades left behind them; and even then the real fighting men did little injury, sneaks and dead-heads being the principal plunderers. It would take a volume to describe the acts of outrage; neither station, age nor sex was any protection; Southern men and women were as little spared as Unionists; the elegant mansion of General Robert E. Lee's accomplished niece and the cabin of the negro were alike ransacked; John Deane, the first civilian ever made a State prisoner by Mr. Lincoln's Government, had his watch and money robbed from his person, in the open street of Potosi, in broad day, as unceremoniously as the German merchant at Fredericktown was forced, a pistol at his ear, to surrender his concealed greenbacks. As the citizens of Arkansas and Northern Texas have seen in the goods unblushingly offered them for sale, the clothes of the poor man's infant were as attractive spoil as the merchant's silk and calico or the curtain taken from the rich man's parlor; ribbons and trumpery geegaws were stolen from milliners, and jeweled rings forced from the

➤Francis M. Cockrell.➤
Steel engraving, mid- to late nineteenth century. Missouri History Museum.

fingers of delicate maidens whose brothers were fighting in Georgia in Cockrell's Confederate Missouri brigade.

It was not until days after the incidents above given and many like them, had notoriously occurred, after the outrages had got almost beyond control, and his own staff loudly murmured their disgust and alarm at the condition of affairs, that General Price, in the fifth week of the campaign, ordered the organization of provost guards. To the control of these, a position requiring the most energetic activity and relentless sternness, he assigned a youthful officer of amiable disposition, who had been recently wounded and being thus disabled from riding his horse, was compelled to make the rest of the campaign in a buggy.

The natural result ensued, and the disorders still continued. They may be judged of by the facts that at Boonville, the hotel occupied as General Price's own headquarters, was the scene of public drunken revelry by night; that guerrillas rode unchecked, in open day, before it, with human scalps hanging to their bridles, and tauntingly shaking bundles of plundered greenbacks at our needy soldiers; and that in an official letter to him there, which he left unanswered and undenied, I asserted that while "the wholesale pillage in the vicinity of the army had made it impossible to obtain anything by purchase, stragglers and camp followers were enriching themselves by plundering the defenseless families of our own soldiers in Confederate service." On still darker deeds I shudderingly keep silent.

Under his unmilitary management, numerous wagons which the soldiers believed to contain untold wealth of plunder by staff officers and dead-heads, had dangerously augmented his train, so that it numbered over five hundred vehicles, and, shockingly controlled and conducted, often stretched out eight or ten miles in length. Marched in the center of the army, flanked, preceded or followed by a rabble of dead-heads, stragglers and stolen negroes on stolen horses, leading broken down chargers, it gave to the army the appearance of a Calmuck horde. The real fighting soldiers, badly fed, badly marched, and getting little rest in a noisy disorderly camp where their horses, blankets, pistols and even the spurs on their boots were often stolen from them in their sleep, scarcely disguised their apprehension that the odious train would occasion disaster to the army, and they were plainly reluctant to shed their blood to save the plunder it conveyed.

All these causes, and many others it would be tedious to mention, had visibly affected the tone, spirits and efficiency of the troops. Military men had forebodings of disaster to an army that General Price's mismanagement had converted into an escort for a caravan; God-fearing men trembled lest, in heaven's anger at the excesses which had marked the campaign, some thunderbolt of calamity should fall upon our arms.

It did fall, and like a thunderbolt.

As the army left the Osage or Marais des Cygnes, Marmaduke's division and Fagan's were in the rear of the train, Tyler's brigade guarded it, Shelby's division was in the advance. A force of Federal cavalry, estimated by most who fought with it at twenty-five hundred, and without artillery closely followed us. To gain time for the enormous train to pass on safely, it was deemed necessary to form rapidly, and, without dismounting receive the attack; the ground was unfavorable, but the alternative was to sacrifice the rear of the petted but detested train. The two divisions were mainly the same heroic Arkansans and Missourians, well disposed and readily disciplined, who had, under the immediate direction of their own officers, aided in driving the well trained troops of Steele from the Washita valley; but under General Price's direct command they had become seriously demoralized. The enemy, not mounted riflemen but real cavalry using the saber, charged our lines. It matters little to inquire which company or regiment first gave way; the whole six large brigades, were in a few minutes utterly routed, losing all their cannon, Marmaduke, Cabell, [Col. W. F.] Slemons and [Lt. Col. William Leader] Jeffers were captured, "standing with the last of their troops;" Fagan, almost surrounded, escaped by sheer luck; Clark owed his safety to his cool intrepidity and his saber. So of other officers of less rank.

Seated in his ambulance, in which he had remained most if not all of that morning, at the head of the train, General Price was six or eight miles off when all this happened. Cabell had informed him the night before that the enemy was actually attacking our rear; he believed that experienced officer mistaken. Marmaduke had sent him word that morning that about three thousand Federal cavalry threatened our rear; he thought that Marmaduke, having called on Fagan for support, could

⊷Joseph O. Shelby.⊶
Halftone, 1861–1865. Missouri History Museum.

manage them. After a day's march of only sixteen miles the army was ordered, to the general astonishment, to go into camp on the Little Osage, and had already commenced doing so, when news of the rout reached General Price. He sent for Shelby and besought that clear-headed and heroic young general to "save the army."

And Shelby did it. Like a lion in the path of the triumphant Federals, he gathered around him his two brigades, depleted in previous successive fights, harassed and weary, but still defiant. Those merry madcaps were in fighting trim; chased a few days before by an overwhelming Federal force they had luckily disembarrassed themselves of all demoralizing superfluities. The astonished foe recoiled before [Col. Sidney Drake] Jackman leading a reckless charge of his fearless brigade; Jeff Thompson, commanding Shelby's own, displayed his fire and dash as in 1861; Fagan and Clark rallied their scattered divisions. Both parties retired from the field as the setting sun cast his rays on the Camden of our revolution. No wiser or better than our forefathers, who reviled Washington, we also have our Gates.

Thus much has been necessary to protect the reputations of our captive generals, and show that no blame can attach to them. But the present is as fit an occasion as any to allude to some other points of that campaign.

I leave to some more graphic pen than mine to describe the horrors and perils of the long retreat—General Price's sweeping reduction of all transportation but his own; the security given us by Fagan's forethought in obstructing the fords of the Marmiton; the frantic flight of the train for over sixty miles, from the Marmiton to Carthage, without a halt to feed or water; the abandonment of the entire stock of salt for the private soldier, medicines and spirits for the sick, and bandages for the wounded, while headquarter messes preserved their cushions and pillows, their coffee and whisky, their pots and their pans; the defeat at Newtonia of the very force which had so lately defeated us; brave soldiers dropping dead from exhaustion, neglect, sickness and famine, and lying unburied on the prairie; weary stragglers slaughtered by the savage Indian; war-worn veterans feeding for days on beef without salt or bread, or eating steaks cut from mules fallen dead in the road, or starving altogether; sick and wounded soldiers deprived of a Government wagon, in order to carry negroes in it; small pox showing its ghastly face; staff servants and slaves brought along on speculation, fattening on wheaten biscuit, while sick soldiers were hungering after bread; General Price, smilingly sitting in front of his headquarters in a house, and sipping his toddy, while his medical department had no spirits where-

with to revive the failing strength of the sick and wounded, lying in
the open air in the damp Arkansas river bottom; these, and many other
equally strange events may attract the attention of some future historian. He would not do full justice to his subject unless he ascertains
and reports whether in that dreary march of weeks over mountains and
desert prairies, in snows and storms of bleak November, General Price
ever left his cushioned ambulance or well-sheltered quarters to inspect,
visit, or mingle among his faithful troops, suffering from war, pestilence,
and famine, to cheer their sinking spirits by word, look, or gesture, or
above all, ever observed in any way the noble maxim of Napoleon's
general, Marshal Marmont, that "the chief of an army must provide for
the well being of the soldier, and know, on important occasions, how
to partake of *his* sufferings and privations."

Nor should that historian fail to note the warm, liberal, and hospitable reception of our war-worn army by the noble people of Northern Texas, at the very moments when they had to guard their stables
nightly against the sneaking thieves who infested it or ran away in
advance of it, to sell (for specie only), the goods and chattels they had
stolen from Southern homes; and even when they were forced to listen
to the ungrateful tirades of some army demagogue, who had made that
long campaign without a graze on person, horse, or clothes.

It would be affectation to conceal the consciousness, that the statements here made, will appear almost incredible. State pride, old political
and personal association, and confidence in the assertions of General
Price and his friends, concerning his military habits and abilities, especially in connection with a Missouri campaign, had led me to disregard
the almost universal judgment of military men upon him, and to exert
with persistent zeal, as the President, Secretary of War, and Commander
of this department well know, whatever of official or personal influence I had, to obtain his transfer to Arkansas, and his assignment to the
command of the late expedition to Missouri. I had never previously
been with him on a campaign; and no one who reads of the facts here

stated, can be filled with more unmixed amazement than I was, on witnessing most of them and having evidence of the others. Stupendous as has been the boldness of the attempts to mislead the press and forestall public opinion concerning that campaign, the main facts are gradually leaking out in such hideousness, that any attempt of official reports to veil it, of a court of inquiry to whitewash it, or of a court martial to bury it, will only recoil. But having aimed at the most impartial accuracy, and desiring to do injustice to no one, I am perfectly willing to take General Price, if he desires it, before his own troops, and, freely discussing his campaign, call out from among his own officers and soldiers, witnesses of what has here been stated, and much more besides.

Though the expedition has failed to accomplish the grander objects aimed at, yet the good results inevitable under even the worst management, have been obtained. It produced some diversion in favor of Forrest, and enabled thousands of our citizens to join our ranks; some came out with the army and others are gradually finding their own way to our lines. Thus the army of the department is really stronger than ever. The old troops will, with proper discipline, soon again be the magnificent brigades which in September last crossed the Missouri line. They will be even improved by disasters which have shown them, not only as Holy Writ teaches, that "the robbery of the wicked shall destroy them," but that it also endangers an army that tolerates it. The blow (it is to be hoped, a mortal one), which the disasters of the expedition have given to that system of LOOSE DISCIPLINE, which has occasioned all our defeats, will greatly improve the efficiency of the whole Trans-Mississippi army; and the total collapse of General Price's military reputation may mitigate the nuisance of politician generalship.

The moral power of our State in the Confederacy is vastly increased by the fact that thousands from our sister States, for the first time visiting our populous central counties have heard the pulsations of the great heart of Missouri, and cheerfully testify, that it is sound and true to our cause, even after three years of oppression by the enemy, and imagined desertion by their Southern brethren.

Events have made my official station one of oppressive responsibilities. Elected in time of peace, in a poll of one hundred and fifty-four thousand of Missouri's voters, I am, of all the officers now recognized by either party to this war, the only one whose authority is both derived under her ancient constitution and based on a direct vote of her whole undivided people, while no other political authority now in existence can exhibit either of those special marks of republican legitimacy; and the recent expedition has fully disclosed the fact, before partially known, that thousands even of the Unionists of Missouri, and some in high position, still recognize her ancient government as the only legal one. As the head of that government, though exiled from her soil, and while always advocating just and stern retaliation for wrongs done to its supporters, I can not look calmly on, while the fair State, whose constitution makes me protector of the legal rights of even the vilest criminal within her limits, is made the scene of such excesses as attended that expedition. Usage forbids my here stating what official action I shall take in reference to it, on the facts here stated and others, some of which, the public interests may require to be kept secret. But though powerless to prevent lawless violence heretofore by the enemy or by others, I trust that action will not be unbecoming the constitutional chief magistrate of a civilized, but deceived, insulted, plundered, and outraged constituency.

No wise government will visit on masses of men or subordinate officers punishment, or even marks of displeasure for misconduct, which the former were led into by the absence of control, and the latter endeavored to prevent. But the statesman and the soldier will alike predict, that if the inhabitants still in Missouri are to believe that the generalship and discipline exhibited in the late campaign are the best our Confederacy can furnish, her fate is sealed, and the next Confederate army entering our borders, will be met, even by our own friends, as a band not of brothers but of robbers. The language, if stern, is true. But should the Confederate Government, by some signal public act, evince a deep disgust at the management of that expedition, they will yet rise again to greet our coming; Missouri's stalwart sons will again rush to uphold the Confederate banner; the gentle, but resistless attraction of a just and firm government, discriminating in its punishments, and the subtle political wisdom of a Christian forgiveness, will harmonize the better elements of her population; and at no distant day, regenerated and disenthralled, the noble State will lift her mighty arm, and casting her huge sword into the balance of contending armies, end at once this desolating war.

Thos. C. Reynolds
Governor of Missouri.

Appendix 1: Contemporaneous Material about the Price Expedition

There are several additional notes to be found in the Official Records that also pertain to the relationship between Thomas Reynolds and Sterling Price. Those that particularly pertain to Price's expedition into Missouri are presented here.

The publication of Governor Reynolds's December 17, 1864, letter brought out the following cards (letters to the editor or responses to other letters).

A CARD.

In the Texas Republican, of the 28th of December, 1864, there appears a communication over the signature of one Thos. C. Reynolds, who pretends to be, and styles him self in it, the Governor of the State of Missouri.

The communication purports to defend two gallant and distinguished officers against charges alleged to have to been made against them, but which I had never heard made by either officer or soldier. In reality, it was intended to be a violent and malignant attack upon myself, as the officer in command of the late expedition to Missouri.

So far as the communication pays tribute to the gallantry displayed by the officers and soldiers engaged in that expedition, I heartily concur in it. So far as it relates to myself, however, I pronounce it to be a tissue of falsehoods.

Sterling Price.

Governor Reynolds on General Price's Card.

Marshall, Texas, January 12, 1865

In the card published by General S. Price in the Shreveport News of the 10th inst., after his departure from that city for Central Texas, he silently declines an offer in my letter of 17th of December last to "take him before his own troops and call out from among his own officers and soldiers witnesses of what has there been stated, and much more besides." After such a shrinking, his coarse general denial will have less weight with thinking men, than a specific answer to even any single allegation in that detailed statement of his campaign, and is in fact merely a specimen of the bluster by which he has been accustomed to keep down discussion of his public acts. That farce is about played out.

As to the slanders on Generals Marmaduke and Cabell, I refer to their staff officers.

He concurs in my tribute to the gallantry of his officers and soldiers. It was made at his expense; I am glad he bears it cheerfully.

General Price describes me as one who "pretends to be Governor of the State of Missouri." The Federals take the same view of my position; but he has the distinction of being the first man in our lines to publish his concurrence with them in it.

As the Missouri executive recognized by the Confederate Government, I have deemed it both my right and my duty officially to publish, in reference to the late campaign in that State, a statement of facts which are admitted to have shocked the public conscience. I reaffirm it. To the Confederate authorities it belongs to determine whether a truculent denial by the accused is, in their system, an acquittal, or whether they will take any action on it.

Thos. C. Reynolds,
Governor of Missouri.

OR, ser. 1, vol. 41, pt. 3, p. 976

FRANKLIN COUNTY, Mo., October 2, 1864—9 p. m.

General S. PRICE:

My DEAR GENERAL: I am much obliged by the regard shown me in your urging me today to avoid the risks of being in the advance of your army, but on mature reflection I have concluded to remain with General Shelby. I trust my whole career heretofore will show that I am above any vulgar desire for a reputation for mere animal courage or recklessness at the expense of duty, but in an army endeavoring to restore him to the executive chair the proper place of a Governor of Missouri is in the front; besides, as I have taken it heretofore, a change now might be misconstrued, and official caution should not go to the extent of effecting personal character, so necessary in the executive of a people who can recover their liberties only by risking their lives and fortunes. General Shelby suggests that [John T.] Coffee's regiment and Slayback's battalion be formed into a command for General Thompson.

Permit me to urge this on you. It would give me personally great pleasure.

I remain, general, very truly, yours,

Thos. C. Reynolds.

OR, ser. 1, vol. 41, pt. 4, p. 1123

SHREVEPORT, LA December 24, 1864.

Maj. Gen. STERLING PRICE, Provisional Army, C. S.:

GENERAL: The enclosed publication★ I have deemed necessary to vindicate Generals Marmaduke and Cabell against injurious charges and to place the late Missouri campaign in a proper light before the public. In performing my imperative official duty in reference to that expedition I desire to avoid giving unnecessary pain to any one. I therefore frankly state to you that, believing myself fully acquainted with all the facts in relation to the return of your son, General Edwin Price, by your advice, within the Federal lines in 1862, his subsequent

---

★ The *Marshall (TX) Republican* article on p. 134.

course, and the communications between you and him, I design to make a memoir of those facts to the President of the Confederate States, and on it and the management of the late expedition to ask from him an order that you cease to be an officer in the provisional army of those States. Such a request (and still more such an order) would perhaps necessitate the giving of more or less publicity to that memoir. With a disposition to enable you to avoid the disagreeable discussions it would occasion, I propose that if you will at once resign your commission in that army and your position of Missouri bank commissioner (assigning, if you think proper, whatever reasons for those steps you may judge best, and such as will not necessitate controversy), and abstain hereafter from any interposition, directly or indirectly, in the military or political affairs of the Confederate States or the State of Missouri, that memoir will be sent as a paper to remain in the secret archives of the Government and not used unless necessary to meet such an interposition, or an attack by yourself, or any of your friends, on the Confederate authorities or myself for the action of any of us in this matter. I presume it will be in accordance with your own feelings, as it is with mine, that any future intercourse between us shall be only in writing, confined to indispensable official business and an answer to this letter.

I am, general, very respectfully, &c.,

Thos. C. Reynolds,

Governor of the State of' Missouri.

From the Thomas C. Reynolds folders at the Missouri History Museum

Shreveport, La, 3rd April, 1865.

Major O. M. Watkins

Dear Sir:

On the verbal communication made to me by you on Friday last concerning the view of Col. Musser and yourself in reference to proposing some mode of adjusting the relations between Gen. S. Price & myself, I have consulted with some friends in whose judgment I have confidence. Their concurrent opinion, and my own, is that, under existing circumstances, an endeavour of that kind might only lead to further controversy, and should be avoided. It is due to myself to add (and you may state it in any quarter where you think it will not be misconstrued) that I have no disposition to widen the breach already existing, and I respectfully suggest that, if circumstances shall occasion Gen. Price & myself to meet, in official intercourse or otherwise, a reciprocal observance of that courteous demeanour which is due to society, or to official propriety, would seem to me to be, in the existing condition of public affairs, perfectly consistent with a preservation of the present position of each party to the controversy.

Appreciating the patriotic motives which have prompted Col. Musser & yourself in this matter, I remain, Dear Sir,

Very respectfully yours,

Thos. C. Reynolds.

Head Quarters, Shelby's Division
Unofficial Lanesport, Ark. Dec. 7, 1864.
Dear Governor,

I am sorry that our parting was not more agreeable and that our conversation, which I desired and intended should be private and friendly, should have been interrupted and perverted as it was.

I was very sincere in my friendship in the matter I spoke about but I am more afraid that my desire will have had the opposite effect from that intended for Crisp(?), or someone, who heard the conclusion of your remarks, has reported them to Genl. Price, probably with exaggerations and perversions. Every Missourian will regret a controversy of an unpleasant nature between Genl. Price and yourself, and none more than I, for I am proud to rank you both among my personal friends, and questions strictly of a public nature, still lead to private ill feeling, and God knows, we Missourians cannot afford a "divided front," either towards the Enemy or towards our friends. I hope Dear Governor, that you will still reconsider the determination you expressed, at our parting, and will "let the dead bury the dead"—and let your time and talents, be used only for the future. You know my opinion of General Price, for I have freely expressed it on proper occasions. My opinion has not been changed by the result of our Expedition. Nor has yours. Others that did not, will now think as we have thought, and no more Cavalry Expeditions will be under his direction. This will be all that should be desired, and you can let the laurels that have heretofore been placed upon his brow, quietly rest there—whether deserved or not— and when they are only taken from the common enemy let them still be piled on, if any one chooses to do so.

All furloughs have been revoked by order of Genl. Magruder, and Genl. Price has gone to Washington to have a personal interview with Genl. Magruder. The Head Quarters of this Corps is now at Richmond, Ark., about fifteen miles from here. Our Divisions are strung along Red River to find Corn. I was to remain here, but I have already consumed the forage and will move down stream tomorrow. [Brig. Gen. Richard M.] Gano's Brigades are near here in Winter Quarters and we must leave them what corn is near their camp. [Brig. Gen. John Austin] Wharton's Cavalry are also below us, so there will be an immense number of horses to be fed this winter between here and Fulton.

There are Couriers between here and Shreveport and I hope to hear from you occasionally. I will write whenever there is news from Missouri—very many of the men are coming in daily, but no news of importance is received. I have not yet seen [James S.] Rains.

Respects to Bragg, Charley Polk and other friends.

Yours Most Respectfully,

M. Jeff Thompson.

To His Excellency T. C. Reynolds.

OR, ser. 1, vol. 41, pt. 4, p. 1093

HEADQUARTERS DISTRICT OF ARKANSAS,

Washington December 2, 1864.

General JAMES S. RAINS,

Commanding Missouri State Guards:

GENERAL: I am instructed by the commanding general to say to you that he directs you to move your command to Laynesport, reporting your arrival there both to Major-General Price and Governor Rey nolds. As it is probable that Governor Reynolds will soon definitely arrange with General Smith the future distribution of your command, no further orders will be given you from these headquarters unless in case of emergency.

Very respectfully, your obedient servant,

Ed. P. Turner,

Assistant Adjutant-General.

CITY OF MEXICO, 17ᵀᴴ MAY, 1866

Hon. Thomas C. Reynolds,

Sir: In answer to your letter of yesterday, and after carefully re-perusing your published letter of 17ᵗʰ December, 1864, in the <u>Marshall Republican</u>, in relation to the Missouri campaign of that year, we state the following.

From the entrance of General Sterling Price's army into Missouri till its return to Texas, in that year, we were constantly with the division of Genl. Joseph O. Shelby, on whose staff you also served, as a volunteer aide, throughout that campaign. All the facts stated in that published letter, in regard to the operations of that division, we know to be correctly given: the other statements of that letter, in regard to that campaign, its events and management, the circumstances attending it, the sufferings and neglect of the soldiers in the retreat to Texas, as well as in regard to the opinions and feelings of the officers and men at the time, we believe, mainly from our own knowledge and partly from statements of others at the time, to be entirely true and impartial.

When your letter appeared it was the subject of much attention in our division and elsewhere; and while there was great variety of opinion as to the expediency of the controversy, and the compassion for General Price personally, we must say that the letter itself was universally admitted to be true, both in substance and in details; indeed we never heard any one pretend to deny this.

You can make such use of this letter as you may deem necessary. Knowing ourselves to be perfectly impartial in the controversy between you and Gen. Price, we make this statement of facts, merely as one due to you.

We remain, Sir,

Very respectfully yours,

John N. Edwards
R. J. Laurence

In addition to the foregoing I state that the facts related in your letter before mentioned, concerning the causes of Gen. Shelby's delay at Potosi, his reaching Caledonia, the pursuit of Gen. Ewing, the march from Pilot Knob to Jefferson, the general conviction of the case with which that city could have been taken, the opinions freely expressed that St. Louis could have been taken, the occurrences at Boonville, the army's being scantily supplied on the Missouri River, the injury to recruiting on account of the distrust of the people in regard to Gen. Price's remaining in the State or making a successful campaign, the general management and military habits of Gen. Price, the disorder in the army, the order of march, and the result of it at Boonville, the outrages and plundering, especially by "dead heads" and stragglers, the organization and management of the provost guard, the train and the dissatisfaction and alarm of the army on account of it, the conversation in which (in my hearing) Gen. Price called on Gen. Shelby to "save the army," the position and course of Gen. Price on that occasion, the repulse of the Federals, in the afternoon of that day, and the flight of the army on the next day;—are all within my own personal knowledge, and are truly and impartially stated in that letter; indeed, many additional and more shocking circumstances could have been mentioned, on the same subjects. The feeling of the army was such that, on one night soon after our crossing the Arkansas River on our retreat, fears were had of an attack by some of Clarke's Missouri cavalry on the supplies of food and liquor known to be in the wagons of Gen. Price and his staff, and Gen. Shelby, by order of Gen. Price, furnished a guard to protect them. On that retreat I never knew or heard of Gen. P's leaving his ambulance or his immediate camp.

John N. Edwards.

I also have personal knowledge of the correctness of all the above except the remark of Gen. Price about "saving the army," but I heard of it soon after it was made, and it was the subject of general remark.

R. J. Laurence.

City of Mexico

July 3, 1866

Hon. Trusten Polk,

St. Louis, Mo.

Dear Sir:

I heard lately that letters had been received from you in this country to the effects that you were annoyed by suits claiming damages from you for alleged depredations committed in the Confederate campaign in Missouri in 1864. If my evidence can be of any service in the defense of those suits, it is cheerfully at your disposal. It so happens that I can testify to your opposition to those depredations, and especially to a conversation with you at Richwoods in which you urged measures to arrest them.

The course towards you amply confirms an opinion I have frequently expressed since the close of the late war, that if the U.S. government sincerely desires a restoration of harmony between the lately opposite parties, it should not merely grant an amnesty, but embody in the U.S. Constitution, an act of oblivion, both in civil and criminal actions, in relation to all belligerent acts on either side.

Please remember me to our common friends and believe me,

Very truly yours,

Thos. C. Reynolds,

(Hotel San Carlos)

OR, ser. 1, vol. 41, pt. 3, p. 975

O.A.K. HEADQUARTERS,

Saint Louis, Mo., October 1, 1864.

To THE MEMBERS OF THE ORDER OF
AMERICAN KNIGHTS OF THE STATE OF MISSOURI:

SIR KNIGHTS: Morning dawneth. General Price with at least 20,000 veteran soldiers is now within your State. Through your supreme commander (and with the approbation of the supreme council) you invited him to come to your aid. He was assured that if he came at this time with the requisite force you would co-operate and add at least 20,000 true men to his army. He has hearkened to your prayer and is now battling for your deliverance. Sons of Liberty, will you falsify your plighted word—I know you will not. You are strong in numbers—full 30,000 strong—and your influence is potent. It requires but prompt action on the part of the members to insure the ultimate triumph of our cause. As you value your property, your liberties, your lives, and your sacred honor, fail not to give a helping hand in this crisis. Under and by virtue of the authority vested in me by section [——] of the code of the O.A.K.'s, authorizing the appointment of a major-general to command the members called into the military service, I shall appoint that brave and true soldier, Missouri's favorite son, Maj. Gen. Sterling Price, military commander of the O.A.K.'s of the State of Missouri.

All able-bodied men of the O.A.K.'s are hereby called upon and required to render military service in behalf of our cause. All true knights will yield prompt obedience to time orders amid commands of General Price. Meantime do all possible damage to the enemy.

Seize all arms and munitions of war within your power. Take possession of and hold all important places you can, and recruit as rapidly as possible. If you cannot sustain yourselves fall back upon the army of Occupation. In townships and counties where you cannot concentrate on account of the presence of the enemy repair singly or in squads without delay to the army, or to points where your brethren may be marshaling their forces, and in all cases be ready to obey the commands of your chieftain and unite with the forces when an opportune moment offers. Ye knights, who belong to the militia, a change of government is now impending and you possess peculiar advantages for doing good service, and it is believed you will not fail to act efficiently.

You joined the militia that you might the better protect yourselves under Radical rule. Now prepare to strike with the victorious hosts under General Price and aid in the redemption of the State. Already hundreds of militiamen, arms in hands, have taken position beside the brave and gallant soldiers under General Price. In no event permit yourselves to be arrayed against your brethren. I enjoin it upon the district and county commanders and the grand seniors to be vigilant and active in the discharge of their respective duties. Let each one feel that upon him depends the successful issue of this contest, and that it is a paramount duty to immediately enter the service. I address you perhaps for the last time. You have honored me and given me your confidence. I have endeavored to merit as I appreciate that consideration. Danger has not deterred me from the discharge of duty, and the period of my intercourse and co-labors with you and brethren of other States. I shall ever revert to [it] with feelings of pleasurable emotion. I have rejoiced to note the unanimity of sentiment and earnestness of purpose evinced to put forth every effort, with force of arms if need be, to establish the great principles of liberty and free government and States rights, so soon as the event which is upon us transpired. Brethren, the time for action has come. We must now meet the hosts of the tyrant in the field and sustain our friends and our cause. Be assured I shall buckle on my armor, and I trust I shall greet many thousands of you in the camp of our friends. If we do not sustain General Price, and our cause in consequence fails, all will be lost. We must fight. Honor and patriotism demand it. Then remember your solemn oaths. Remember the sacred obligations resting upon you and resolve, individually and collectively, to do your duty knowing it full well.

Until otherwise ordered headquarters of the O.A.K.'s will be hereafter in the army of General Price.

All officers of the O.A.K.'s are charged to use the utmost dispatch in communicating this letter to the members. Absence from the city prevented an earlier issue of this communication. Remember our motto: "Resistance to tyrants is obedience to God."

Given under my hand and seal of the O.A.K.'s of the State of Missouri, this 1st day of October, A. D. 1864.

John H. Taylor,
Supreme Commander of the State of Missouri.

[Editor's note: Apparently, few OAKs answered this call. At about the same time that this call was issued, the news of the debacle at Pilot Knob arrived in St. Louis. Members of these kinds of organizations appeared to draw their own conclusions from the news and decided, for the most part, to stay home.]

The transcript of the Court of Inquiry held in Shreveport beginning on April 21, 1865, is found in the Official Records, series 1, volume 41, part 1, pages 701–729, and is titled "Record of the Price Court of Inquiry" and Official Records, series 1, volume 48, part 1, page 1415.

OR, vol. 41, pt. 1, pp. 701–729
Record of the Price Court of Inquiry.

PROCEEDINGS OF A COURT OF INQUIRY CONVENED AT SHREVEPORT, LA., BY VIRTUE OF THE FOLLOWING SPECIAL ORDERS:

SPECIAL ORDERS, HDQRS. TRANS-MISSISSIPPI DEPARTMENT,

No. 58. Shreveport, La., March 8, 1865.

XVI. At the instance of Maj. Gen. Sterling Price a Court of Inquiry is hereby appointed to meet at Washington, Ark., at 12 m. [noon] on Monday, the 3rd day of April, 1865, or as soon thereafter as practicable, to investigate the facts and circumstances connected with the recent Missouri expedition under his command. The Court will give its opinion upon the facts which may be developed.

Detail for the Court: Brig. Gen. Thomas F. Drayton, Provisional Army, C. S.; Brig. Gen. E. McNair, Provisional Army, C. S.; Col. P. N. Luckett, Third Texas Infantry; Maj. O. M. Watkins, assistant adjutant-general, judge-advocate.

Should it become necessary during the investigation for the Court to change the place of meeting it will do so, notifying department headquarters thereof.

By command of General B. Kirby Smith:

H. P. Pratt,

Captain and Assistant Adjutant-General.

SPECIAL ORDERS, HDQRS. TRANS-MISSISSIPPI DEPARTMENT,

No. 81. Shreveport, La., April 5, 1865.

VI. Paragraph XVI, Special Orders, No. 58, current series, Department Headquarters, is so amended as to make Shreveport, La., the first place of meeting of the Court of Inquiry instituted at the insistence of Major-General Price.

By command of General E. Kirby Smith:

P. B. Leeds,
Major and Acting Assistant Adjutant-General.

FIRST DAY
SHREVEPORT, LA,
April 21, 1865—10 a.m.
The Court met pursuant to the foregoing orders:

Present, Brig. Gen. Thomas F. Drayton, Provisional Army, C. S.; Brig. Gen. E. McNair, Provisional Army, C. S.; Col. P. N. Luckett, Third Texas Infantry. Maj. Oscar M. Watkins, assistant adjutant-general, judge-advocate.

Maj. Gen. Sterling Price, Provisional Army, C. S., appeared before the court.

The judge-advocate read the orders convening the Court and asked Major-General Price if he had any objection to any member named in the detail. He replied, none.

The Court was then duly sworn in the presence of Major-General Price by the judge-advocate, and the judge-advocate was duly sworn by the president of the Court.

Major-General Price asked of the Court to be allowed the assistance of Col. Richard H. Musser, Ninth Missouri infantry, as his military friend. The Court was then cleared for deliberation and the request of Major-General Price granted.

The hour of 12 m. having arrived adjourned to meet to-morrow at 10 a.m.

SECOND DAY.
SATURDAY, April 22, 1865—10 a.m.
At a Court of Inquiry then held at Shreveport, La., pursuant to adjournment.

Present, Brig. Gen. Thomas F. Drayton, Provisional Army, C. S.; Brig. Gen. E. McNair, Provisional Army, C. S.; Col. P. N. Luckett, Third

Texas Infantry; Maj. O. M. Watkins, assistant adjutant-general, judge-advocate.

Maj. Gen. S. Price appeared before the Court.

The proceedings of yesterday read.

The judge-advocate then introduced as evidence an official copy of the letter of instructions from General E. Kirby Smith, commanding Trans-Mississippi Department, to Maj. Gen. Sterling Price, directing him to make the campaign in Missouri. Said official copy is dated August 4, 1864, and is hereunto attached and marked Exhibit A.

Capt. T. J. MACKEY, corps of engineers, was then sworn, no other witnesses being present.

Examined by the JUDGE-ADVOCATE:

Question. Were you in the campaign of 1864 in Missouri under command of Major-General Price?

Answer. I was.

Question. State in what capacity you served, when you joined the command, when the march began, the route it pursued, and the places where the enemy were encountered and with what results, from the time you joined the command until the end of the campaign.

Answer. I was chief engineer on the staff of Major-General Price. Joined the command at Princeton, Ark., on the 29th August, 1864. The march began from Princeton August 30, 1864, moving west of it to Dardanelle, on the Arkansas River. Reached Dardanelle on the 6th day of September, 1864. I was then directed by Major-General Price to prepare pontoons for the passage of the river, provided no practicable ford could be found. Inquiring for the usual fords from citizens, I learned that they were impracticable. A practicable ford was found by me a half mile southeast of Dardanelle—a ford three or three feet and a half in depth, the river 290 or 300 yards in width. Ammunition was removed from caissons ordnance stores necessarily raised in the wagons. We crossed without accident and marched fourteen miles to the vicinity of Dover, in Arkansas. From thence Major-General Fagan moved east to Springfield, Ark., with his division. At Dover a council of war was held. I was not present. There the object of the campaign was then developed. The roads from Dardanelle to Batesville, Ark., and from Dardanelle to Springfield, Mo., fork at Dover. The main body of the army, with headquarters, moved by way of Clinton, Ark., crossing the White River at O'Neal's Ferry, about eighteen miles above Batesville. At Batesville, or near there, Major-General Price and staff made a junction with Major-General Fagan's force. At O'Neal's Crossing Major-General Marmaduke, with his division, moved by an upper route direct to Powhatan. The road was rough and a difficult one, and was adopted because of the forage and subsistence that it furnished. Headquarters with General Fagan's division moved from Batesville, fourteen miles, to Powhatan, Ark, which point it reached on the 15th September, 1864, where it was joined by Generals Marmaduke and Shelby. Moved from Powhatan to Pocahontas on the 16th, a distance of eighteen miles. At Pocahontas we halted two days for the purpose of reorganizing, many recruits being then in camp, and to distribute ordnance to the different divisions. At that point two or more brigades were organized and added to Major General Fagan's division, under Colonels [Archibald S.] Dobbin and [Thomas H.] McCray, and one brigade, under Colonel [Thomas R.] Freeman, added to Major-General Marmaduke's division, and a brigade, under Colonel Jackman, to General Shelby's division. These four brigades were chiefly of recruits from Arkansas and Missouri. At this point, by direction of General Price, I prepared four or five maps indicating the routes by which the different Divisions should move on entering Missouri, it having been determined by General Price to move by three routes to Fredericktown, Mo., 140 miles from Pocahontas. General Price directed me to lay the routes down clearly, so that the subordinate commanders could always communicate with him readily and know where he was. From Pocahontas General Price, with Major-General Fagan's division, moved direct to Fredericktown by Greenville, the middle route. Major-General Marmaduke moved by

Poplar Bluff; Dallas, and Bloomfield, by the longest route to the same point. Brigadier-General Shelby moved upon the left. This route leads through Patterson. He encountered the enemy in the vicinity of Doniphan and defeated him without loss to himself, capturing a few prisoners and the telegraph office with its instruments. He again engaged the enemy at Patterson, defeated him, capturing a few prisoners without loss to himself. Prior to this engagement the enemy had burned the town of Doniphan. Doniphan is in Missouri, twenty miles from Pocahontas. General Shelby's engagement at Doniphan was on the 19th, the day after leaving Pocahontas.

On the 22nd General Shelby engaged the enemy at Patterson. The three divisions made their junction at Fredericktown, Mo., on the 24th day of September, 1864. At that point General Shelby had an engagement with the enemy, defeating him with little loss. A very few prisoners taken on the 23rd of September, the day before the junction.

On the morning of the 26th General Shelby, by Major-General Price's order, moved from Fredericktown and in the direction of Saint Louis and the Iron Mountain Railroad. He moved in a northwesterly direction about forty-five miles to cut the road at Mineral Point. General Shelby's order was to burn bridges and depots. He destroyed the two bridges at this point. I learned this officially in the discharge of my duties as an engineer.

On the morning of the 26th September Major-General Price, with Major-Generals Marmaduke's and Fagan's divisions, moved west on the road leading from Fredericktown to Pilot Knob, Mo., to the Saint Francis River, where the army halted at a point nine miles distant from Pilot Knob. Major-General Fagan moved forward the same day with his division to Arcadia, two miles distant from Pilot Knob, leaving his train at the Saint Francis. I started to move with him, was ordered back by General Price for the purpose of repairing the bridge, 400 feet in length, across the Saint Francis. I had assigned an officer of engineer troops to that duty. General Price desired me to attend to it myself, as it was the only practicable crossing in his rear. Heard heavy firing in the direction of Arcadia the same day, Major-General Fagan driving in the enemy's outposts.

On the morning of the 27th General Price moved to the front about eight miles with General Marmaduke's division. Found Major-General Fagan in possession of Arcadia and Ironton. These are small towns about three-quarters of a mile east. We found the enemy in position in the vicinity of Pilot Knob.

On the 27th Generals Fagan's and Marmaduke's divisions assaulted Pilot Knob and were repulsed. On the night of the 27th the enemy evacuated their work, blowing up their magazine. We followed early on the morning of the 28th, General Price with Major-General Fagan's division reaching Potosi, thirty-two miles north of Pilot Knob, on the 29th of September. Major-General Marmaduke moved on the left northwest on the 28th, following the enemy in the direction of Cuba, a point on the railroad between Saint Louis and Springfield, Mo. Brigadier-General Shelby had already moved from Potosi on the 28th by General Price's order in the direction of Pilot Knob. On reaching Caledonia, twelve or thirteen miles distant from Pilot Knob, he moved west to cut the enemy's line of retreat upon Cuba. Headquarters with Major-General Fagan's division moved by Richwoods to Saint Clair, thirty-five miles northwest of Potosi, where they were joined by the divisions of Generals Marmaduke and Shelby. At Richwoods Brigadier-General Cabell left the main command on the 30th and marched to Franklin, thirty miles from Saint Clair, at the junction of the Pacific and Southwest Railroad.

On the 1st October General Price, with Major-Generals Fagan's and Marmaduke's divisions, marched north to the vicinity of Union, where Brigadier-General Cabell rejoined us on the 2nd. At that point Major-General Marmaduke moved northwest to cut the Pacific Railroad, to destroy the bridge at the mouth of the Gasconade, a point on the railroad between Saint Louis and Jefferson City. Major-General

Price continued to move west on the Jefferson City road to the vicinity of Mount Sterling, about fifty miles from Union. At Mount Sterling Major-General Marmaduke joined him on the 5th of October.

On the 6th [7th] the advance engaged the enemy four or five miles from Jefferson City and about thirty-one miles front Mount Sterling, driving him into the city.

On the 7th [8th] retired from Jefferson City, by way of Russellville, to California. Camped at Russellville, seventeen miles west of Jefferson City.

On the 9th moved north on the road to Boonville. Our rear was attacked at California, a point on the railroad between Jefferson City and Boonville. The attack was repulsed.

On the 10th we marched sixteen miles to Boonville, Brigadier-General Shelby in advance, who had an engagement at Boonville, resulting in the capture of between 200 and 300 prisoners, with their arms. Major-General Price, with Major-Generals Marmaduke's and Fagan's divisions, reached Boonville on the 10th, where the command remained two days.

The enemy making demonstrations on our force at Boonville from the direction of Tipton on the 11th, they were repulsed and pursued for eighteen miles.

During the night of the 12th the command moved from Boonville on the road to Lexington to Chouteau Springs, twelve miles from Boonville. The next day, the 13th, Major-General Marmaduke's division, under the command of Brigadier-General Clark, was detached and moved in the direction of Glasgow, a town on the north bank of the Missouri River, crossing that stream at Arrow Rock. General Price, with Major-General Fagan's division and Brigadier-General Shelby's division, proceeded on the 14th to Jonesborough, about twenty-eight [miles] from Boonville. From that point Brigadier-General Shelby moved with a part of his division and a battery in the direction of Glasgow, to a point on the south bank of the Missouri River, opposite Glasgow.

On the 15th General Price, with Major-General Fagan's division, moved to Keiser's, on the Salt Fork of the La Mine River, seventeen miles from Jonesborough and thirty from Glasgow.

On the 14th, from Jonesborough, Brigadier-General Thompson, with a brigade of Brigadier-General Shelby's division, moved south to Sedalia on the Pacific Railroad. On the night of the 17th and on the 18th all detachments rejoined Major-General Price, who had remained on the La Mine with General Fagan's division.

On the 18th the command marched twenty-two miles to Waverly. Our advance, under Brigadier-General Shelby, engaged and defeated the enemy at that point.

On the 19th the army marched twenty-six miles, engaging the enemy in force in the vicinity of Lexington, and defeated him.

On the 20th we moved twenty-two miles west in the direction of Independence in pursuit of the enemy, who had engaged us on the day before.

On the 21st we engaged the enemy in force on the Little Blue, eight miles east of Independence, defeating him and inflicting on him heavy loss. On that night we entered Independence, having marched twenty-six miles during the day. The command moved west twelve miles on the 22nd, skirmishing with the enemy on the Big Blue, eight miles west of Independence, the enemy contesting our passage of the stream.

On the 23rd engaged the enemy in force in the vicinity of Westport and defeated him. From this point we moved south twenty-four miles to the Middle Fork of Grand River, in the vicinity of which we had a skirmish with the cavalry of the enemy.

On the 24th we moved thirty-three miles to Blooming Grove, Kans., on the Marais des Cygnes.

On the 25th Major-Generals Fagan's and Marmaduke's divisions were attacked eight or nine miles from Blooming Grove, near Mine Creek, in the rear of the train, and routed by the enemy. On the afternoon of the 25th we defeated the enemy that had routed Major-Generals Fagan and Marmaduke after the enemy had been re-enforced by 2,500 cavalry from Fort Scott. This occurred between the Osage and Marmiton Rivers, and eight or nine miles from the previous fight of that day, the army marching about twenty-eight miles on that day and camped at Redfield Post-Office, on the Marmiton.

On the night of the 25th we destroyed about one-third of our train and a portion of our ordnance stores.

On the 26th the entire force, with the train, marched to Carthage, fifty-eight or sixty miles.

On the 27th marched twenty-two miles to Shoal Creek.

On the 28th marched to Newtonia, seventeen miles, encamping three miles south of Newtonia. Near this place we engaged the enemy in force and routed him. From Newtonia, on the 29th, we marched twenty-six miles to the vicinity of Pineville.

On the 30th from thence to Maysville, Ark., on the line of the Cherokee Country, a distance of twelve miles.

On the 31st we reached Illinois River, in the Cherokee Nation, twenty-six miles from the last encampment.

On the 1st of November we arrived at Boonsborough, or Cane Hill, in Arkansas. From this point Major-General Fagan was sent with his division on the following day to attack the enemy at Fayetteville, Ark., eighteen or twenty miles east of Cane Hill, where the main army remained until the 4th, when, being rejoined by Major-General Fagan, we marched fourteen miles on that day and camped in the Indian Territory.

On the 5th eighteen miles and on the 6th twenty miles, to the Arkansas River, which was crossed at Pheasant Bluffs on the 7th; marched four miles.

On the 8th Major-General Fagan, with his division, moved southeast by way of Ultima Thule to Washington. Brigadier-General Shelby had on the day before moved southwest to the North Fork of the

Canadian River. General Price, with General Marmaduke's division, marched ten miles on the 8th.

On the 9th nine miles.

On the 10th twelve miles.

On the 11th fourteen miles.

On the 12th two miles, to Gaines' Creek, where there was pasturage and subsistence. On the 13th sixteen miles, to Perryville, in the Choctaw Nation, where we remained until the morning of the 15th, when we marched seventeen miles.

On the 16th seven miles.

On the 17th fourteen miles to the vicinity of Little Boggy, where Colonel [Charles H.] Tyler left the main body with his brigade of recruits, moving southeast in the direction of Doaksville.

On the 18th the main army moved ten miles, to Boggy Depot.

On the 19th nine or ten miles, to Leflore.

On the 20th nine miles, to Little Blue.

On the 21st fourteen miles, to Island Bayou.

On the 22nd sixteen miles, crossing Red River at Kemp's Ferry into Texas, General Marmaduke's division there took the river route to Clarksville, Tex., eighty-five miles distant, where it joined the main body, which had marched through Bonham. This junction occurred on the 28th or 29th. We then moved thirty-six miles to Laynesport, Ark., where the expedition rested, the main army having marched 1,438 miles exclusive of the movements of detachments.

The hour of 2.30 p. m. having arrived the Court adjourned to meet on Monday next, the 24th instant.

THIRD DAY.

MONDAY, April 24, 1865, 9 a.m.

At a Court of Inquiry then held at Shreveport, La., pursuant to adjournment.

Present, Brig. Gen. Thomas F. Drayton, Provisional Army, C. S.; Brig. Gen. E. McNair, Provisional Army, C. S.; Col. P. N. Luckett, Third Texas Infantry; Maj. O. M. Watkins, assistant adjutant-general and judge-advocate.

Maj. Gen. S. Price appeared before the Court.

The proceedings of the second day read.

Examination of Capt. T. J. MACKEY, corps of engineers, continued by JUDGE-ADVOCATE.

Question. State the character of the road from Camden to Dardanelle.

Answer. From Camden to Princeton, for fifteen or sixteen miles crosses through a bad flat; the other portion of the road to Princeton, about the same distance, tolerably good, but at that time heavy rains having fallen all the roads were bad. From Princeton to Tulip, nine miles, very good road. From Tulip, the march of the next day, twenty-five miles on the Benton road, the road was good, with the exception of the last five miles, which led over a rocky and broken country. The march of the next day (the 1st of September), of eighteen miles, the road followed a rocky ridge, rough, but practicable for heavy trains. The march of the next day (2nd), crossing the Goose Pond Mountain, the ascent being easy, but the road was rough. The march of the 3rd, of fifteen miles, led over a mountainous country. On the 4th the country passed (fifteen miles) was rough, but the roads practicable. The 5th we marched sixteen miles, the character of the road being but little changed. On the 6th fourteen miles were traversed, the road being about the same to Dardanelle.

Question. How was the weather when the march from Camden to Dardanelle was made?

Answer. We had two rainy days between Princeton and Dardanelle.

Question. Was there, within your knowledge, any delay in the march between these points not occasioned by the character of the roads or weather?

Answer. There was, the march being regulated by the supply of forage, which had to be collected by detachments on our flanks and front. There was a delay of some hours on the 4th September, until Major-General Fagan, who had moved in the direction of Benton and who was in our rear, could come up. I know of no other, unless the marches were shortened, because of the condition of the draught horses, which was bad, but not worse than I have observed in all of the trains of the department for the last three years.

Question. Was there any delay in crossing the river at Dardanelle not caused by the necessity of raising the ordnance stores to prevent their damage, the character, of the ford being considered?

Answer. I know of none.

Question. State the general character of the roads pursued from Dardanelle to Pocahontas.

Answer. The country was broken and rocky, the roads practicable for heavily loaded wagons, with easy fords, with gravel and rocky bottoms.

Question. How was the weather during the march between these points?

Answer. Generally good, but some days extremely hot.

Question. Do you know of any delay in reaching Pocahontas not occasioned by the character of the roads, the conditions of the draught animals, or the state of the weather?

Answer. I know of none.

Question. Give the general character of the roads from Pocahontas to Fredericktown and the state of the weather during the march between those points, and state if there was any delay in the march.

Answer. The country rolling; roads tolerably good; the streams all easily crossed; the weather good; I know of no delay.

Question. State whether or not there was any halt at Fredericktown; if you say there was, state its length and how the army was engaged during the time.

Answer. We halted about two days. The army was encamped. A considerable amount of property, consisting of boots, shoes, clothing, &c., captured and purchased, was being distributed and recruits being received and organized, one or two companies being formed. Major-General Marmaduke was marching. He, having a longer route to pursue, did not overtake us till the day we left Fredericktown. Six or seven forges were engaged during the halt in shoeing horses and mules and repairing the transportation.

The Judge-Advocate here handed the witness a diagram of Pilot Knob and its approaches, which is hereunto attached and marked Exhibit B [see next page] and asked:

Question. Is that an accurate diagram of the country it purports to represent?

Answer. It is. It was drawn from a sketch made by me on the spot.

Question. You have stated that on the 26th September Major-General Fagan drove in the enemy's outposts. State where that outpost was, and the character of the enemy's works.

Answer. The outpost was Fort Curtis and vicinity, a decimated earth-work, commanding the road from Arcadia to Fredericktown, having a command of about fifty feet above that road.

Question. State in what direction the garrison of Fort Curtis retired.

Answer. North to Pilot Knob, distant a mile and three-quarters.

Question. What time on the 27th September were the enemy again encountered? Who commanded? State whether or not any reconnaissance of the enemy's position and strength was made, and if so by whom made and with what result.

Answer. We arrived in the vicinity of Pilot Knob about 10 a.m. I informed General Price, who commanded in person, that I would make a reconnaissance, and with a guide proceeded to the crest of Shepherd's Mountain to a point about 1,500 yards distant from the work on Pilot Knob. The work was then firing south-east at our

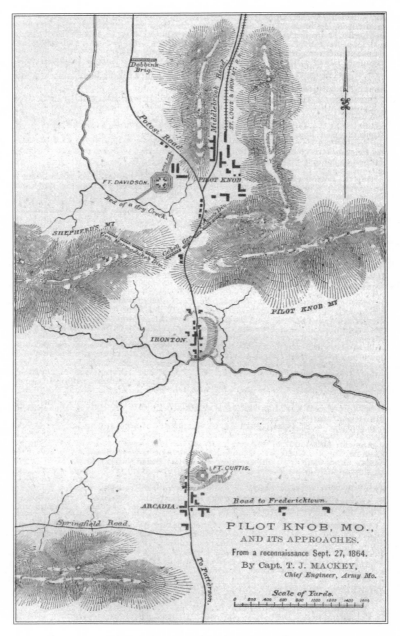

Pilot Knob, Missouri, and Its Approaches.
From the Official Records, ser. 1, vol. 41, pt. 1, p. 708. Missouri History Museum.

sharpshooters, who were showing themselves on Pilot Knob Mountain. I remained in that position but a minute or two, having been driven down by the fire of sharpshooters of the enemy. I observed that the work was situated in an open plateau, the ground between the work and the mountain being free from obstructions, and the road from Pilot Knob to Potosi running almost due north from the work; the armament of the work consisting apparently of eight heavy guns. There appeared to be but a slight ditch around it. The work being enveloped in smoke, I could not see very distinctly. I returned from the mountain and informed General Price of the location of the work; that the ditch was slight the work appearing to have been embanked from the interior. I stated to General Price that the work was commanded by Shepherd's Mountain, the key to the position, in which opinion he concurred with me, he having consulted a map of the situation made previously by the engineers of General Hardee. I did not then, nor do not now regard the ditch of that work as being a serious obstacle to a successful assault. The work was an irregular octagonal earth-work, called Fort Davidson, the faces being from thirty to thirty-five yards each with a bomb-proof magazine, the garrison apparently being about 1,000 men. It was largely over-garrisoned. There was no bomb or splinter proof shelters for troops. The guns were in barbette. I then suggested the following plan of attack of the position, which was to place six or eight field pieces on the crest of Shepherd's Mountain by hand, stating that the guns could be placed in position in about two hours on a point 1,200 or 1,500 yards from the work and about 300 feet above it; that proper support should be assigned for those pieces; that while that was being done the work should be invested by the remaining troops of the two divisions of Generals Marmaduke and Fagan, with the remaining four pieces of artillery; that I thought the route north in the direction of Potosi would be the natural line of retreat of the enemy if driven from the work. General Price concurred with me.

Question. State what dispositions were made by Major-General Price; what orders were given by him within your hearing for the conduct of the battle, and then state how the battle was fought and with what result.

Answer. General Price ordered an assault to be made; I do not know by whom the dispositions were made. The troops were formed in the following Order: Marmaduke's Division on the north slope of Shepherd's Mountain, about 800 or 900 yards distant from the work; Fagan's Division on Marmaduke's right, its left resting on Shepherd's Mountain on a prolongation of Marmaduke's line, its right resting on the west slope of Pilot Knob Mountain, both divisions masked by the timber on the mountain and about equidistant from the work, Fagan a little nearer to it. Dobbin's brigade of about 1,500 or 1,600 men was in position about a mile due north of the work on the road to Potosi. He was in position several hours before the line of attack was formed. Two field pieces were placed in position on Shepherd's Mountain about 1,250 yards from the work. The other guns, eight field pieces, including two or three rifles, were in reserve with a regiment dismounted at Ironton, three-fourths of a mile southeast of Pilot Knob. General Price observed to the staff officers of Generals Marmaduke and Fagan that there must be a perfect concert of action in the assault; that the movements of both divisions must be simultaneous; that they must attack together, and enjoined that Generals Marmaduke and Fagan should communicate freely with him and with each other to secure perfect harmony of action. General Price had previously, and three or four hours before the assault was made, dispatched couriers to be mounted on the best horses to Brigadier-General Shelby, then believed to be at Potosi to march immediately for Pilot Knob with the double object of cutting the enemy's line of retreat, and operating against any force that might assist the garrison. These dispositions were complete between 2 and 3 p.m., when a few rounds, five or six in number, were fired from the guns in battery on Shepherd's Mountain. Fagan's division debouched upon the plateau at a point about 500 yards distant from the work, where his whole line came under fire. Marmaduke debouched upon the plateau about 600 yards from the work. Several (say five) minutes later Fagan's division, after advancing about 100 yards on the plateau, broke in the most disgraceful manner, and before it had experienced any material loss, with the exception of Cabell's brigade, which was on the extreme left, which moved steadily across the plateau at double-quick and delivering its fire under the fire of five or six heavy guns, two six-inch Coehorn mortars, and two or three 2-pounder steel skirmish guns which swept the gorge of the work upon which Cabell's right was moving; the enemy attempting to raise the drawbridge, but the ropes breaking the gorge was left open. The enemy's chief attention was directed to Cabell's brigade, which having reached a point in the vicinity of the ditch, and meeting with very heavy loss, fell back in very great disorder up the slope of Pilot Knob Mountain. Marmaduke, while Cabell was moving as described, moved from the southwest and west faces of the work, his command delivering its fire as it advanced. After having passed about 200 yards on the plateau in which the work is situated under fire of several of the guns of the work with but little effect on its line, the entire division halted and laid down on the dry bed of a creek about 250 or 300 yards from the work just before Cabell's line broke. About 4 o'clock in the afternoon the fight concluded, Marmaduke's division continuing to remain in the bed of the creek sheltered from the fire, the other troops retiring in great disorder, General Price using every effort to rally the troops in person.

Question. What was the force under command of Major-General Marmaduke, and what was the force under Major-General Fagan, and what were their respective losses in the assault on Fort Davidson?

Answer. Marmaduke's division I estimated at 3,000 or 3,500, Fagan's about 4,000. Fagan's loss in killed and wounded was about 350 officers and men, and Marmaduke's about 75 or 80, perhaps somewhat less. My estimate is based from observation of the field after the fight. This includes the reserves.

Question. How long have you been a soldier?

Answer. With the exception of brief intervals, for nineteen years, and was educated for the profession; and since May, of 1861, in the armies of the Confederacy.

Question. How long in your opinion would it have required the ten guns of General Price's army on the crest of Shepherd's Mountain to have forced the surrender of Fort Davidson?

Answer. Fifteen or twenty minutes, if using shells and the practice good.

Question. How long did it take to move the two guns that were in position on the crest of Shepherd's Mountain to their position?

Answer. About an hour and a half or two hours; perhaps a little longer.

Question. State if the fight was renewed on the following morning (28th September); and if not, why not?

Answer. The fight was not renewed, the enemy having evacuated the fort during the night. About 2:30 or 3 in the morning we were advised of his evacuation by the explosion of his magazine. The enemy retired by the Potosi road undisturbed.

Question. State at what time General Price's army was reformed and started in pursuit.

Answer. Very early in the morning of the 28th, some of the troops moving at daylight.

Question. State how the enemy were observed during the night, if at all, and what dispositions were then made to intercept the retreat on the following day, and with what result.

Answer. I have no personal knowledge of how they were ob-served by night. Until that time they were observed by Major-General Marmaduke's division and Colonel Dobbin's brigade. On the morning of the 28th our army was moved on the Potosi road in pursuit. I heard General Price ordering the pursuit to be vigorous; I know not with what result, as I was ordered to remain at Fort Davidson to destroy it and its armament.

Question. What fell into the hands of our army at Pilot Knob?

Answer. The fort, with its killed and wounded; its armament, consisting of 4 32-pounder guns, 4 24-pounder howitzers on garrison carriages, 4 6-inch Coehorn mortars, 4 steel 2-pounder skirmish guns, together with many hundred rounds of fixed ammunition for these guns; a large amount of ammunition for small-arms, and about eight or ten days' rations for 1,000 men; some 100 or 200 blankets; also the foundry, furnaces, and all the work-shops of the Pilot Knob Iron Company; the towns of Arcadia, Moulton, and Pilot Knob, and 2,000 pounds of coffee, with a large amount of supplies in those three towns.

The hour of 3 p.m. having arrived the Court adjourned to meet tomorrow, the 25th instant, at 9 a.m.

FOURTH DAY.
TUESDAY, April 25, 1865—9 a.m.
At a Court of Inquiry then held at Shreveport, La., pursuant to adjournment.

Present, Brig. Gen. Thomas F. Drayton, Provisional Army, C. S.; Brig. Gen. E. McNair, Provisional Army, C. S.; Col. P. N. Luckett, Third Texas Infantry; Maj. O. M. Watkins, assistant adjutant-general and judge-advocate.

Maj. Gen. S. Price appeared before the Court.

The proceedings of yesterday read.

The JUDGE-ADVOCATE then continued the examination of Capt. T. J. MACKEY, corps of engineers.

Question. You have stated that in crossing the Blue River our army encountered resistance. State the character of the resistance, what obstacles to our crossing were interposed by the enemy, and how the crossing of our army was effected.

Answer. The enemy had felled the timber around the ford on the road leading to Westport for 500 yards, making a very formidable entanglement. General Price in person designated a path up the bank, which was very bold, by which a part of his cavalry (Shelby's), after having dismounted, ascended the opposite bank, driving the enemy back. He then ordered me to cut a road through the entanglement without delay, so that his artillery could pass. This road was cut by 90 or 100 axmen in about one hour and a half. A portion of our troops then advanced under the immediate direction of General Price. The enemy fell back to the vicinity of Westport. Our loss very light; theirs not known to me.

Question. When the affair on the Marais des Cygnes prairie occurred (on the 25th of October) where was General Price during the engagement?

Answer. He was with the leading division (Shelby's), five or six miles from the field, his usual position when there was no reason to apprehend an attack in rear.

Question. State whether or not, at Boonville, Mo., there was any engagement with the enemy, and, if you say there was, state the relative position of the two armies and their relative strength and the result.

Answer. We arrived at Boonville on the 10th of October. In the afternoon of the 9th of October General Shelby dashed into Boonville, capturing a garrison of about 300 men, who were behind barricades with their arms. On the 10th General Price entered Boonville at the head of the army, Fagan's division encamping on the east and southeast of the town, observing the approaches upon Boonville from those directions; Marmaduke's division south of the town, about three-fourths of a mile distant from Boonville, its left resting on the Tipton road connecting with Cabell's brigade of Fagan's right. Heavy pickets thrown out in the direction of Tipton. Shelby's division was west of the town. On the next day, the 11th, the position of the troops not being materially changed, the enemy made a demonstration from the direction of Tipton, driving in our pickets on that road. From the extent of the enemy's line observed by me I estimate their force in our immediate front at 2,500 men, some of them were dismounted. After a personal reconnaissance I reported it to Major-General Price on the field as my opinion that this was the advance of a large force. They had opened with artillery in advancing. Their advance was engaged by Cabell's brigade and checked. The enemy fell back a mile or two and General Price sent various detachments to observe his strength and position. The enemy fell back in the course of the night, and on the following morning was again in the vicinity of the town, south and west of it. General Price ordered Brigadier-General Shelby to turn the enemy's left, while Major-Generals Marmaduke's and Fagan's divisions pressed him on the right and center. Before the enemy could be turned effectually he fell back after a severe engagement with a part of Brigadier-General Shelby's division. He was pursued for eighteen or twenty miles in the direction of Tipton by Major-General Fagan's and a part of other divisions.

Question. Did you hear any general at Boonville propose to General Price to go out and crush the enemy? If so, state who the general was and the plan proposed to General Price.

Answer. I heard no general press General Price to attack the enemy, but heard General Fagan in a very undecided manner express to General Price an opinion that the enemy should be attacked. He proposed no plan.

Question. What was the character of troops opposed to General Price in Missouri and Kansas—regulars, volunteers of long service, new organizations of volunteers, or militia?

Answer. I ascertained their character from prisoners taken from various commands. Some were veteran troops from Atlanta, some from near Nashville and Vicksburg; also a large number of militia from Missouri and Kansas.

Question. You have stated that at some times short delays in the march of the army were occasioned by the necessity of removing obstructions from the road. State what measures were adopted by General

Price to make those delays as short as possible. Whether or not there was an organization of a pioneer corps; and, if there was, how it was controlled and managed.

Answer. There were parts of two companies of engineer troops, numbering in the aggregate seventy-five men, under my orders. A company of pioneers was attached to Fagan's division not under my orders. These were but poorly supplied with working implements. When we were crossing at Dardanelle I was directed by General Price to fully equip them as speedily as possible. I converted three of the pontoons into wagon bodies, forming an engineer train, and a fourth pontoon converted into a wagon body to the pioneers of Fagan's division. After crossing the Missouri line all these troops were speedily fully equipped. On the day that we crossed the Arkansas River General Price ordered that the engineer troops should march in advance of the army to remove obstructions, repair bridges, &c. Fagan's company of pioneers moved always with the division, but was ordered while in Missouri by General Price to move in the front of the army under my direction, which order was obeyed for one day only. Fagan's pioneers were the most efficient in that army. The engineer troops were ragged, and many of them unshod.

Question. Was the failure to comply with this order reported to General Price and, if so, state what measures, if any, he adopted to enforce its observance.

Answer. I reported the fact to Colonel Maclean, the assistant adjutant-general on General Price's staff, who stated that he would issue another order. I know not that it was issued.

Question. State whether or not the army was ever detained because of the engineer or pioneer troops being from the front of the army. If so, how long, and what occasioned their absence from the fronts?

Answer. Sometimes it was detained for an hour or two from this cause in Arkansas and Missouri; sometimes from mistakes of their own officers, mistaking a detachment to guard our flanks for the advance guard of the main army. The officer in command of engineer troops assigned by department headquarters was a confirmed cripple, and his physical incapacity to discharge the duties of his office occasioned some mismanagement of those troops. On one occasion, I think at the crossing of the Osage, where it was necessary to cut a roadway, the train was detained four or five hours by the absence of General Fagan's pioneers, whose captain reported to me as an excuse that they were eight miles behind by order of General Fagan.

Question. How long in all was the march of the army from Princeton to Fredericktown delayed because of the improper organization or management or disposition of the engineer and pioneer troops, and their want of proper implements?

Answer. About three days.

Cross-examined by Maj. Gen. S. PRICE:

Question. State if Princeton was not the place of rendezvous for the army south of the Arkansas River.

Answer. It was.

Question. State if the army under my command was not detained in organizing it, arranging transportation, and the issuing of necessary supplies until a late hour on the day I reached Tulip.

Answer. It was.

Question. State, if you know, why the route by Dardanelle was taken instead of the route east of Pine Bluff.

Answer. First, because the route east of Pine Bluff furnished but a scant subsistence. The Saline River and Bayou Bartholomew crossed on that route, both unfordable, the bottoms being very bad, and the country between the Saline and Arkansas Rivers on that route had been in a great measure exhausted of its supplies by our army and that of the enemy. Second, the great probability of having our crossing of the Arkansas River disturbed by the gun-boats of the enemy on that stream.

Third,—in the event of crossing of that stream safely we would have had to cross the White River either at Jacksonport or Batesville. Had we moved directly upon Batesville we should have marched twenty-five or thirty miles over a long prairie, a bog in the rainy season and a desert in the dry. In addition, we would have had to cross the high, rocky spurs of mountains, almost impracticable for loaded wagons, with the enemy in position on our left flank at Little Rock and Pine Bluff within from twenty-five to thirty miles of our line of march; also on our right flank at Devall's Bluff. Fourth. Had we marched by Jacksonport, we could have found no better ford within twenty miles of the place as reported from previous reconnaissances. This route in distance is some sixty miles the shortest. The upper route was taken because, first, it could supply forage and subsistence; second, the road practicable, better bottoms of streams, not wide; third, it masked the real object of the campaign, indicating Fort Smith as the objective point and threatening Little Rock itself, and the passage of the Arkansas safe from disturbance by gun-boats, and a greater probability of finding the river fordable above than below Little Rock.

Question. Was it not necessary to raise the quartermaster's and commissary stores in the wagons as well as the ammunition at Dardanelle?

Answer. I did not observe that, but in some cases I observed that ordnance stores were raised.

Question. What is your professional opinion of the necessity of carrying pontoons along when navigable streams are to be crossed in the line of march?

Answer. I think it eminently proper. The organization of the army is not complete without a pontoon train. This judgment is derived from the teachings of all masters of the art of war and from my knowledge of the streams to be crossed, which were liable to sudden freshets. I deem the pontoon train essential to that army, especially as its subsistence was always in advance, as in the case of the Army of Missouri.

Question. Was any delay occasioned by taking along the pontoons?

Answer. No material delay; sometimes a brief delay to the rear guard by the breaking of the coupling poles.

Question. Was the pontoon train an encumbrance?

Answer. It was not.

Question. State the nature and character of the Arkansas.

Answer. From Dardanelle to its mouth it varies in width at ordinary stages of water from 200 to 400 yards, tortuous in its course, and liable to sudden rises from heavy rains above, with but few fords, quicksand bottom. Navigation above Little Rock very precarious; fords changing materially in the course of the day.

Question. Were you acquainted with General Price's chief of staff Colonel Maclean?

Answer. I was for many years.

Question. Are you acquainted with his general reputation as an engineer and soldier?

Answer. I am.

Question. Tell the Court what was Lieutenant-Colonel Maclean's reputation as an engineer and a soldier.

Answer. He stood in the front rank of his profession as a civil engineer. His reputation was very high as a soldier.

Question. What do you know of the diligence of General Price in availing himself of Colonel Maclean's skill as an engineer, as well as your own, and his habits as to consulting maps, getting information as to the country, use of guides, and general judiciousness of his disposition for the marches?

Answer. It was the habit of General Price to avail himself of maps made by Colonel Maclean constantly, and also the published maps of the country. I was seldom consulted upon that head. His habit was to secure the service of guides and assign an officer to their special direction in cases where he did not himself know the country. The army was never without a guide to my knowledge, and it was a matter of special inquiry with me constantly. The order of march was invariably furnished at night to the generals of divisions, stating the hour at which the army would move, the position of each division en route, the position of trains, and general officers informed of the point to which we would move each day, and the position of the commanding general. Special instructions, usually verbal, were given by the commanding general for covering the flanks of his army to prevent attack, the strength of the rear and advance guard regulated by the reported movements of the enemy. There was a standing order to march at daylight, unless otherwise specially ordered.

Question. Do you know of an order to General Fagan to make a thorough reconnaissance of Ironton and vicinity on the 26th of September, 1864?

Answer. General Price issued such an order on the Saint Francis on that day.

Question. Do you know what information Major-General Fagan communicated to Major-General Price on his arrival in the vicinity of Ironton?

Answer. I heard General Fagan express his opinion of the strength of the position of Pilot Knob to General Price, and stated that he could take it with his division alone in twenty minutes by assault, and urged that the assault he made. He stated that the enemy might send a large detachment by railroad from Saint Louis and relieve the garrison and the work unless we acted promptly; that the strength of the garrison was small.

Question. What was the information in relation to the enemy having forced prominent citizens into the fortifications, and was not that information urged as a reason why the place should not be shelled?

Answer. Information was furnished General Price in my presence by citizens of Ironton and Arcadia that the enemy had forced Southern residents, old and young, including boys, into the work from the college of Arcadia. These citizens urged that he should not shell the work.

They also stated to General Price that these citizens in the work would not fire upon our column assaulting the work.

Question. Do you know of the message sent by Major-General Marmaduke from Shepherd's Mountain to Major-General Price while in full view of the enemy's works at Pilot Knob? Or state what was said by Major-Generals Marmaduke or Fagan or both of them to General Price about the assault?

Answer. I do. An officer of General Marmaduke's staff reported to General Price that he was instructed by General Marmaduke to report that in his (General Marmaduke's) opinion that with two guns on Shepherd's Mountain, where he then stood, he could take the works in a few minutes. I am not positive of the precise words.

Question. Did Major-General Price order the assault on the work at the earnest solicitation of Major-Generals Fagan and Marmaduke? State what you know.

Answer. He did.

The witness here desired to correct his testimony in answer to the question previously propounded by the judge-advocate, which reads as follows:

Question. How long in all was the march of the army from Princeton to Fredericktown delayed because of the improper organization or management or disposition of the engineer and pioneer troops, and their want of proper implements?

To which the witness replies: About one day.

FIFTH DAY.
WEDNESDAY, April 26, 1865—9 a.m.
At a Court of Inquiry then held at Shreveport, La., pursuant to adjournment.

Present, Brig. Gen. Thomas F. Drayton, Provisional Army, C. S.; Brig. Gen. E. McNair, Provisional Army, C. S.; Col. P. N. Luckett, Third

Texas Infantry; Maj. O. M. Watkins assistant adjutant-general and judge-advocate.

The Court was cleared at the instance of the judge-advocate.

The judge-advocate then asked an order of the Court to summons [*sic*] Governor Thomas C. Reynolds as a witness.

The Court after mature deliberation directed the judge-advocate to issue the summons desired.

Maj. Gen. Sterling Price then appeared before the Court.

The cross-examination of Capt. T. J. MACKEY continued by Major-General PRICE:

Question. Did you examine the works at Pilot Knob, more particularly Fort Davidson, after the action?

Answer. I did, very carefully.

Question. State your professional opinion of the practicability of ditch and parapet for assault. State reasons.

Answer. The ditch offered but a slight obstruction and could have been readily passed and parapet mounted. The ditch was ten feet in width, depth, six feet four inches, the command of the work eight feet. The scarp and exterior slope had been very much washed; the inclination of the exterior slope very gradual, so that it could be easily mounted. I tested the practicability of mounting it by taking a musket in my hand after we were in possession of the work, springing into the ditch and running up the exterior slope to the crest of the parapet. I repeated this with fifteen men, each with a musket in his hand, no man having any assistance from his comrade. I called the attention of Major-General Price and Brigadier-General Clark to the experiment while I was making it.

Question. If there had been prompt co-operation of the two assaulting divisions what would have been, in your professional opinion, the result?

Answer. I am satisfied that the work would have fallen upon their first assault.

Question. State your professional opinion as to under what circumstances there is the greatest amount of casualty and loss of life to an assaulting column.

Answer. When the column of attack wavers and begins retiring.

Question. Were you present after part of General Fagan's column fell back and was rallied; and did you hear General Fagan ask permission to renew the assault? State what was said by Generals Fagan, Price, and Cabell.

Answer. I was. I did hear General Fagan ask permission to renew the assault. I heard General Fagan state that he could take it by another assault, and that his (General Price's) escort ought to take part in the assault; that he had thrown his own escort in. General Price stated that he would not renew the assault. Cabell remarked to General Price that it was a damned wise decision.

Question. During the two days' stay at Boonville, was the ferryboat constantly employed in crossing recruits to the army from North Missouri?

Answer. It was.

Question. Did you see General Price's command in several successful battles? State where and when.

Answer. I did. At Lexington, Mo.; on the Little Blue; in the vicinity of Independence; at Westport; in the valley of the Osage, on the 25th of October, 1864; at Newtonia, Mo., all during the fall campaign of the Army of Missouri in 1864.

Question. Did General Price dismount the larger portion of his troops before battle; and what were his usual dispositions before battle?

Answer. He invariably dismounted the larger portion of his troops. His usual dispositions were to form his line of battle in two ranks, dismounted, when with nine brigades, one to be kept mounted on each flank, artillery posted on line of battle or on the nearest commanding ground, supports designated for batteries, reserve of one or two brigades at about half or three-fourths of a mile, varying according to the character of the ground.

Question. Were you present when General Price received information that the enemy was moving at the Marais des Cygnes on the rear of his column? If so, did General Price return immediately at half speed, first ordering General Shelby to the rear with his old brigade under Brigadier-General Thompson?

Answer. I was. General Price returned as stated, and such orders were given to General Shelby in my presence.

Question. Were you with General Price when he met the retreating column at the Marais des Cygnes? State where it was, in what order, and where was the train.

Answer. I was not with General Price when he met the retreating column on the Marais des Cygnes.

Question. What other dispositions did General Price make with the unarmed troops after the Marais des Cygnes affair, and what was the result?

Answer. On the day of the Marais des Cygnes affair, while we were engaging the enemy between the Marmiton and the Osage, and while we were being pressed heavily by the enemy, General Price formed about 5,000 or 6,000 unarmed men and moved with them upon the enemy's right under a fire of shell, and the enemy gave way upon the advance of this force.

Cross-examination concluded.

The Court was then cleared to consider of questions suggested by a member.

Major-General Price again appearing before the Court, the witness, Capt. T. J. MACKEY, was re-examined by the JUDGE-ADVOCATE:

Question. How far were the pontoons carried, and were they ever used?

Answer. They were carried to Dardanelle, where four of the eighteen were converted into wagon bodies and the others burned.

Question. Was this information as to the enemy having forced into Fort Davidson prominent citizens of the vicinity subsequently confirmed; and, if so, how?

Major-General Price here objected to this question, and assigned the following reasons:

The question is improper because it is not necessary that the information should have been absolutely true. It is sufficient that the information should have reached the commanding general through the only channel by which that officer could acquire a knowledge of the state of things, from citizens of the country who were well affected toward our army. If it appeared to be true, and was in accordance with the enemy's custom, that citizens should be pressed into their fortified places, especially sympathizers with General Price's cause, it is sufficient. It is a well-established principle of military criticism that a general is not to be judged by the state of facts that actually existed at the given time, but by such facts as appeared to him to exist from the best information he could gain.

The Court was then cleared for deliberation, and decided that the question be put.

The witness proceeded to answer:

After the retreat of the enemy I met a few citizens who were in the fort during the fight, who stated that they had been forced into it. The dead bodies of persons in citizens' dress were found in and around the work. These persons were identified as citizens by women after the fight.

By a MEMBER:

Question. What was the state of discipline in General Price's army during the campaign?

Answer. Not very good.

Question. You have already testified to the causes of delay during the march between Princeton and Potosi. Please state how many days were lost, and could this delay have been provided against?

Answer. Four or five days. This is only an approximate estimate, including delay from all causes. I think this could not have been provided against by any means within the control of the commanding general.

Question. How many cannon were fired at Fort Davidson from Shepherd's Mountain, and with what effect? What description of guns and caliber?

Answer. Two or three pieces. On the day of the assault two shells burst in or at the work. I cannot state with what effect, nor can I give a description of the guns.

Question. Were fascines or other material prepared for facilitating the passage of the ditch?

Answer. None whatever. After the assault, I prepared a number of scaling ladders.

Question. You say that General Price on the morning of the 28th August ordered the pursuit of the enemy, who had evacuated Fort Davidson during the night. Do you know if any of them were over-taken and captured? If so, how many?

Answer. I cannot say of my own knowledge that they were over-taken.

Question. To what point did the enemy retreat, by what road, and when did he reach his destination?

Answer. He retreated to a point on the Southwest Branch of the Pacific Railroad. He moved from Pilot Knob along the Potosi road. In the vicinity of Caledonia he took the road to Steelville. I cannot say when he reached his destination.

Question. Did General Shelby return in time from Potosi to take any measures for intercepting or pursuing the retreating Federals?

Answer. He did not return in time to intercept them. He pursued them.

Question. When you felt convinced that the officer in command of the engineer company was a confirmed cripple, did you report the fact to Major-General Price; and if so, what action did he take?

Answer. I reported the fact to General Price, who stated that I had better put some other officer in command and that he would approve it.

Question. Did General Price have any of the Hannibal and Saint Joseph Railroad destroyed; and if so, how many miles of it?

Answer. He ordered the destruction of it in my presence. I know not if the order was executed or not.

Question (by a MEMBER): Did General Price give instructions for the destruction of any of the railroads in North Missouri? And if so, state what roads and then state the number of miles of each that were destroyed and where.

Answer. He did, of the North Missouri Railroad and the Hannibal and Saint Joseph. I cannot state the number of miles of each that were destroyed and where.

Major-General Price then asked the permission of the Court to propound to the witness the questions which follow. The Court was cleared, and after deliberation decided that the questions be asked.

Whereupon Major-General Price again appeared before the Court.

Question. You state the discipline of the command was not good. Does this statement relate to the time of General Price assuming the command or subsequently?

Answer. To both.

Question. Was the discipline at any time worse than usual with troops of that character in an enemy's country?

Answer. It was not.

Question. What was the character of the troops which joined General Price at the second rendezvous in North Arkansas?

Answer. General Shelby's old brigade and a large body of recruits, consisting of citizens of that section, conscripts, absentees without leave from their commands, and deserters, and but a few volunteers. Shelby's command was never in a high state of discipline, but reliable in battle. They were the right arm of the army. The larger parts of the command that joined us there were of recruits, conscripts, and absentees.

Question. Do you know of General Price sending a detachment from Boonville to destroy the Peruque bridge, on the North Missouri Railroad; and if so to whom were the orders given. Give the names and character.

Answer. They were given to Colonels Anderson and [William C.] Quantrill. They were the most distinguished partisan leaders, and were the terror of the enemy in that section and accustomed to operating on railroads.

The hour of 2 o'clock having arrived, the Court adjourned to meet at 9 a.m. tomorrow, the 27th instant.

SIXTH DAY.

THURSDAY, April 27, 1865—9 a.m.

At a Court of Inquiry then held at Shreveport, La., pursuant to adjournment.

Present, Brig. Gen. Thomas F. Drayton, Provisional Army, C. S.; Brig. Gen. E. McNair, Provisional Army, C. S.; Col. P. N Luckett, Third Texas Infantry; Maj. O. M. Watkins, assistant adjutant-general and judge-advocate.

The record of the previous day's proceedings was read.

The judge-advocate stated to the Court that on yesterday he had sent a summons to appear as a witness to Governor Thomas C. Reynolds, as directed by the Court, a copy of which is hereunto attached and marked Exhibit E [not found] to which summons said Governor Reynolds replied by the following letter:

SHREVEPORT., LA., April 27, 1865.

Maj. O. M. Watkins,

Assistant Adjutant-General, Judge-Advocate, &c.:

MAJOR: Your letter of yesterday, informing me that the Court of Inquiry ordered at General Price's instance desired my attendance as a witness, has been received. Although the order convening the Court does not direct any investigation of the statements published by me in reference to General Price, yet as it was occasioned by them, and I have been and may hereafter be in consultation with you in reference to the inquiry, delicacy prompts me to exercise my legal right of declining to testify in the case. I do so with the greatest respect to the Court and yourself.

I am, major, very respectfully, yours,

Thos. C. Reynolds.

The judge-advocate submitted this letter to the Court and asked that the Court be cleared to consider it. The Court was accordingly cleared.

The Court decided that it had not the right to compel the attendance of Governor Reynolds, as he did not belong to the line or staff of the army.

General Price appeared before the Court.

The judge-advocate represented to the Court that he was in no way connected with the campaign to be investigated. That when it was conducted he was serving far from the scenes of its operations, and that when ordered on the Court he had no knowledge of the matters to be investigated, with the exception of what could be gleaned from unofficial and ex parte statements contained in the newspapers of the day. That Governor Reynolds, of Missouri, served throughout the campaign, and that Major-General Price, in his cross-examination, makes reference to charges contained in a letter or circular published by Governor Reynolds before this Court was asked for or ordered. He therefore requests the Court to permit Governor Reynolds to be present during the taking of such testimony as the Court may not deem necessary to be kept from the knowledge of one of his high official position in order that the judge-advocate for his own information may consult with him more intelligently on the facts and circumstances to be scrutinized by the Court.

The Court was cleared for deliberation. The request of the judge-advocate was refused, inasmuch as Governor Reynolds does not appear in the attitude of prosecutor, and the Court sits with its doors closed at all times to all persons except those absolutely necessary for the transaction of its business.

General Price again appeared before the Court.

The judge-advocate announced the decision of the Court.

Maj. JAMES R. SHALER, assistant adjutant-general, was then sworn and examined by the judge-advocate, no other witness being present:

Question. Were you in the campaign in Missouri in the autumn of 1864 under command of Major-Gen. Price; and if so, in what capacity you served, when you joined the command, and when you left it?

Answer. Yes; I was the inspector-general of that army and on the staff of Major-General Price. I served in that capacity on the staff of Major-General Price from May, 1864, to December of that year.

Question. State the organization of the army under command of Major-General Price while operating in Missouri in September and October of 1864 at the beginning of the campaign, and give any material changes that were made during the campaign.

Answer. At the commencement of the march it was composed of Major-General Fagan's division and a battalion of three companies; Major-General Marmaduke's division of one brigade of Missouri troops and a battalion of six companies, and a brigade of Louisiana troops ordered to report to General Marmaduke, but failed to do so. Upon the arrival of the army at Pocahontas, the army was reorganized, and upon leaving that place was composed of three Divisions. Major-General Fagan's, composed of four brigades and a battalion of three companies, Major-General Marmaduke's of two brigades, and Brigadier General Shelby's of two brigades. To Brigadier General Cabell's and Colonel Slemon's brigades, in Major-General Fagan's Division there were attached two pieces of artillery, making four in all for the Division. Major General Marmaduke's division had a battalion of artillery attached to it composed of two batteries, three pieces in each battery. Brigadier-General Shelby's division had one battery of four pieces and one company as a body guard of the commanding general of the army. After arriving at Boonville a brigade of Missouri recruits of two regiments was formed and placed under the command of Colonel Tyler and became part of Marmaduke's division. Besides these there were companies of partisan troops reported by their leaders to General Price, but never became a part of the regular organization.

Question. State the caliber and character of the artillery in the Army of Missouri.

Answer. I cannot state it with accuracy. They were field pieces, some of them rifled. Two of Brigadier General Shelby's pieces were Parrott guns; the caliber I do not recollect.

Question. State the discipline of the troops when the campaign began and during it to its conclusion.

Answer. There was no discipline when it began and during the campaign, and at its conclusion there was all the disorder that must necessarily obtain in an undisciplined command.

Question. Were any measures adopted by General Price to secure discipline? If there were, state what measures.

Answer. Yes; orders were issued by General Price which, if carried out, would have secured order; but it was impossible to carry them into execution literally with such a command.

Question. State whether or not any depredations or outrages were committed by the soldiers of General Price's command during the campaign; and if so, state their character and general extent.

Answer. Yes, there were. The soldiers commenced plundering at Arcadia, and from there throughout the whole expedition. Wherever supplies were to be found there was more or less plundering. There seemed to be a desire upon the part of the troops generally not to molest persons of Southern proclivities, but whenever persons disposed to be favorable to the Federal cause were found their property was taken. All kinds of property was taken.

Question. State whether these outrages were committed by soldiers while on the march under the eye of their officers, or by what class of soldiers.

Answer. They were generally committed by soldiers who left the column, some straggling and some under permission of their immediate commanders. The captains of companies, regimental, brigade, and division commanders all gave permission to scout, and by such parties many depredations were committed.

Question. Were any measures adopted by General Price to prevent these outrages? If so, state what they were, and were any efforts made by him to punish such offenders ? If there were, state the character of such efforts.

Answer. A provost guard was organized in each brigade and a provost-marshal-general appointed for the army. Provost-marshals of brigades reported to their provost-marshals of divisions, and they to the provost-marshal-general, who was directed by Major-General Price to call for whatever number of troops he required to prevent these outrages. Stringent orders were repeatedly given with reference both to stragglers and to private property, directing their arrest in all cases. In case of resistance on their part, that they should be shot down. In many instances General Price in person directed the arrest of persons with stolen property in their possession. General Price instituted a court-martial at or about Pocahontas. There were no other measures adopted that I can think of at present.

The hour of 3 p. m. having arrived, the Court then adjourned to meet again on to-morrow, the 28th instant, at 9 a.m.

SEVENTH DAY.

The Court assembled at 9.15 a.m. on Friday, April 28, 1865, pursuant to adjournment.

Present, Brig. Gen. Thomas F. Drayton, Provisional Army, C. S.; Brig. Gen. E. McNair, Provisional Army, C. S.; Maj. O. M. Watkins, assistant adjutant-general and judge-advocate.

Maj. Gen. Sterling Price appeared before the Court.

Col. P. N. Luckett, Third Texas Infantry, was absent.

The proceedings of yesterday were read, after which the judge-advocate read to the Court the following note—

Shreveport, LA., April 28, 1865.

Maj. O. M. WATKINS,

Judge-Advocate, &c.:

Major: Colonel Luckett was quite sick this morning and will not be able to attend Court today.

I am, very respectfully, your obedient servant,

C. M. Taylor,

Surgeon, Provisional Army, C. S.

and asked that the Court adjourn because of the illness of Colonel Luckett until Monday next. The Court then adjourned to meet again at 9 o'clock on Monday next, the 1st of May, 1865.

EIGHTH DAY.

The Court met at 9 a.m. on Monday, May 1, 1865, pursuant to adjournment.

Present, Brig. Gen. Thomas I. Drayton, Provisional Army, C. S.; Brig. Gen. E. McNair, Provisional Army, C. S.; Maj. O. M. Watkins, assistant adjutant-general and judge-advocate.

Maj. Gen. S. Price appeared before the Court.

Proceedings of the seventh day were read.

The judge-advocate stated to the Court that he was informed by Surg. C. M. Taylor that Colonel Luckett was still too ill to attend Court.

The Court then at 9.15 a.m. adjourned to meet at 9. a.m. on to-morrow, the 2ᵈ day of May, 1865.

NINTH DAY.

The Court met at 9 a.m. on Tuesday, May 2, 1865, pursuant to ad-journment.

Present, Brig. Gen. Thomas F. Drayton, Provisional Army, C. S.; Brig. Gen. E. McNair, Provisional Army, C. S.; Maj. O. M. Watkins, assistant adjutant-general and judge-advocate.

Maj. Gen. S. Price appeared before the Court.

Col. P. N. Luckett, Third Texas Infantry, absent.

The judge-advocate read the proceedings of yesterday, and also the following note from Surg. C. M. Taylor:

OFFICE OF DIRECTOR, GENERAL HOSPITAL

Shreveport, La., May 1, 1865.

Maj. O. M. WATKINS,

Judge-Advocate:

MAJOR: I have been prescribing for Colonel Luckett for some time past, and I am satisfied that he will not be able to continue as a mem-ber of the Court without serious injury to his health, and I have rec-ommended that he apply for leave of absence for sixty days, and have given a certificate upon which he will base his application.

I am, very respectfully, your obedient servant,

C. M. Taylor,

Medical Director, General Hospital, Trans-Mississippi Department.

Whereupon the Court was cleared for deliberation, and resolved to proceed with the investigation of the case now before it.

Major-General Price again appeared before the Court.

The JUDGE-ADVOCATE continued the examination of Maj. JAMES R. SHALER, assistant adjutant-general's department:

Question. Did any recruits join the command of General Price during the campaign? If so, state how many and the number that returned with him to Arkansas, and what measures were adopted by General Price to recruit.

Answer. Yes; many. I think as many as 10,000. From 5,000 to 7,000 returned with us from Arkansas. General Price gave to persons applying authority to organize companies and regiments. I know of no other measure. The difficulty was not to get troops, but to organize them.

Cross-examined by Maj. Gen. S. PRICE:

Question. What number of armed troops entered the State of Missouri under General Price's command?

Answer. About 7,000.

Question. What was the number and character of the unarmed troops?

Answer. About 2,000 unarmed troops, mostly deserters.

Question. State what sort of troops constituted General Price's command with which he entered Missouri; what character of persons they were composed, and how officered.

Answer. About 5,000 of the troops were of the usual character of Confederate cavalry. The remainder were deserters and conscripts, officered by men of their own kind, to some extent. This does not apply to brigade commanders.

Question. Do you know of any marauders being executed summarily? State when and where and in what manner.

Answer. Yes; I know of two certainly, and I think more having been shot down summarily for marauding by Colonel Freeman. I don't recollect when or where. Colonel Freeman notified me officially that when these men were arrested and brought to Colonel Freeman's quarters they admitted that they had been marauding, and one said that he would do the same thing again, whereupon he, Colonel Freeman, shot them. I cannot be precise as to the details.

Question. Do you know of General Price's complimenting Colonel Freeman for his shooting these men, and in what terms?

Answer. General Price expressed his approval of Colonel Freeman's conduct, but I do not remember whether Colonel Freeman was present or not.

Question. Did you hear General Price say if in his power he would make Colonel Freeman brigadier for that act?

Answer. I don't remember having heard him say so.

Question. Do you know of any officers being punished by General Price for participating in outrages?

Answer. Many were placed in arrest, from colonels of regiments down. I don't know what was done with them subsequently.

Question. Were these permissions to scout you mention as given by captains, regimental, and brigade commanders in accordance with General Price's orders?

Answer. They were in violation of them.

Question. Was it not absolutely necessary that the different commands should sometimes spread over a large extent of country on horseback to procure forage?

Answer. Yes.

Question. Was an additional provost guard ordered up at Arcadia and placed under command of Colonel Tyler, an old army officer?

Answer. Yes.

Question. You say the difficulty was not to get recruits, but to organize them. Was there any difficulty in subsisting, protecting, and arming them? State what.

Answer. Yes; there was great difficulty, as arms could not be procured. The unarmed men in the command interfered materially with the rapidity and effectiveness of its movements.

Question. Was not much the larger half of the troops unarmed from the time he reached Central Missouri?

Answer. I think so. I don't think that the armed men at any time during the campaign exceeded 8,000 or 9,000 in number.

Cross-examination by Major-General Price concluded.

Re-examined by the JUDGE-ADVOCATE:

Question. You say that these permits to scout, given by company, regimental, or brigade commanders were in violation of General Price's orders. State what measures, if any, were adopted by General Price to prevent their continuance, and whether or not any officer or officers were punished for having given such permission.

Answer. I know of no measures except reiterated orders from General Price and his staff officers forbidding such permissions. I don't know that any officers were punished for giving such permission.

The re-examination by the judge-advocate was here concluded.
By a MEMBER:

Question. What prevented an earlier movement of General Price from Camden?

Answer. Want of ordnance stores, which were to have been received from Shreveport.

Question. When did they arrive?

Answer. I can't give the precise date, but it was on the 27th or 28th of August. A considerable portion crossed the Ouachita River on Sunday, which I think was the 28th.

Question. What was the strength of Dobbin's brigade when at Pilot Knob? How did it happen that Colonel Dobbin did not intercept the enemy on his retreat from Fort Davidson?

Answer. I do not recollect, nor can I tell how it happened that the retreat was not intercepted.

Question. Were you in a position on the night of the 27th and 28th of September, 1864, to know whether sentinels and pickets were posted so as to detect the earliest movements of the enemy, aggressive or retreat?

Answer. I was not.

Question. Do you know that troops were stationed to watch the enemy in the fort and give notice of his movements at the earliest moment?

Answer. Yes; troops were stationed on the road leading along the Iron Mountain Railroad toward Saint Louis, and also upon the road by which the enemy eventually retreated toward Caledonia, and orders were sent to Brigadier-General Shelby to move down upon the Caledonia road, which, had he received, would have intercepted the retreat of the enemy.

Question. What was the nearest point to the fort that any of these troops were posted on the route by which the enemy retreated?

Answer. I don't know.

Question. Were you at the battle of Marais des Cygnes? Was the order of battle a judicious one? To what cause do you attribute the disasters of the day? Who was the immediate commander at Marais des Cygnes?

Answer. I was conducting the train, was with it when it was parked, about nine miles from where the fight began.

Question. Were the different foraging parties sent out during the march placed under the charge of commissioned officers?

Answer. Many times they were not.

Question. Why was it so difficult to carry out General Price's orders for the enforcement of discipline among the troops?

Answer. Because they were undisciplined troops, and also the command being always in motion it was impossible to inaugurate any system of discipline or punishment, and because there was a large number of unarmed men who seemed to think themselves not amenable to orders.

Question. Were any officers or soldiers punished or shot for marauding or straggling by sentence of a court-martial?

Answer. None that I know of.

Question. Did any disaster occur in the campaign attributable to a want of confidence or distrust in the leadership of the major-general commanding the expedition?

The judge-advocate objected.

The Court was cleared for deliberation and the objection was sustained.

Major-General Price appeared again before the Court.

Question. Was there any distrust or want of confidence in the leadership of Major-General Price on the part of the troops of the campaign?

Answer. Not that I know of.

Question. Were the orders issued by General Price in regard to the discipline of the troops in his command obeyed; and if not, did he, General Price, enforce obedience?

Answer. No, sir. General Price depended upon his division commanders to enforce his order, the composition of the command and the disposition of the troops being such as to render it impossible for him to attend to the enforcement of orders himself.

Question. What was the practice of General Price in the employment of guides on the march, and who had charge of them?

Answer. His practice was to procure guides from the different commands who were thoroughly acquainted with the country in which he was operating, and he was more particular about that than any other branch of my department of the army. I had charge of the guides myself and reported with them to the commander of the advance division.

The examination of Maj. James R. Shaler, assistant adjutant-general's department, was here concluded.

Capt. T. T. TAYLOR, assistant adjutant-general, was sworn by the JUDGE-ADVOCATE and examined by him, no other witness being present:

Question. State whether or not you served in the autumn campaign of Major-General Price in the year 1864; and if so, state in what capacity you served, when you joined the command, and how long you remained with it.

Answer. I served with it as an attaché to the inspector-general's department; joined the command about the 28th or 29th of August, and remained until we reached Richmond in Arkansas, I think in the latter part of December.

Question. Were you assigned specially to the discharge of any duties during that time? If so, state to what duties.

Answer. At the beginning of the campaign and until we reached the Arkansas River, I was directed by Colonel Shaler, the inspector-general, to attend the train and look after its movements. After we crossed the Arkansas I sometimes selected camps, but was not specially assigned to any particular duty.

Question. How were the orders of the major-general commanding published to the army during the campaign?

Answer. Through the adjutant-general's department. On the battle-field sometimes General Price gave orders himself and through his staff.

Question. State whether or not you ever heard an order of the major-general commanding read to the troops during the campaign.

Answer. I don't know that I ever did, I not being with the troops, but at General Price's headquarters.

Question. Did you ever ride along the lines of march to ascertain how the march was conducted?

Answer. Yes.

Question. State whether you did so frequently or not.

Answer. I did frequently.

Question. What was the character of the discipline of the troops during the march; whether or not there was any delay in the march? And if you say there was, state what caused it.

Answer. It was bad. Yes, there was delay. I don't know the reason of it.

The examination-in-chief was here concluded.

Cross-examined by Major-General PRICE:

Question. Had you not been acting as assistant to Colonel Shaler before the command started from Camden, and did you continue to do so on the campaign?

Answer. Yes.

Question. What was, in your knowledge, the diligence of Major-General Price in preserving order on the march, both as relates to the troops and the train?

Answer. There was great diligence.

Question. State the character of the troops. State what efforts General Price made to preserve good order and discipline.

Answer. The troops were undisciplined, and General Price frequently gave me personal instructions to prevent the straggling of the troops and the closing up of the train. I think I rode two horses to death in carrying out these instructions.

Question. Do you know of any court-martial being held at Richwoods and elsewhere on the expedition into Missouri?

Answer. I know that it was held at several points on the road.

Question. Do you know of any soldiers being executed for marauding on the expedition? State how many, when and where.

Answer. Not of my own knowledge.

Question. Did you hear any officer make any report to General Price concerning the execution of men for marauding? If so, state what officer; state what was reported and what General Price did or said.

Answer. Yes, I heard Colonel Freeman, commanding brigade in Marmaduke's division, report to General Price in person that he had himself shot some men—I don't know how many, two I think—whom he had caught robbing. General Price said that if he had it in his power he would make him a brigadier for it.

Question. Do you remember any further particulars of the report than you have stated?

Answer. No, not to General Price.

Re-examined by the JUDGE-ADVOCATE:

Question. You have stated in answer to questions propounded during the cross-examination that you rode along the lines of the army during its march very often, and that General Price used great diligence in preserving order during the march; now state whether or not he took measures to correct every evil resulting from a want of order in the march that was officially reported by you to him.

Answer. He did.

Question (by a MEMBER). To what causes do you attribute the bad discipline of the army, as already stated by you?

Answer. To the fact that two-thirds of the army were deserters from commands south of the Arkansas River, and to the want of the enforcement of discipline by subordinate generals.

The examination of Captain Taylor is here concluded.

The hour of 3 p.m. having arrived the Court adjourned to meet again at 9 a.m. on Wednesday, the 3rd day of May, 1865.

TENTH DAY.

WEDNESDAY, May 3, 1865—9 a.m.

The Court met pursuant to adjournment.

Present, Brig. Gen. Thomas F. Drayton, Provisional Army, C. S.; Brig. Gen. E. McNair, Provisional Army, C. S.; Maj. O. M. Watkins, assistant adjutant-general and judge-advocate. Col. P. K. Luckett, Third Texas Infantry, absent.

Major-General Price appeared before the Court.

The record of the proceedings of yesterday were read.

The judge-advocate then read to the Court the following order and letter from department headquarters.

SPECIAL ORDERS, HEADQUARTERS TRANS-MISSISSIPPI DEPARTMENT,

No. 104. Shreveport, La., May 2, 1865.

VIII. The Court of Inquiry instituted at the instance of Major-General Price by Paragraph XVI, Special Orders, No. 58, current series, Department Headquarters, will on receipt of this order adjourn to Washington, Ark., and there resume its sessions.

By command of General E. Kirby Smith:

P. B. Leeds,

Major and Acting Assistant Adjutant-General.

Maj. O. M. WATKINS.

HDQRS. TRANS-MISSISSIPPI DEPARTMENT, ADJUTANT-GENERAL'S OFFICE,

Shreveport, May 3, 1865.

Brig. Gen. T. F. DRAYTON,

Provisional Army, C. S., President Court of Inquiry, Shreveport:

GENERAL: I am directed by the general commanding to say the Court of Inquiry of which you are president will finish with the witness it may now have on the stand before adjourning to Washington as directed in the order of yesterday, but that no new witnesses will be called here.

I am, general, very respectfully, your obedient servant,

S. S. Anderson,

Assistant Adjutant-General.

The Court then at 10 a.m. adjourned to meet at Washington, Ark., on Monday, the 8th instant at 12 m., or as soon thereafter as practicable.

Oscar M. Watkins,

Major, Assistant Adjutant-General and Judge-Advocate.

HEADQUARTERS TRANS-MISSISSIPPI DEPARTMENT,
Shreveport, La., May 19, 1865
I certify the above to be the original of the proceedings of a Court of
Inquiry, ordered from department headquarters in case of Major-General Price.
C. S. West, Major and Assistant Adjutant-General.

Major-General Price asks the indulgence of the Court and their
patient consideration of the following:

The investigations up to the time of their summary interruption
by the general commanding the department had developed enough of
the history of the campaign into Missouri for his individual vindication and to relieve him from that feeling of delicacy which impelled
him to forbear presenting anything to the Court that would put him in
the attitude of seeking delay in this investigation, but it must be apparent to the Court that the range given by the order calling them places
him continually at a disadvantage. Although the Special Orders, No. 58,
Paragraph XVI, recites that a court of inquiry is called at the instance
of Major-General Price, that order mentions no imputation, charge,
or transactions into which it is made your duty to inquire, unless it be
considered that a campaign of nearly ninety days, in which over forty
battles and skirmishes were fought, and nearly 11,500 miles traversed
by the army under his command, is a transaction of such a character
as the commanding general may be authorized to order a court of inquiry into at the instance of an officer who may desire it.

He desires here to remark that courts of inquiry in the army are
instituted for the vindication of officers who have a right to demand
them, and in all instances in demanding them the custom of the service
and all analogies of the law would indicate that the applicant should
himself indicate what transaction, charge, or imputation he desires investigated. And further, it is proper to remark that courts of inquiry, except when ordered by the President, are exclusively, for the vindication

of the personal honor of officers who ask them, and courts-martial are instituted solely for their prosecution and punishment, which are tribunals to be called into being at any and all times at the discretion of the commanding general. While it is the right of every officer to demand a court of inquiry into any charge, imputation, or transaction against him it is still in the discretion, and is conceived to be in the line of duty, of the commanding officer of the department to determine if in his opinion the charge, transaction, or imputation is of such a character as will in the letter and spirit of the Articles of War warrant and authorize him in calling the court, and to grant or refuse it. If there is not such a state of facts brought officially to the knowledge of the commanding general as will bring the applicant within the Articles of War, the good of the service and other high considerations would impel him to deny what an over-sensitive jealousy of his reputation might induce an officer to demand. The granting of a court of inquiry is, under such circumstances, tantamount to an official statement that some transaction to be inquired into and explained, charge, or imputation, is before the reviewing officer and affecting his mind to the prejudice of the officer at whose instance he grants the inquiry. When such is the case the letter asking the court, or something indicating the particular transaction, should be laid before them both for their edification and the advantage of the officer whose honor and reputation is to be affected by the result of the inquiries.

Major-General Price stands ready to vindicate his own acts, but does not propose to vindicate the conduct of every single officer and man who accompanied him on his campaign last fall into Missouri. So far as respects himself personally as an officer and a gentleman, he desires everything brought to light concerning it; but as he could only exercise human diligence and human energy, and was forced to rely on the zeal and discretion of junior officers for such support as would with good fortune be successful, he cannot be fairly bound to defend all his juniors, who, not having asked for an inquiry, are not before this

Court. Much less can it become him, and still further is it from his desire, to investigate such disasters to his command in Missouri as were accompanied with the loss or captivity of the brave and valuable officers who commanded immediately at the time.

Major-General Price requests that the Court will determine the course they may feel it their duty to pursue in the progress of this investigation, and that he may be advised of such determination and make his dispositions in accordance. He calls attention to the second clause of the Articles of War under which all courts of inquiry are authorized and instituted, which relates to the danger of courts of inquiry being perverted and used for the destruction of military merit, and relies on the high tone and integrity of his brother officers, uninfluenced by other than considerations of the most manly and soldierly character, for his complete vindication. He must as in duty bound to himself insist that courts of this character can only legitimately be called into being and dissolved by commanding officers of departments, and that any unasked-for interference with their deliberations at any stage, so as to govern or direct any steps in the investigation, or produce delays, are without warrant and calculated to do him injustice and wrong.

EXHIBIT A.

HEADQUARTERS TRANS-MISSISSIPPI DEPARTMENT,
Maj. Gen. S. PRICE, Shreveport, La., August 4, 1864.
Commanding District of Arkansas:
GENERAL: You will make immediate arrangements for a movement into Missouri, with the entire cavalry force of your district. General Shelby should be instructed to have his command in Northeast Arkansas ready to move by the 20th instant. You can instruct him to await your arrival with the column immediately under your command. A brigade of Louisiana troops, under Colonel [Isaac F.] Harrison, has been ordered to report to you. They should be added to General Mar-

maduke's command, and with his old brigade constitute his division. General Clark should be transferred to the command of Marmaduke's old brigade. Colonel Greene should be left in Arkansas, together with the other regimental commanders whose mutinous conduct has already proved them unfitted for command.

General Shelby's old brigade, increased by the one raised in East Arkansas, can be organized into a division under his immediate command. General Fagan will command the division composed of Cabell's and [William A.] Crawford's brigades. These skeleton organizations are best adapted for an expedition in which a large addition to your force is expected. These weak brigades should be filled by the regiments raised in Missouri, and you should scrupulously avoid the organization of any new brigades. You will carry a supply of ammunition for General Shelby's command in Northeast Arkansas, and should yourself be provided with ammunition sufficient for the expedition. You will scrupulously avoid all wanton acts of destruction and devastation, restrain your men, and impress upon them that their aim should be to secure success in a just and holy cause and not to gratify personal feeling and revenge. Rally the loyal men of Missouri, and remember that our great want is men, and that your object should be, if you cannot maintain yourself in that country, to bring as large an accession as possible to our force. Your recruits will in all probability be mounted; deal frankly with them, and let them understand that mounted organizations, made there through necessity, are liable to be dismounted on their arrival in our lines, where forage and subsistence will not admit the maintenance of so large a cavalry force. Make Saint Louis the objective point of your movement, which, if rapidly made, will put you in possession of that place, its supplies, and military stores, and which will do more toward rallying Missouri to your standard than the possession of any other point. Should you be compelled to withdraw from the State, make your retreat through Kansas amid the Indian Territory, sweeping that country of its mules, horses, cattle, and military supplies of all kinds.

The division of General Fagan, the senior officer of your command, should be increased as soon as practicable.

By command of General Kirby Smith:

W. R. Boggs,

Brigadier-General and Chief of Staff.

[Editor's note: This court of inquiry did not complete its work. There was never any verdict rendered. On May 3, 1865, it was directed to transfer its proceedings to Washington, Arkansas, to continue hearing testimony. This did not occur. A final memo, dated May 19, certified the foregoing as the official proceedings. Protests of General Price did not prevail. While the court was meeting, the Confederacy fell. First [Robert E.] Lee (April 9), then [Joseph E.] Johnston (April 18) surrendered. Only the Trans-Mississippi District remained. News of Lee's surrender and the flight of the Confederate government reached Shreveport in the third week of April. Some in the Trans-Mississippi, including Price and Reynolds, wanted to continue the struggle, but most units were melting away through desertions. Guerrillas abounded, and the roads were unsafe. The news of Johnston's surrender reached Shreveport on May 8. On May 26, the Trans-Mississippi District was surrendered at New Orleans. On June 2, Price announced the surrender to Missouri troops that were stationed in Shreveport. And on that evening, he set out on his trip to exile in Mexico. Others fleeing to Mexico met him at San Antonio and included E. Kirby Smith, Thomas Reynolds, and Joseph O. Shelby, along with several hundred of his men who preferred exile to surrender. On July 4, they crossed the Rio Grande River into Mexico.]

Appendix 2: Background Material for Reynolds's Manuscript

A number of documents, mainly from the Official Records, pertain to various aspects of the Civil War in Missouri and Arkansas and provide additional information to support the original Reynolds text, that is, events before the Price expedition to Missouri of 1864. These are presented below in chronological order and are numbered, with brief descriptions:

1. OR, ser. 1, vol. 2, p. 798, armaments from Confederate States of America (CSA) to Missouri.

2. OR, ser. 1, vol. 3, p. 375, Harney-Price Agreement.

3. OR, ser. 1, vol. 53, p. 692, Thomas Reynolds to Jefferson Davis, June 3, 1861.

4. OR, ser. 1, vol. 53, p. 696, Jackson Proclamation, June 12, 1861.

5. OR, ser. 1, vol. 53, p. 721, CSA aid to Missouri.

6. OR, ser. 1, vol. 53, p. 722, Claiborne Jackson to Sterling Price, August 10, 1861.

7. OR, ser. 1, vol. 53, p. 730, Price Proclamation, August 20, 1861.

8. OR, ser. 1, vol. 17, pt. 2, p. 279, William Tecumseh Sherman to John Rawlins, October 18, 1862.

9. OR, ser. 2, vol. 4, pp. 642, 742, Hamilton Gamble to Samuel R. Curtis, October 22, 1862; Edward Bates to Gamble, November 21, 1862.

10. OR, ser. 1, vol. 22, pt. 2, p. 780, Reynolds to James Seddon, January 31, 1863.

11. OR, ser. 1, vol. 22, pt. 2, p. 781, Seddon to E. Kirby Smith, February 3, 1863.

12. OR, ser. 1, vol. 22, pt. 2, p. 781, Seddon to Smith, February 5, 1863.

13. OR, ser. 1, vol. 22, pt. 2, p. 782, Reynolds to Seddon, February 5, 1863.

14. OR, ser. 1, vol. 22, pt. 2, p. 783, Seddon to John Pemberton, February 6, 1863.

15. OR, ser. 1, vol. 53, p. 870, Reynolds to Price, May 18, 1863.

16. OR, ser. 1, vol. 53, p. 852, Davis to Smith, March 18, 1863.

17. OR, ser. 1, vol. 53, p. 871, Reynolds to Price, May 25, 1863.

18. OR, ser. 1, vol. 22, pt. 2, p. 863, Theophilus H. Holmes to Price, June 8, 1863; Price to Holmes, June 9, 1863.

19. OR, ser. 1, vol. 22, pt. 2, p. 935, Smith to governors, July 13, 1863.

20. OR, ser. 1, vol. 22, pt. 2, p. 935, Reynolds to Seddon, July 20, 1863.

21. OR, ser. 1, vol. 22, pt. 2, pp. 941–943, Price to Smith, July 23, 1863; Thomas Snead to James Fagan, July 23, 1863; General Orders No. 6, July 23, 1863; Snead to John S. Marmaduke, July 23, 1863.

22. OR, ser. 1, vol. 53, p. 918, Reynolds to Price, December 4, 1863.

23. OR, ser. 1, vol. 53, p. 998, Reynolds to Price, June 2, 1864.

24. OR, ser. 1, vol. 53, p. 999, Price to Reynolds, June 9, 1864.

25. OR, ser. 1, vol. 41, pt. 2, p. 1011, Reynolds to Price, July 18, 1864.

26. OR, ser. 1, vol. 41, pt. 2, p. 1020, Price to Reynolds, July 22, 1864.

27. OR, ser. 1, vol. 41, pt. 2, p. 564, Ethan A. Holcomb to Clinton B. Fisk, August 4, 1864.

No. 1. OR, ser. 1, vol. 2, p. 798 (n. 37)

Extracts from the proceedings of the Advisory Council of the State of Virginia.

Friday, May 3, 1861.

Judge Cooke, the special messenger from the governor of Missouri, having again appeared before the council and urged what he believed to be the extreme importance, in the present juncture of affairs in that State, of a favorable response to the application presented by him yesterday, at least so far as may secure the delivery to him at the Portsmouth navy-yard of the heavy ordnance he asked for.

Advised unanimously that General Gwynn be instructed to furnish, upon the order of the governor of Missouri, the heavy ordnance called for in his requisition, provided that the order can be filled without detriment to the public service at Norfolk, in all twenty-two pieces, ten 24 and 18-pounder siege guns, four 8-pounder howitzers, six 8 or 10-inch mortars, and two 8-inch columbiads.

John J. Allen,
Francis H. Smith,
M. F. Maury,
Ro. L. Montague.

No. 2. The Harney-Price Agreement

OR, ser. 1, vol. 3, p. 375 (n. 23)

Saint Louis, May 21, 1861.

The undersigned, officers of the United States Government and of the government of the State of Missouri, for the purpose of removing misapprehensions and allaying public excitement, deem it proper to declare publicly that they have this day had a personal interview in this city, in which it has been mutually understood, without the semblance of dissent on either part, that each of them has no other than a common object equally interesting and important to every citizen of Missouri—that of restoring peace and good order to the people of the

State in subordination to the laws of the General and State Governments. It being thus understood, there seems no reason why every citizen should not confide in the proper officers of the General and State Governments to restore quiet, and, as among the best means of offering no counter-influences, we mutually recommend to all persons to respect each other's rights throughout the State, making no attempt to exercise unauthorized powers, as it is the determination of the proper authorities to suppress all unlawful proceedings, which can only disturb the public peace.

General Price, having by commission full authority over the militia of the State of Missouri, undertakes, with the sanction of the governor of the State, already declared, to direct the whole power of the State officers to maintain order within the State among the people thereof, and General Harney publicly declares that, this object being thus assured, he can have no occasion, as he has no wish, to make military movements, which might otherwise create excitements and jealousies which he most earnestly desires to avoid.

We, the undersigned, do therefore mutually enjoin upon the people of the State to attend to their civil business of whatsoever sort it may be, and it is to be hoped that the unquiet elements which have threatened so seriously to disturb the public peace may soon subside and be remembered only to be deplored.

Sterling Price,
Major–General Missouri State Guard.
Wm. S. Harney,
Brigadier-General, Commanding.

No. 3. OR, ser. 1, vol. 53, p. 692 (n. 27)

MEMPHIS, TENN., June 3, 1861.
His Excellency JEFFERSON DAVIS,
President of the Confederate States of America:
Sir: You are doubtless partially aware of the present condition of Mis-

souri. As shown by the proclamation of General Harney, herewith enclosed, it is the fixed purpose of the United States Government to suppress her State sovereignty, prevent by force the arming and disciplining of her militia and the assembling of her Legislature or her sovereign convention for any purpose unacceptable to the Lincoln Administration. This fixed policy has already been exhibited in several instances, particularly in the affair at Camp Jackson, near Saint Louis, accounts of which I herewith enclose. The answer made by General Harney to the writ of habeas corpus issued by the U.S. district judge for the eastern district of Missouri, in the case of Emmett MacDonald (an extract from which is herewith enclosed), shows clearly the intention of the U.S. authorities to act under a "higher law," and disregard even the Constitution of the United States itself in their attempt to reduce Missouri to the condition of a subject province. The position assumed by her General Assembly in this matter is shown in the resolutions (herewith enclosed) unanimously adopted by both branches of that body. The people, however, are unorganized but not entirely unarmed. Good judges assure me that 60,000 rifles and shotguns are in the hands of true Southern men in our State, and my own knowledge of our people convinces me that at least two-thirds and possibly three-fourths of the voters of Missouri desire a speedy union with the Confederate States but in our present condition it is impossible to call together our convention or take a popular vote on the question. That body cannot now direct any such vote for the plain reason that the U.S. authorities have the will and physical power to prevent the polls from being opened; nor can either the General Assembly or the convention sit in safety or tranquility except under the protection of a friendly armed force. It is to the Confederate States alone, to her sister Southern States, that Missouri can look for the necessary aid for that purpose. Missouri being still nominally one of the United States, no legal or constitutional express authority exists in any one to invite your Government to send us aid. No duties or powers are entrusted to the Governor in view of any such emergency. The manifold civil duties he has to perform at the capital of the State require his presence, and the necessity of his avoiding acts compromising his position toward the United States Government, or endangering his person and the State records, is apparent to any one who is aware how greatly the interests and convenience of the people depend on the Governor's attention to those civil duties. It cannot, therefore, be expected that he should assume, without express direction of the Constitution, duties of a military and quasi-international character.

On mature consideration, examination of the laws and constitution of Missouri, and consultation with leading men of mature judgment and sound patriotism, I have come to the conclusion that, in the absence of any provision of our constitution applicable to such a state of affairs, the high moral duty of leading an armed effort to redeem the State from subjection, and its Governor and other authorities from virtual captivity, devolves not upon the Governor, but upon me. As lieutenant-governor I am, by our constitution, president of the senate, and I am also by law president of the General Assembly when in joint session.

That body has adjourned to meet at the capital on the third Monday of September next. As their presiding officer I am the only person armed with power by law to arrest disturbers of their deliberations when they are in actual session, and I conceive it to be but a small extension of this authority for me to take necessary measures to put down those who intend to disturb those deliberations by possibly even preventing a session. To wait until the General Assembly meets and attempt to punish such disturbance after it is committed would be sheer folly, as it would have been committed by a force sufficient to defy punishment. Moreover, I have entirely reliable information that an attempt on my part to perform the duties of presiding officer of the senate would be prevented by the U.S. authorities; and even if the information be incorrect, I do not consider it becoming the dignity of a free State that one of its principal officers should exercise his powers virtually at the sufferance of a military dictator claiming the right to suspend even the writ of habeas corpus. I believe history will furnish examples of protection given to such an officer in such an emergency by friendly foreign powers; and should no precisely similar example exist, I feel assured that the public opinion of your Confederacy, as well as that of Missouri, would fully justify you in extending protection to the presiding officer of a body which, as the General Assembly of Missouri has done, has unmistakably evinced its sympathy with your cause.

Under this sense of duty to the General Assembly and people of Missouri I intend to return to the State, and, as soon as I can do so with a reasonable prospect of success, call around me such of her citizens (and I know they can be counted by tens of thousands) who are willing to join me in the attempt to free her from the military rule now imposed upon her. To do so without meeting with prompt expulsion (more injurious to our cause than it would be not to make the attempt at all) is impossible, unless I am accompanied by an army of the Confederate States.

Officially, as presiding officer of the General Assembly, I hereby request the aid of your Government, and invite it to send with me a body of C. S. troops sufficient to prevent a failure at the start, and to serve as a nucleus around which the Missourians may gather to form a home force to protect their menaced liberties. If you are willing to accept this invitation, the conditions and extent of the assistance can be settled hereafter in a personal interview or otherwise.

Hoping for a prompt, and, if possible, favorable answer, I have the honor to be, Mr. President, very respectfully, your obedient servant,

Thomas C. Reynolds,
Lieutenant-Governor of the State of Missouri.

No. 4. OR, ser. 1, vol. 53, p. 696 (nn. 18, 20, 28)
A PROCLAMATION.

To the PEOPLE OF MISSOURI:

A series of unprovoked and unparalleled outrages have been inflicted upon the peace and dignity of this Commonwealth and upon the rights and liberties of its people by wicked and unprincipled men, professing to act under the authority of the United States Government. The solemn enactments of your Legislature have been nullified, your volunteer soldiers have been taken prisoners, your commerce with your sister States has been suspended, your trade with your own fellow-citizens has been and is subjected to the harassing control of an armed soldiery, peaceful citizens have been imprisoned without warrant of Law, unoffending and defenseless men, women, and children have been ruthlessly shot down and murdered, and other unbearable indignities have been heaped upon your State and yourselves.

To all these outrages and indignities you have submitted with a patriotic forbearance which has only encouraged the perpetrators of these grievous wrongs to attempt still bolder and more daring usurpations. It has been my earnest endeavor under all these embarrassing circumstances to maintain the peace of the State and to avert, if possible, from our borders the desolating effects of a civil war. With that object in view I authorized Major-General Price several weeks ago to arrange with General Harney, commanding the Federal forces in this State, the terms of an agreement by which the peace of the State might be preserved. They came, on the 21st of May, to an understanding, which was made public. The State authorities have faithfully labored to carry out the terms of that agreement. The Federal Government, on the other hand, not only manifested its strong disapprobation of it by the instant dismissal of the distinguished officer who on its part entered into it, but it at once began and has unintermittingly carried out a system of hostile operations in utter contempt of that agreement and in reckless disregard of its own plighted faith. These acts have latterly portended revolution and civil war so unmistakably that I resolved to make one further effort to avert these dangers from you. I therefore solicited an interview with Brigadier-General Lyon, commanding the Federal army in Missouri. It was granted, and on the 10th instant, waiving all questions of personal and official dignity, I went to Saint Louis, accompanied by Major-General Price.

We had an interview on the 11th instant with General Lyon and Col. F. P. Blair, Jr., at which I submitted to them this proposition:

That I would disband the State Guard and break up its organization; that I would disarm all the companies which have been armed by the State; that I would pledge myself not to attempt to organize the militia under the military bill; that no arms or munitions of war should be brought into the State; that I would protect all citizens equally in all their rights, regardless of their political opinions; that I would repress all insurrectionary movements within the State; that I would repel all attempts to invade it, from whatever quarter and by whomsoever made, and that I would thus maintain a strict neutrality in the present unhappy contest, and preserve the peace of the State. And I further proposed that I would, if necessary, invoke the assistance of the U.S. troops to carry out these pledges. All this I proposed to do upon condition that the Federal Government would undertake to disarm the home guards which it has illegally organized and armed throughout the State, and pledge itself not to occupy with its troops any localities in the State not occupied by them at this time.

Nothing but the most earnest desire to avert the horrors of civil war from our beloved State could have tempted me to propose these humiliating terms. They were rejected by the Federal officers. They demanded not only the disorganization and disarming of the State militia and the nullification of the military bill, but they refused to disarm their own home guards, and insisted that the Federal Government should enjoy an unrestricted right to move and station its troops throughout the State whenever and wherever that might, in the opinion of its officers, be necessary, either for the protection of the "loyal subjects" of the Federal Government or for the repelling of invasion, and they plainly announced that it was the intention of the Administration to take military occupation under these pretexts of the whole State, and to reduce it, as avowed by General Lyon himself, to the "exact condition of Maryland."

The acceptance by me of these degrading terms would not only have sullied the honor of Missouri, but would have aroused the indignation of every brave citizen, and precipitated the very conflict which it has been my aim to prevent. We refused to accede to them, and the conference was broken up. Fellow-citizens, all our efforts toward conciliation have failed. We can hope nothing from the justice or moderation of the agents of the Federal Government in this State. They are energetically hastening the execution of their bloody and revolutionary schemes for the inauguration of a civil war in your midst; for the military occupation of your State by armed bands of lawless invaders; for the overthrow of your State government, and for the subversion of those liberties which that government has always sought to protect, and they intend to exert their whole power to subjugate you, if possible, to the military despotism which has usurped the powers of the Federal Government.

Now, therefore, I, C. F. Jackson, Governor of the State of Missouri, do, in view of the foregoing facts and by virtue of the powers vested in me by the constitution and laws of this Commonwealth, issue this my proclamation, calling the militia of the State, to the number of 50,000, into the active service of the State, for the purpose of repelling said invasion, and for the protection of the lives, liberty, and property of the citizens of this State; and I earnestly exhort all good citizens of Missouri to rally under the flag of their State for the protection of their endangered homes and firesides, and for the defense of their most sacred rights and dearest liberties.

In issuing this proclamation, I hold it to be my solemn duty to remind you that Missouri is still one of the United States; that the executive department of the State government does not arrogate to itself the power to disturb that relation; that that power has been wisely vested in a convention, which will at the proper time express your sovereign will, and that meanwhile it is your duty to obey all the constitutional requirements of the Federal Government; but it is equally my duty to advise you that your first allegiance is due to your own State, and that you are under no obligation whatever to obey the unconstitutional edicts of the military despotism which has enthroned itself at Washington, nor to submit to the infamous and degrading sway of its wicked minions in this State. No brave and true-hearted Missourian will obey the one or submit to the other. Rise, then, and drive out ignominiously the invaders who have dared to desecrate the soil which your labors have made fruitful and which is consecrated by your homes!

Given under my hand as Governor and under the great seal of the State of Missouri at Jefferson City this 12ᵗʰ day of June, 1861.

Claiborne F. Jackson.

No. 5. OR, ser. 1, vol. 53, p. 721

AN ACT to give aid to the people and State of Missouri.

The Congress of the Confederate States of America do enact, that to aid the people of the State of Missouri in the effort to maintain, within their own limits, the constitutional liberty which it is the purpose of the Confederate States in the existing war to vindicate, there shall be, and is hereby, appropriated, out of any moneys in the Treasury not otherwise appropriated, $1,000,000, to supply clothing, subsistence, arms, and ammunition to the troops of Missouri who may co-operate with those of the Confederate States during the progress of the existing war; said sum to be expended under the discretion of the President of the Confederate States for the purposes aforesaid.

Approved August 6, 1861.

No. 6. OR, ser. 1, vol. 53, p. 722

MEMPHIS, August 10, 1861.

Major-General PRICE:

GENERAL: I have only time to write you a line, not knowing that the bearer intended leaving for your camp until a moment since. Since my last dispatch I have been to Richmond, and though I could get no arms, I have secured an appropriation of $1,000,000 to buy arms, munitions of war, and clothing for our troops. They have also passed other acts, all looking to our independence and our ultimate admission into the Confederate States. They are sending us all the men and arms they can, and ere long I trust you will see in Missouri many thousands of the noblest sons of the South to battle in the ranks of our Missouri soldiers in one common glorious cause, determined to bleach their bones upon the plains of our State sooner than submit to the yoke of Lincoln and his horde of vagabonds who are fighting for $13 per month.

I still have hope that we shall soon have a supply of new arms, but we are certain to have all the arms and all the men now in the South that can be spared from Virginia. I shall try to get off tomorrow to join Pillow at New Madrid, and proceed with him to the camps of Thompson and Hardee, in the direction of the Southwest Branch of the Pacific road, and thence to join you and McCulloch at such a point as the strength of our forces and the position of the enemy will justify us in undertaking. The exact number of these several forces combined I cannot tell, but if my information is correct it cannot fall much, if any, short of 20,000, with good arms and a large supply of ammunition. Many of these troops are well drilled, and commanded by skillful and experienced officers. We hear that you fought a successful battle with Lyon on the 3rd instant; but we hear so many false rumors over the wires that I credit nothing till I know the truth. Our friends everywhere in the South are in the finest spirits, and all are determined to give Missouri all the aid in their power. I send you a copy of my proclamation and declaration in answer to the proceedings of the convention; the balance must be settled by bayonets.

My regards to General McCulloch, and say to him that I have two suits of clothes for him. I also send him a copy of the proclamation, &c.

Yours, truly,

C. F. Jackson

No. 7. OR, ser. 1, vol. 53, p. 730

PROCLAMATION.

JEFFERSON CITY, August 20, 1861.

To the PEOPLE OF MISSOURI:

FELLOW-CITIZENS: The army under my command has been organized under the laws of the State for the protection of your homes and firesides and for the maintenance of the rights, dignity, and honor of Missouri. It is kept in the field for these purposes alone, and to aid in accomplishing them our gallant Southern brethren have come into our State. With these we have achieved a glorious victory over the foe, and scattered far and wide the well-appointed army which the usurper at Washington has been more than six months gathering for your subjugation and enslavement. This victory frees a large portion of the State from the power of the invaders and restores it to the protection of its army. It consequently becomes my duty to assure you that it is my firm determination to protect every peaceable citizen in the full enjoyment of all his rights, whatever may have been his sympathies in the present unhappy struggle, if he has not taken an active part in the cruel warfare which has been waged against the good people of this State by the ruthless enemies whom we have just defeated. I therefore invite all good citizens to return to their homes and the practice of their ordinary avocations, with the full assurance that they, their families, their homes, and their property shall be carefully protected. I at the same time warn all evil disposed persons who may support the usurpations of anyone claiming to be provisional or temporary Governor of Missouri, or who shall in any other way give aid or comfort to the enemy, that they will be held as enemies and treated accordingly.

Sterling Price,
Major General, Commanding Missouri State Guard.

No. 8. OR, ser. 1, vol. 17, pt. 2, p. 279 (n. 38)

HEADQUARTERS DIVISION OF MEMPHIS,

Maj. JOHN A. RAWLINS, Memphis, October 18, 1862.

Assistant Adjutant-General, Jackson, Miss.:

DEAR Sir: I am this moment in receipt of the general's letter of the 11th. From some cause there is unusual delay in the letters to and from. I have had several messengers in from the interior of late. Holly Springs is occupied in force, with camps at Davis' Mill, 9 miles south of Grand Junction; at Cold water, and the Chewalla Creek, east of Holly Springs. Van Dorn and Price were both at Holly Springs yesterday, expecting Pemberton, who is to command all. This is from Ex-Brig. Gen. Ed. Price, son of the rebel general, who has resigned, and whom I have permitted, on certain letters of General [John M.] Schofield and Governor Gamble, to return to Missouri. He came in this morning. He came through Oxford a day or two since. There was nothing said of General Joe Johnston being there with 40,000 from the Virginia army. I have heard from many that [Confederate general Daniel] Ruggles has joined from below with some 4,000 men, supposed to be reorganized regiments of the returned prisoners sent to Vicksburg by us so opportunely for them.

I have no doubt that in and around Holly Springs is now assembled all the forces they can collect together, and it behooves General Grant to keep his men near enough for concentration.

General Curtis, on the supposition that Missouri was in danger, has taken one-half of the Helena force back to Saint Louis to be sent to the Iron Mountain; the fact is that there is no considerable force in Arkansas threatening Missouri. [Union] General [Eugene A.] Carr has the other half; say 9,000 men, and expects help from me. I will write him to strengthen his defenses, and no force will attempt to storm his fort where he has heavy ordnance. He has a larger force than I have, and I have a much more important place to defend than Helena is. The boats navigating the river are now assailed above and below. I have sent a force above to Island 21, and now comes a call to send some to a post below. We will have to do something more than merely repel these attacks. We must make the people feel that every attack on a road here will be resented by the destruction of some one of their towns or plantations elsewhere. All adherents of their cause must suffer for these cowardly acts.

I propose to expel ten secession families for every boat fired on, thereby lessening the necessity for fighting boats for their benefit, and will visit on the neighborhood summary punishment. It may sometimes fall on the wrong head, but it would be folly to send parties of infantry to chase these wanton guerrillas.

So far as the city of Memphis and neighborhood is concerned all is well. Guerrilla bands are being called into Holly Springs, where the enemy is doubtless concentrating for some effort. We are ready for them here.

I rather fear for [Tennessee towns] Bolivar and Jackson. Pemberton's command, though is confined to Mississippi and Louisiana, and to assume the offensive he would have to enter Tennessee.

Your obedient servant,

W. T. Sherman,

Major-General, Commanding.

No. 9. OR, ser. 2, vol. 4, pp. 642–643, 742 (n. 38)

SAINT LOUIS, October 22, 1862.

Major General CURTIS:

GENERAL: In February last General Edwin W. Price, a son of General Sterling Price, was captured in this State and was brought to this place. He was afterwards paroled by General [Henry] Halleck, limiting the Parole to the county of Chariton, where be resided. He was treated with confidence as an officer by General Halleck. From Colonel [William E.] Moberly, who commands the enrolled militia, as well as from others I receive the assurance that General Price always kept his parole strictly as an officer of integrity was bound to observe it. Colonel Moberly informed me that upon one occasion when an attack by guerrillas was threatened upon the post under his command the danger coming to the knowledge of General Price he gave the colonel information of the danger. He was exchanged about two weeks since for General Prentiss. When he was about to leave for the South he called upon me and gave me the assurance it was not his purpose to bear arms again but that as soon as be reached the south he would resign his commission and return home and would here employ all the influence he possessed with the disloyal people to keep them at peace with the Government.

He now calls upon me and shows me that be has resigned his position as brigadier and he expresses the purpose to exert all his influence to prevent any further hostile demonstration as far as he can by those who have hostile feelings to the Government. He seeks to be protected in his person and Property, and if it were necessary will give his parole of honor for his peaceful conduct. I have confidence that General Price will keep any promise he may make and would have no hesitation in applying to the President for a pardon as was given by him to General Watkins. In the meantime it might be desirable if you should concur in the propriety of the course I recommend that you should give to General Price a safeguard to secure him against molestation in his person and property. If you desire it he will report to you at once. In fact he prefers to be the bearer of this letter. Be good enough to signify your wishes upon this subject to him.

Very respectfully, your obedient servant,

H. R. Gamble.

ATTORNEY-GENERAL'S OFFICE, November 21, 1862.

His Excellency H. R. GAMBLE, Governor of Missouri.

SIR: I have the pleasure to send you herewith the President's full pardon for Edwin W. Price. As it was granted solely upon your representation it is forwarded to you to be used and disposed of at your discretion. I think the proceeding was both humane and politic and I expect good results from it.

I have the honor to be, very respectfully, your obedient servant,

Edward Bates,

Attorney-General.

No. 10. OR, ser. 1, vol. 22, pt. 2, p. 780 (nn. 42, 44, 45)

RICHMOND, VA., January 31, 1863.

Hon. JAMES A. SEDDON, Secretary of War:

DEAR SIR: I will call at 1 p. m. to-day (Saturday) on Mr. [Edward S.] Joynes, to learn, through him, from you, when it will be convenient for you to see me. I enclose for your perusal the documents★ which produced the change of opinion mentioned in my last note. The very decided (and it seems to me injudicious) language used by General Price in the closing paragraph of his Special Orders, No. 82, would indicate that to send him with only a portion of his troops to Arkansas would but increase the imbroglio, and one of the main objects in making any disposition of the subject now is to content him and his men. Since the date of my last note, General Price has telegraphed to Senator Clark that he is on his way here. Major Cabell thinks that the special order above alluded to was not intended to go as far as its language really does, and that the order suggested by me will fully satisfy General Price and his men. If so, I still think it the best solution of the question. On his arrival, something may be determined on to give us the advantage of his presence in Arkansas to recruit our forces without detriment to

---

★ enclosures withdrawn by Mr. Shepherd, February 23, 1863.

the military operations in Mississippi. After settling this difficulty, arising out of misapprehended promises, the best plan will be to manage the Missouri troops on the simple military principle that they should cheerfully go wherever ordered, and so remain until ordered away.

I remain, dear sir, very truly, yours,

Thos. C. Reynolds,
Governor of Missouri.

No. 11. OR, ser. 1, vol. 22, pt. 2, p. 781 (n. 42)

WAR DEPARTMENT, C. S. A.,

Richmond, Va., February 3, 1863.

General E. KIRBY SMITH, Jackson, Miss.:

Arrange, if you can, with General Pemberton for the exchange of General Price and his command for troops under your command to the west of the Mississippi. It is desired that General Price and his command should be transferred as soon as may be, consistently with the safety of General Pemberton's command.

J. A. Seddon,
Secretary of War.

No. 12. OR, ser. 1, vol. 22, pt. 2, p. 781 (n. 42)

WAR DEPARTMENT C. S. A.,

Richmond, Va., February 5, 1863.

General E. Kirby Smith, General Commanding, &c.:

SIR:

I telegraphed you yesterday to Jackson, Miss., requesting you to endeavor to arrange with General Pemberton for exchange of troops from your command on the west of the river for the command of General Price, whom it is the desire of the Department to transfer as soon as existing necessities will allow. I hope that telegram reached you; but, both to guard against mischance and to possess you more fully of the wishes of the Department on this subject, I address you by letter likewise. It has long been contemplated and desired by the Department to transfer General Price, with at least his Missouri troops, across the Mississippi, but unfortunately the exigencies of the service have constantly presented obstacles to the removal. The consequence has been much dissatisfaction and some distrust among the Missouri troops, and it is feared that General Price himself has conceived the idea of injustice done him. It has, too, been a constant subject of complaint and misrepresentation on both sides of the river among all disaffected toward the Government. All this it is important, as soon as possible, to extinguish by the transfer. In addition to these motives, it is believed, as you will readily understand, that General Price's influence and reputation can be made most available for the service of the Government in the Trans-Mississippi Department, and that, besides gathering additional forces at once from Missouri, when the time arrives, as I trust it soon may, for an onward advance toward the north, he, more speedily and effectually than any one else, might arouse the Missouri people to a united and energetic movement to relieve themselves from the thraldom of their present tyrants.

In view of all these considerations, I trust you will exert yourself to concert with General Pemberton for the exchange contemplated, or, failing in that, for the transfer, at the earliest practicable period at all consistent with the safety of his command, of General Price and his Missouri troops to the Trans-Mississippi Department. If important to effect this, you might engage to send at an early period an equivalent force to General Pemberton. Should Vicksburg be successfully defended, as I have strong confidence it will be, then, at least, it is hoped the arrangement can be easily effected.

With high esteem, most truly, yours,

J. A. Seddon, Secretary of War.

No. 13. OR, ser. 1, vol. 22, pt. 2, p. 782 (n. 42)
RICHMOND, VA., February 5, 1863.

Hon. JAMES A. SEDDON,

Secretary of War:

DEAR SIR: Your draught of a letter to General E. K. Smith (herewith returned) I communicated to General Price, and he expresses himself satisfied with it, on the supposition that, of course, instructions equally strong and explicit will be sent to General Pemberton, who will naturally be very anxious to retain troops so valuable as General Price's veterans, unless the wish of the Department is distinctly intimated directly to him. General Price has no wish to leave Vicksburg on the eve of an attack, but he thinks (as I do) that the best mode of weakening that attack would be to send him to make a diversion in Arkansas. It is possible General Pemberton may be able to spare General Price's command at once. Permit me, therefore, to suggest a change in the sentence before the last in your letter, so that it may read thus, "To effect this at once, you might engage to send afterward, at an early period, an equivalent force to General Pemberton." I am glad this imbroglio can be thus arranged, but candor compels me to add that it cannot fail to come up again unless the two lieutenant-generals, to whom it is referred, succeed in effecting the transfer of General Price in time to anticipate any further advance of the enemy in Arkansas. Argue as we will, the people believe he can prevent that advance.

I remain, dear sir, with high esteem, very truly, yours,

Thos. C. Reynolds,
Governor of Missouri.

No. 14. OR, ser. 1, vol. 22, pt. 2, p. 783 (n. 42)

WAR DEPARTMENT, C. S. A.

Richmond, Va., February 6, 1863.

General J. C. PEMBERTON,

General, Commanding, &c.:

SIR: A day or two since I telegraphed, and have since written, General E. Kirby Smith, on his passage through your department, to endeavor to arrange with you for the exchange of troops from his department for General Price's command, or, at least, General Price and his Missouri troops. It has long been contemplated and desired by the Department, as soon as the safety of your command would allow, to transfer General Price, with his Missouri troops, to the Trans-Mississippi Department. Late events increase the wish, and if the matter can be arranged so as not to weaken your army materially, it would be very gratifying to the Department to have it accomplished without further delay. Should you be unable to arrange this exchange, then, as soon as you can spare General Price and his Missouri troops without seriously endangering your command, you are requested to order him and them to the Trans-Mississippi Department, to report to General Smith. Great confidence is felt by the Department that, under your skillful leadership, the attack now being made against Vicksburg will be triumphantly repelled, and it is hoped that then it will be in your power to make safely the desired transfer.

With high esteem, most respectfully, yours,

J. A. Seddon, Secretary of War.

No. 15. OR, ser. 1, vol. 53, p. 870

CAMDEN, Ark., May 18, 1863.

Maj. Gen. S. PRICE,

Little Rock, Ark.:

GENERAL: I had designed to be in Little Rock by this time, but finding most of our State records here, I determined to summon the State officers to this place and make it my temporary headquarters, in order to set in operation the process of arranging the unfinished business of Governor Jackson's administration and determining with them on a more settled location of our State offices. I hope you will favor me with a regular correspondence on the military condition of affairs, and communicate your views to me fully and freely. As the mails are uncertain, I have adopted the plan of numbering my letters, thereby you can at once discover whether they all reach you. Please adopt the same plan in your letters to me. My address here is care of Benjamin T. Powell, esq., Camden, Ark.

I remain, as ever, very truly, yours,

Thos. C. Reynolds.

No. 16. OR, ser. 1, vol. 53, p. 852 (n. 48)

RICHMOND, VA., March 18, 1863.

Lieut. Gen. E. K. SMITH,

Commanding the Trans-Mississippi Department:

MY DEAR SIR: Permit me to present to you my friend, Governor Reynolds, of Missouri, who will have much official connection with you, and to ask for him your special consideration. As a right-minded man of large knowledge and sound views on military questions, he will be found, I venture to predict, both useful and agreeable to you.

Very truly, yours,

Jefferson Davis.

(Copies to Lieut. Gen. T. H. Holmes, Little Rock, Ark., and Lieut. Gen. J. C. Pemberton, Jackson, Miss.)

No. 17. OR, ser. 1, vol. 53, p. 871 (n. 58)

CAMDEN, Ark., May 25, 1863.

General S. PRICE,

Little Rock, Ark.:

GENERAL: I return you my thanks for your letter of the 22nd, just received. I regret that the claimants against the State are so impatient, but you err in supposing that my temporary establishment of the State officers here will be equivalent to deferring indefinitely the payment of those soldiers, &c. On the contrary, it is a step taken with a view to forward their interests. The affairs amid records of the State are scattered and in some confusion. They must be arranged and looked into before any definite policy is determined on. The claims against the State are estimated to exceed $2,000,000, and the Confederate notes in the treasury amount to a small sum. As all claims cannot be paid in current money, a decision has to be made as to which are to be preferred. At Little Rock neither I nor the officers would be allowed any time to attend to business. Here the whole matter can be investigated without interruption and the necessary instructions given to the officers. I have repeatedly declared that the claims of soldiers will be preferred, and when payment is to be made the paymaster will be sent to them. I propose to locate the State officers here or at some other suitable place; my own movements will be regulated by circumstances. I trust that your letter will be the commencement of frequent correspondence between us forwarding the great object we both have at heart, the redemption of Missouri.

I remain, general, as ever, with great respect, your friend and servant,

Thos. C. Reynolds.

P. S.—Although I can now say nothing definite on the subject, yet I may be able to visit Little Rock very soon.

T. C. R.

No. 18. OR, ser. 1, vol. 22, pt. 2, p. 863 (n. 66)

ON THE ROAD, June 8, 1863.

General STERLING PRICE, Commanding Northeastern Arkansas:

DEAR GENERAL: I started this morning to visit you, but my ambulance broke, and I am obliged to return. My object in coming was to see if we could with propriety attack Helena. Please inform me whether the condition of your troops will justify the attempt.

I am, general, very respectfully, your obedient servant,

Th. H. Holmes,

Lieutenant-General.

HEADQUARTERS, Jacksonport, June 9, 1863.

Lieut. Gen. T. H. HOLMES:

GENERAL: I have the honor to acknowledge the receipt of your note written "on the road," dated the 8th of June, and regret that accident prevented your arrival here. In regard to the condition of my troops, I am glad to say that they are now fully rested and in excellent spirits.

General Marmaduke also reports his command to be in efficient condition. He reports to me this morning the following number: Total present, Shelby's brigade, 1,561; Greene's brigade, 1,122; [John Q.] Burbridge's brigade, 1,089, Kitchen's battalion, 286. In all 4,058. Of these, many are out on outpost duty. [George W.] Carter's brigade, now attached to General Walker's command, is reported 1,170 total present. From the most reliable information General Marmaduke can obtain, the enemy have not more than from 4,000 to 5,000 at Helena; and were a movement conducted with celerity and secrecy, by which you could concentrate the commands of Generals Frost and Fagan with this column, I entertain no doubt of your being able to crush the foe at that point.

I have the honor to enclose two communications from Colonel Carter and one from Colonel Coleman, &c.*

[*Sterling Price.*]

No. 19. OR, ser. 1, vol. 22, pt. 2, p. 935 (nn. 60, 64)

HEADQUARTERS TRANS-MISSISSIPPI DEPARTMENT, Shreveport, La., July 13, 1863.

Govs. THOMAS C. REYNOLDS, F. R. LUBBOCK, H. FLANAGIN, and THOMAS O. MOORE:

SIRS: Upon my arrival in this department, in April last, I found headquarters at Little Rock, Ark. I repaired there from Alexandria, and endeavored to impartially survey the field of my labor. After investigation

---

* Not found.

into the past and present condition of the department, I was enabled to form an opinion of what should be my future course. I determined that my most important duties were administrative, and that I must leave, in a great measure, the active operations of the field to my juniors. I selected this as the most central and best point for depots and headquarters.

Vicksburg has fallen. The enemy possess the key to this department. What will be his future operations can only be determined by time. It is my duty to try to anticipate, meet, and if possible thwart, if not defeat, his plans, whatever they may be.

The possession of the Mississippi River by the enemy cuts off this department from aid from and communication with Richmond; consequently we must be self-sustaining and self-reliant in every respect.

My position as commanding general under existing and future state of affairs places me in the way of ascertaining the wants and necessities of the department better than any other person. These are of the most weighty character, and require serious consideration of the wise and patriotic intellects of the States west of the Mississippi. I see the magnitude of the subject and the great responsibilities connected with it.

I am an humble, but by position an important, agent in the defense of a cause that involves all that makes the name of home and country desirable. With God's help and yours, I will cheerfully grapple with the difficulties that surround us, and if you and the reflecting minds of your respective States will sustain me, with prayer to God, and with my every mental and physical effort devoted to the cause, I shall work on hopefully and, I trust, successfully. To do this, however, I must have your personal acquaintance, your confidence, and your individual and combined co-operation, with that of the leading spirits and judicial minds of your States.

I earnestly desire to secure and merit the confidence of the people whose homes I am ordered to defend. I would, then, respectfully suggest that you will meet in conference with me at Marshall, Tex., on the 15th day of August next, and that you will invite the members of the supreme courts of your States to attend with you at that meeting. I desire to have the support and advice of the representative men of the States composing my department.

I have the honor to be, very respectfully, &c.,

E. Kirby Smith,

Lieutenant-General, C. S. Army.

No. 20. OR, ser. 1, vol. 22, pt. 2, p. 935 (nn. 60, 64)

LITTLE ROCK, ARK., July 20, 1863.

Hon. JAMES A. SEDDON, Richmond, Va.:

DEAR SIR: The paymaster-general of Missouri, Col. J. T. Thornton, takes this letter across the Mississippi to mail to you, and will, after a visit on business to Columbia, present you a letter of introduction and bring you information as to affairs here. My position here is satisfactory. When I last wrote you I anticipated great trouble. A firm but conciliatory course, which Colonel Thornton will detail to you, produced a complete alteration in the attitude of General Price and others, and I now have confidence in harmonious action between them and me, in support of the views I expressed in Richmond to you and the President. A system of counterpoises among the military politicians, indispensable to a just exercise of civil authority, will soon be established. The materials for it are ample.

I enclose a copy of an important letter yesterday received from General E. K. Smith, as you may fail to get a copy. Governor Lubbock and I were schoolfellows in Charleston. I shall seek his co-operation in directing the military toward good ends and good measures. Both Governor Flanagin and Governor Moore will, I think, from my knowledge of them, act in no sectional or separatist spirit.

General E. K. Smith has the confidence of everybody, and, in my opinion, is just the man for this department. We are not at all despondent on account of the loss of Vicksburg, but will endeavor to do our full share in the coming struggle.

It gives me great pleasure to notice the high opinion the military and the public generally entertain of your vigor and ability as a war minister.

I write also to Colonel [W. P.] Johnson, by this opportunity, a short letter. Colonel Thornton has confidential verbal messages for you from me, and I think you will not regret giving him a long interview. He has my full confidence, and can be trusted as an intelligent, reliable man.

I remain, dear sir, very truly, yours,

Thos. C. Reynolds

[Governor of Missouri.]

P. S.—If anything should happen to Holmes and Price, old General [John] Roane ranks all other officers here. All tell me Fagan is by far the best of the Arkansas brigadiers, and I think so too; he was distinguished at Manassas, Shiloh, and recently very much at Helena. Let me urge you to have him made a major-general.

No. 21. OR, ser. 1, vol. 22, pt. 2, pp. 941–943 (n. 78)

HEADQUARTERS PRICE'S DIVISION,

Des Arc, Ark., July 23, 1863.

Lieut. Gen. E. KIRBY SMITH, Shreveport.

GENERAL: You will probably have received a communication addressed to me by Dr. Pearson, and by me forwarded to you this day, through district headquarters, with my endorsement upon it. That communication was intended to advise me that our friends in Saint Louis (from which city Dr. Pearson is just returning) believe that the enemy are about to send a force of 60,000 men into this State. The writer who is known to me as a very intelligent and trustworthy gentleman, states, in confirmation of this report, that twelve regiments had already left Saint Louis for Rolla, in Southwestern Missouri, and six regiments for Helena, in this State. This last statement has been fully verified by reports from Helena. It has also been manifest, for three weeks past, that the enemy were concentrating near Ironton, in

Missouri, a heavy force of cavalry and artillery (from 6,000 to 10,000 men), well equipped and supplied with pontoon teams, &c., and plainly intended to operate in this direction, and the latest intelligence shows that this force, the advance of which is even now within this State, is but the advance of a heavy force of infantry. Being myself fully convinced by these and other facts that the enemy is about to advance against us (probably in three columns; one army from Northwestern Arkansas, another down the White River Valley, and the third from the Mississippi) in numbers which we cannot even hope to withstand in the present scattered condition of the troops in this district and department, and believing also that our own forces cannot be concentrated north of the Arkansas either in sufficient numbers or in time to resist the enemy's advance without exposing ourselves to capture or annihilation, or without, at least, sacrificing uselessly thousands of men, when we have not a man to spare, I believe it to be my duty to urge you, very respectfully, but most earnestly, to be pleased to order all troops within this State, at least, to be concentrated upon some line of defense at least as far south as the Arkansas River.

I send a copy of this communication to Lieutenant-General Holmes.

I am, general, with the greatest respect, your friend and obedient servant,

Sterling Price
Major-General.

HEADQUARTERS PRICE'S DIVISION,
Des Arc, Ark, July 23, 1863.
Brig. Gen. JAS. F. FAGAN,
Commanding Searcy:
GENERAL: You will perceive from the enclosed orders that you are to assume command of this division at once. General Parsons will remain here until further orders from yourself or General Price, but is in readiness to move at any hour. General Marmaduke, who is in command

of all the cavalry in your front, has been directed to keep you advised of his movements and of those of the enemy. General Price leaves for Little Rock this after noon, and will report to you early tomorrow. His staff will report to you early to-morrow morning, and will inform you as to condition of their respective departments. Captain [Robert] Collins' company of cavalry (General Price's body-guard) will report to you for duty.

I am, general, &c.,

Thos. L. Snead,

Major and Assistant Adjutant-General.

[Enclosure.]

GENERAL ORDERS,
No. 6. HEADQUARTERS PRICE'S DIVISION,
Des Arc, July 23, 1863.
Major-General Price having been ordered, in consequence of the illness of Lieutenant-General Holmes, to assume command of the District of Arkansas, the command of this division devolves upon Brig. Gen. James F. Fagan, who will act accordingly, and to whom the division staff, except Maj. Thomas L. Snead, will report immediately, at Searcy.

By command of Major-General Price:

L. A. Maclean,

Major and Assistant Adjutant-General.

HEADQUARTERS PRICE'S DIVISION,
Des Arc, July 23, 1863.
Brig. Gen. J. S. MARMADUKE,
Commanding Cavalry, etc., Jacksonport:
GENERAL: General Price has been ordered, in consequence of the illness of Lieutenant-General Holmes, to assume command of the District of Arkansas. The command of this division devolves upon Brigadier-General Fagan, whose headquarters are at Searcy. General

Price wishes you to assume command at once of all the cavalry in your front. The necessary orders will be issued as soon as he gets to Little Rock, whither he starts this afternoon. He expects you to keep yourself thoroughly and correctly informed as to the movements of the enemy, and to advise him of them promptly. He wishes you to delay and annoy them as much as you possibly can, without endangering too greatly the safety of your command, falling back, when compelled to do so, in the direction of Searcy. You will keep General Fagan well advised as to your movements.

I am, very respectfully, your obedient servant,

Thos. L. Snead,

Major and Assistant Adjutant-General.

No. 22. OR, ser. 1, vol. 53, p. 918 (n. 83)

MARSHALL, Tex., December 4, 1863.

General S. PRICE, Camp Bragg, Ark.:

MY DEAR GENERAL: Your favor of the 5th ultimo reached me on the 7th, and various circumstances have prevented my answering it sooner. Finding it impossible to obtain a house in or near Shreveport, or a healthy location for my camp, I had sent it on the 5th toward Marshall, designing to follow it on the 7th, but your letter determined me to remain. By one of those accidents, to which it is my luck to be especially liable, I had scarcely separated myself from my staff before I became overwhelmed with business so as to have no time to answer letters. Quantrill's case, the applications of Brinker and [W. J.] McArthur to enlist the men he brought out, the business connected with Shelby's expedition, and several other matters of Missourians desiring introductions, &c., to General Smith, occupied all my time, unaided as I was by any of my officers, and also feeling, like most men who have passed their fortieth year, a growing disinclination for the labor of penmanship, and especially of recording. Since my arrival here I have been occupied by the labor of seeking quarters and other indispensable business. I trust these circumstances will at least partially excuse my seeming neglect. But if I have been inattentive to answering your letter, I have not been so as to its requests. I conversed with General Smith on the subject of an attempt to recapture Little Rock and found him anxious to do so. General Holmes was also urging it. Affairs in Southern Louisiana then looked menacing, but have since improved. General Smith determined to send for General Holmes to consult on the subject of advancing on Little Rock, and after seeing General Holmes at Shreveport he determined to visit the army of Arkansas. This he has since started to do, and I presume that ere this reaches you, you will have seen him and unfolded your views to him. I earnestly hope that he will find affairs there in such a condition that he can authorize a forward movement. As you are doubtless aware, I have appointed Col. W. P. Johnson C. S. Senator. I hope the publicity unavoidably given to the fact will not lead the enemy to any greater exertions to capture him in his passage across the Mississippi, or impede his exchange as an army officer should he be captured. I trust you will consider the appointment a good one. Senator Johnson, of Arkansas, and Judge Watkins urged me to press you to accept the position. They were obviously biased by their desire to relieve you of your disagreeable position with General Holmes. Indeed, Senator Johnson frankly avowed that desire as one of his main reasons for the advice he gave me. I deemed it unnecessary to inform those gentlemen that I felt confident of the success of Colonel Thornton, whom I sent to Richmond in July last, in obtaining the transfer of General Holmes from this department in a manner honorable and gratifying to him and his friends; but I told them that no Governor of Missouri would be doing his duty in tempting you to leave the army, even if you desired it, and that no personal friend, after a mature consideration of all our circumstances, would advise you to do it, especially for a temporary senatorial appointment. They seemed convinced my view was correct, and I found Major Snead and Major Cabell to agree with me.

Hoping to hear often from you, I remain, my dear general, very truly, yours,

Thos. C. Reynolds.

P. S.—I return you my thanks for a copy of Colonel Shelby's report sent me by your excellent adjutant, Major Maclean, on the 6th ultimo.

No. 23. OR, ser. 1, vol. 53, p. 998

MARSHALL, TEX., June 2, 1864.

General S. PRICE,

Arkansas:

My DEAR GENERAL: I have written you on March 23 and April 11 last, and also a private letter on the 17th ultimo. Not having received any answer I am apprehensive they may not have reached you. I would be specially obliged by your giving me in detail, as requested in the letter of April 11, your opinions about an advance into Missouri, for I am frequently urged to take official action connected with it, and feel embarrassed by the want of that light which your experience and wisdom will throw upon the subject. For instance, General Rains has just visited me for the third time within the past six mouths to suggest plans in relation to the district which he commands as brigadier-general of the Missouri State Guard, and I have given him a letter to General Smith with a view to a consultation between them. His proposition is, that on the recovery of Little Rock, or some other good base for his operations, he should be sent to his district to organize a State force to be used in advance of and [in] co-operation with the Confederate army in redeeming Missouri. He states that a great many Missourians who refuse to join the Confederate army have invited him to this expedition, and from the confidence of the people of that section in him he expects to raise a force of several thousand men. Please give me your views in full about his proposition.

I remain, my dear general, very truly, yours,

Thos. C. Reynolds.

No. 24. OR, ser. 1, vol. 53, p. 999 (n. 89)

CAMDEN, ARK., June 9, 1864.

His Excellency T. C. REYNOLDS,

Marshall, Tex.:

DEAR GOVERNOR: Your kind favor of the 2^d of June and two others of earlier date have been received since I have written to you. Your
letters were received when I was in the field, and since when I was
engaged in thought upon the subject of my report, which is not yet
entirely completed, which excuses you must receive as an apology for
my apparent neglect. I have one other reason, and that is the absence
of Snead, which compels me to do my own writing, and that has not
been my habit. You asked me in one of your letters for copies of letters
suggesting plans to General Smith. I do not feel at liberty to furnish
those letters to you, but I would be pleased that General Smith should
do so if he thinks proper. You also desire me to give you in detail my
opinions about an advance into Missouri. I have but little encourage-
ment to form opinions or plans for our future military movements.
None have been adopted that have been suggested by me. I, however,
do not complain. Perhaps it was best that they were not adopted; no-
body will ever know. And my plans are to attract the less attention in
the future, for the reason that I am being thrown farther from the chief
in command of the department by the promotion of my juniors over
me; but let that be as it may, I shall go on and endeavor to discharge
my duty to my country, to my command, whatever it may be, and to
myself. I shall hope to deserve the approbation of my country, and if I
get it I should surely be satisfied. You are aware that we have just closed
a brilliant campaign in my district. It would give me pleasure to make
you familiar with all the circumstances connected with it. Suffice it to
say for the present that the cavalry is entitled to the credit of our suc-
cesses. My infantry having been taken from me to assist General Taylor,
I was compelled to meet General Steele's forces (13,000 strong) with
my cavalry force alone. We captured 1,500 of his troops, killed 1,000,

wounded a great many, and captured 700 of his wagons; had driven him into Camden as a place of refuge before the infantry returned. I feel satisfied that if I could have had the troops with me that went to Louisiana, when I first met Steele, I should have made another Lexington affair of it. If we could have followed on to the Arkansas River, as I desired to do, I believe it would have been attended with results similar to the Lexington battle, and the door would now have been open to Missouri. You will say all this has passed. What for the future? I believe that the concentration of our troops on Red River has relieved Texas, that the concentration in the Arkansas Valley will relieve Red River, and a concentration in Missouri will relieve the whole Trans-Mississippi Department south of it. I believe, as General Rains suggests, that we should send good recruiting officers in advance of the army, supported by a cavalry force to enable him to organize their recruits, and they should be joined by the army before the enemy would have time to concentrate a force to overwhelm them. I have not heard from our friend Shelby lately. I fear for him. I had expected to have supported him with the army on the other side of the Arkansas River before this. I requested Col. Sam. Woodson (ex-Member of Congress from Missouri) to call and see you at Marshall. He promised to do so. He says there are 20,000 men in Saint Louis alone now armed and waiting to join me.

Very respectfully, your obedient servant,

Sterling Price,
Major. General.

No. 25. OR, ser. 1, vol. 41, pt. 2, p. 1011 (n. 94)

MARSHALL, TEX., July 18, 1864.

General S. PRICE,

Camden, Ark.:

MY DEAR GENERAL: A close scrutiny of the meager intelligence we have from Northern amid Southern sources would lead to the apprehension that our affairs in the eastern half of our Confederacy are in a critical condition. Major Cabell writes me that the President and Secretary of War are impatient for an advance into Missouri. This would indicate a similar apprehension on their part. On the retreat of Steele I understood we were getting up a large supply train for an advance on Little Rock, and I have been impatiently awaiting intelligence that the train had been completed; but whether owing to want of energy in the proper officers or to other causes this preparation seems to progress slowly. Your campaign in the summer of 1861 showed that an advance into Missouri powerfully aids in relieving Tennessee. When here in March last you expressed the opinion that the recovery of the Arkansas Valley ought to precede an advance to reoccupy our State. But could not a powerful diversion be made by cavalry alone without awaiting the recovery of Little Rock? Even if compelled to return, it might gain time for us in Georgia or avert an attack on Mobile by compelling the enemy to send large forces to Missouri. If successful in maintaining itself the cavalry might be re-enforced by infantry from Arkansas and by recruiting within our State. But the main point of view from which I suggest such an expedition is, that it may take off some of the pressure on us in Virginia and Georgia. On the return of General Smith to Shreveport I design to suggest his consideration of such a diversion in case [Union general Edward R. S.] Canby's attitude at New Orleans does not threaten a speedy advance up Red River.

The main object of this letter is to learn from you at your earliest convenience in a few lines whether you approve of such an expedition; whether you would be willing to take command of it (which is specially desirable), or whether it should be entrusted to Shelby alone. I presume his command (said to be between 3,000 and 4,000 strong) and a brigade from Marmaduke's are all that could be spared, but your name would largely increase it on its entrance into Missouri.

Early's expedition in Virginia and Maryland is not reassuring. If a design to induce Grant to send troops after him, it will fail. It looks very much like the style of military blundering usual with Bragg—a repetition of the strategy by which last winter he sent off Longstreet to Knoxville, and thereby so weakened himself as to let Grant overwhelm him near Chattanooga. If induced by a scarcity of provisions at Richmond, produced by Grant's raids on our railroads west of that city, it is almost alarming. It cannot be from a surplus of force on our side in Virginia, for, if so, why was he not sent to Johnston? The latter seems barely able to hold his own. He would surely not have given up the Etowah Iron-Works and the great manufacturing region of North Georgia unless their defense had been desperate. Activity, energy, and running some risk in this department by an inroad into Missouri may turn the scale in his favor.

Thanking you greatly for the <u>Saint Louis Democrat</u> of the 2nd instant, I remain, very truly, yours,

Thos. C. Reynolds.

No. 26. OR, ser. 1, vol. 41, pt. 2, p. 1020 (n. 94)

CAMDEN, ARK., July 22, 1864.

Governor T. C. REYNOLDS,

Marshall, Tex.:

MY DEAR GOVERNOR: Your favor of the 18th reached me yesterday. I thank you for the suggestions it contains. In view of the importance of an early expedition into Missouri you ask whether it could not be made by cavalry alone in the event of unavoidable delay in the advance of the whole army and the recovery of Little Rock, and whether I approve of such an expedition and would be willing to take command of it. I consider such an expedition practicable, and in the contingency you suggest desirable and important. If it is not General Smith's purpose to concentrate the troops and take possession of the Arkansas Valley I would like to take command of the expedition. You will see from the paper I enclose you that our forces are in possession of Platte City, and that our cause is in the ascendant in many parts of the State.

It is significant that a company of State troops, sent to defend Platte City, went over in a body, with their arms, to the Confederates. My opinion is that the people of Missouri are ready for a general uprising, and that the time was never more propitious for an advance of our forces into Missouri. Our friends should be encouraged and supported promptly. Delay will be dangerous. Unsustained, they may be overwhelmed by superior numbers, become dispirited, and, finally, disheartened and hopeless. I have confidence of the happiest results from the expedition you suggest. In my judgment, the reports of expeditions being fitted out by General Canby to penetrate the Trans-Mississippi Department by way of Red River or other routes are canards, intended to deceive and mislead and to prevent an advance in Missouri. Please send the paper of the 13th to General Smith, if he has returned. You can also show him this hastily-written letter.

Yours, truly,

Sterling Price.

No. 27. OR, ser. 1, vol. 41, pt. 2, p. 564

KEYTESVILLE, August 4, 1864.

General [Clinton B.] Fisk:

DEAR SIR: I take this opportunity to inform you of the condition of Chariton County at this time. I arrived home last night and am informed that there has not been a time within the last three weeks but what there has been bushwhackers in this county, and frequently within two or three miles of this place. There are three gangs, one led by Anderson, one by [Clifton D.] Holtzclaw, and one by a man by the name of Jackson. Each company has from forty to seventy men, well armed and well drilled, and the most of them desperate men. All of the Union men of the county are in the military camps or have fled the county; the larger portion of them are here and at Glasgow; there are a few in Bowling Green Prairie, in Bernhardt's company. Some neighborhoods are nearly deserted. A few of those who are classed as sympathizers have left. There are but few loyal men in the county that have not been robbed of their horses. Brig. Gen. E. Price, of the Confederate States of America, and fifth corporal in Moberly's militia, on Friday last had an interview with Captain Holtzclaw, and made a speech to the men. He (Price) on Saturday made a speech in Brunswick, where he said that he three years ago enlisted Holtzclaw into the Confederate service (here the speaker was loudly cheered). Price also said that he recognized many of his old neighbors and friends; that they were Confederate soldiers and had been driven into the bush by [Joseph] Stanley's and the Brookfield company. There is not a man in Stanley's company but thinks they are treated badly. They went into the company as an independent volunteer organization with the understanding that William E. Moberly nor no other rebel sympathizer would have any control over it. You could not to-day get one of Stanley's men or a half a dozen other loyal men to serve under him by volunteering. At the time that he reported to Colonel [Lewis P.] Miller that there was no trouble in the county Holtzclaw was in the vicinity of Keytesville only the day before. Price had had his interview with him; on the same day Anderson was in the north side of the county robbing and murdering, and yet he, Moberly, informs you that all is quiet. Such villainy and falsehood cannot escape the ear of the citizens, especially the loyal men if it is not seen by those in authority. The loyal men here are anxious to know whether they will get any protection or not. If there will be none many talk of leaving the State, or at least removing their families where they will be safe.

E. A. Holcomb.

Appendix 3: Members of the Confederate Congresses from Missouri

The following information is from Arthur Roy Kirkpatrick, "Missouri, the Twelfth Confederate State" (Ph.D. diss., University of Missouri–Columbia, 1954).

Cong'l District	Provisional Congress (to Feb. 1862)	First Confederate Congress (1862–1863)	Second Confederate Congress (1864–)
Senate	Brig. Gen. John B. Clark[1]	Clark[3]	George G. Vest
Senate	Robert L.Y. Peyton[1]	Peyton[4] (d. Sept. 1863)	Col. Waldo P. Johnson
House of Representatives			
First	William M. Cooke	Cooke (d. Apr. 1863)	Maj. Thomas L. Snead
Second	Thomas A. Harris, Jr.	Harris	Nimrod L. Norton
Third	Casper W. Bell	Bell	John B. Clark
Fourth	Aaron H. Conrow	Conrow	Conrow
Fifth	George G. Vest	Vest	[Vest][5]
Sixth	Thomas W. Freeman	Freeman	Peter S. Wilkes
Seventh	Dr. John Hyer[2]	vacant	Robert A. Hatcher

1. Clark and Peyton, by resolution, were named delegates at large to the unicameral Confederate Provisional Congress.
2. Named, but never served.
3. By lot, received two-year term.
4. By lot, received four-year term.
5. Vest was re-elected to Fifth District, but resigned to take Senate seat. The district's seat was never filled.

Notes

1. A good, short biography of Sterling Price may be found in Lawrence O. Christensen, William E. Foley, Gary R. Kremer, and Kenneth H. Winn, eds., *Dictionary of Missouri Biography* (Columbia: University of Missouri Press, 1999). Three others are Albert Castel, *General Sterling Price and the Civil War in the West* (Baton Rouge: Louisiana State University Press, 1968); Ralph R. Rea, *Sterling Price, the Lee of the West* (Little Rock, AR: Pioneer Press, 1959); and Robert E. Shalhope, *Sterling Price: Portrait of a Southerner* (Columbia: University of Missouri Press, 1971).

   The author of this document, Thomas Caute Reynolds (1821–1887), has received less attention as far as complete biographies are concerned, but he has been the subject of several articles, one of the best of these by Robert E. Miller, "One of the Ruling Class, Thomas Caute Reynolds: Second Confederate Governor of Missouri," *Missouri Historical Review* 80 (July 1986): 422–448. In addition, a doctoral dissertation was written by James G. Downhour, "Thomas C. Reynolds, Missouri's Forgotten Governor" (Southern Illinois University–Carbondale, 2002).

   There are two other, less available sources for information on Missouri's Confederate government: a 1949 master's thesis ("Missouri's Secessionist Government, 1861–1865") and a 1954 doctoral dissertation ("Missouri, the Twelfth Confederate State"), both by Arthur Roy Kirkpatrick at the University of Missouri–Columbia.

2. There is a good discussion of Price's role in the Mexican-American War as part of the Doniphan expedition and as governor of New Mexico in Shalhope, *Sterling Price: Portrait of a Southerner*, 56–77.

3. A short biography of Francis "Frank" Blair Jr. may be found in Christensen et al., *Dictionary of Missouri Biography*.

4. A short biography of B. Gratz Brown may be found in Christensen et al., *Dictionary of Missouri Biography*.

5. "Mr. Russell, Commissioner from Mississippi," had been sent to Missouri during the secession crisis. He addressed a joint session of the Missouri State Senate and House of Representatives on January 18, 1861, and pleaded the case for Missouri to join with the rest of the slave states in seceding from the Union.

6. Thomas L. Price, 1809–1870, served as the first mayor of Jefferson City, Missouri, and also was elected lieutenant governor in 1849. The title "general" came from his commissioning as major general of the militia in 1847. Unlike Sterling Price, he remained loyal to the Union and was elected to the U.S. House of Representatives in 1862, replacing the expelled John W. Reid.

7. James S. Green, 1817–1870, won election to fill four years of an unexpired term in the U.S. Senate and strongly espoused the cause of the South and slavery. His term ended in 1861, and he returned to work with Claiborne Jackson and Thomas Reynolds to achieve secession of the state. However, unlike Jackson and Reynolds, Green remained in St. Louis during the war.

8. Willard P. Hall, 1820–1882, represented the St. Joseph region in the U.S. House of Representatives but was unsuccessful in his contest for the Senate seat won by James Green in 1857. After the secession crisis in Missouri and the departure of Governor Claiborne Jackson and Lieutenant Governor Thomas Reynolds from the state, the state convention created a provisional government with Hamilton Rowan Gamble as governor and Willard Hall as lieutenant governor. Upon the death of Gamble in 1864, Hall assumed the governorship.

9. Trusten W. Polk, 1811–1876, was elected governor of Missouri in 1856, but in 1857 resigned upon his election as U.S. senator. He strongly supported the Southern, pro-slavery Democratic Party positions and because of that was expelled from the U.S. Senate in 1862.

10. John S. Phelps, 1814–1886, was elected to the U.S. House of Representatives in 1844 and represented southwest Missouri for eighteen years. He achieved great power in the House, becoming chairman of the Ways and Means Committee, and was named to become Speaker of the House. However, this did not happen because Northerners feared someone from a slave state, while Southerners considered him pro-Union because he was born in Connecticut. When the Civil War began, he sided with the Union and worked actively to defeat the attempts of Governor Jackson to achieve secession. He led a Union regiment at the battle of Pea Ridge, Arkansas, and, in 1862, was named by President Abraham Lincoln to be the military governor of Arkansas. Phelps, a Democrat, was defeated in the election for governor of Missouri in 1868, mainly due to the draconian laws enacted by the Radical Republicans in Missouri. After the new constitution of 1875, Phelps was easily elected governor.

11. "Trimming" in the sense used here appears to mean "disloyalty to one's principles for immediate gain." Today, the dictionary defines a "trimmer" as one who chooses to modify a position or opinion.

12. Ezra J. Warner, *Generals in Blue* (Baton Rouge: Louisiana State University Press, 1992), 286. Lyon is Nathaniel Lyon (1818–1861), brigadier general of the volunteers and the leader of the "attack" on Camp Jackson, May 10, 1861, in St. Louis. He was killed at the battle of Wilson's Creek, Missouri, August 10, 1861.

13. Robert M. Stewart, 1815–1871, was elected in a special election to fill the governorship that had been vacated by the election of Trusten Polk to the U.S. Senate. He tended to be considerably more moderate than the Southern wing of the Democratic Party. After Claiborne Jackson succeeded him, he was elected as a delegate to the state convention that decided that Missouri should not secede from the Union. At that time, he declared himself to be an unconditional Unionist.

14. For descriptions of the Camp Jackson affair, there are three versions recommended: Thomas L. Snead, *The Fight for Missouri* (New York: Charles Scribner's Sons, 1886; reprinted by Two Trails, Shawnee Mission, KS, 1997), 158–176; John McElroy, *The Struggle for Missouri* (Wash-

ington, DC: National Tribune Co., 1909), 67–87; and Jay Monaghan, *Civil War on the Western Border, 1854–1865* (Lincoln: University of Nebraska Press, 1955; reprinted by Bison Books, 1984), 129–132.

15. "The military bill," also called "the Militia Act," appears in *Laws of the State of Missouri: Passed at the Called Session of the 21ˢᵗ General Assembly* (Jefferson City, MO: J. P. Ament, Public Printer, 1861), 1–43.

16. *Laws of the State of Missouri, Called Session*, 48. The "rebellion act," passed by the called session of the legislature, read as follows:

"AN ACT to authorize the Governor of the State of Missouri to suppress rebellion and to repel invasion.

"WHEREAS, information has been received that the city of St. Louis had been invaded by the citizens of other States, and a portion of the people of said city are in a state of rebellion against the laws of the State, whereby the lives and property of the good people of the State are endangered; therefore,

"Be it enacted by the General Assembly of the State of Missouri, as follows:

"1. That the Governor of the State of Missouri is hereby authorized to take such measures, as in his judgment he may deem necessary or proper to repel such invasion or put down such rebellion.

"This act shall take effect from its passage.

"Approved May 10, 1861."

17. "Parsons, Peyton, Colton Green" were Mosby M. Parsons (1822–1865), Robert Ludwell Yates Peyton (1827–1863), and Colton Greene (1832–1900). Parsons's biography may be found in Ezra J. Warner, *Generals in Gray* (Baton Rouge: Louisiana State University Press, 1992), 228. Peyton served in the Missouri State Guard only a short time and resigned December 13, 1861, to take a seat in the Confederate House of Representatives. Peyton's biography is found in Richard C. Peterson et al., *Sterling Price's Lieutenants: A Guide to the Officers and Organization of the Missouri State Guard* (Shawnee Mission, KS: Two Trails, 1995), 252n, and in Carolyn M. Bartels, *The Forgotten Men: Missouri State Guard* (Shawnee Mission, KS: Two Trails, 1995), 288. Greene's biography may be found in Bruce S. Allardice, *More Generals in Gray* (Baton Rouge:

Louisiana State University Press, 1995), 104; and in Peterson et al., *Sterling Price's Lieutenants*, 33n.

18. Warner, *Generals in Gray*, p. 188. Captain Little was Lewis Henry Little (1817–1862), who fought in the Mexican-American War but resigned his commission May 7, 1861, to serve first in the Missouri State Guard and then in the Confederate army. He served on Price's staff, and then served as brigadier general, commanding a division at Iuka, Mississippi, where he was killed.

19. This proclamation to the people of Missouri is found in *The War of the Rebellion: A Compilation of the Official Records of the Union and Confederate Armies*, ser. 1, vol. 53 (Washington, DC: Government Printing Office, 1880–1901), p. 696, and is reproduced in appendix 2, no. 4.

20. Governor Jackson's proclamation was finally issued on June 12, 1861. See OR, ser. 1, vol. 53, p. 696, reproduced in appendix 2, no. 4.

21. In St. Louis, the *St. Louis Republican* was the Democratic Party's newspaper and the *St. Louis Democrat* was the Republican Party's newspaper.

22. Warner, *Generals in Blue*, 208. William S. Harney (1800–1889) was one of four generals in the U.S. Army at the beginning of the Civil War. His attempts to reach accommodation with Sterling Price and the state militia forces caused him trouble in Washington, DC. He had been out of the city of St. Louis at the time of the Camp Jackson affair and, upon resuming control in St. Louis shortly after the affair, he issued a number of proclamations attempting to calm the fears of the populace. See OR, ser. 1, vol. 3, pp. 370–372.

23. Generals Harney and Price met on May 21, 1861, in St. Louis and drafted and signed an agreement in which Price agreed to keep order in outstate Missouri and, with order achieved, Harney agreed to make no military movements in the state. See OR, ser. 1, vol. 3, p. 375, reproduced in appendix 2, no. 2.

24. Continuing reports of outrages occurring against Union supporters in outstate Missouri were arriving in St. Louis, and queries by General Harney to General Price were parried with claims of no knowledge of such problems. This resulted in the replacement and recall of Gen-

eral Harney (OR, ser. 1, vol. 3, pp. 381, 383) and the command of the region being assumed by General Lyon. On June 11 , 1861, a meeting was held at the Planter's House Hotel in St. Louis between Governor Jackson, General Price, and Colonel Thomas Snead (Price's aide-de-camp) on one side and Colonel Frank Blair, General Lyon, and Major H. A. Conant (Lyon's aide-de-camp). The stormy meeting ended with Lyon ordering the State officials "out of his lines" and essentially declaring war upon the State forces. Three additional descriptions of this meeting and the Harney-Price Agreement are to be found in McElroy, *The Struggle for Missouri*, 109, 112; Snead, *The Fight for Missouri*, 198–200; and Monaghan, *Civil War on the Western Border*, 134–135.

25. Ben McCulloch (1811–1862) served as a colonel in the Texas State troops and was named brigadier general in the Confederate army, commanding in Arkansas. He worked with Sterling Price at Wilson's Creek and was killed at the battle of Pea Ridge.

26. "Lyon's violation of that treaty in the Potosi affair and at St. Louis" consisted of a scout to Potosi, Missouri, in response to complaints of mistreatment of Unionists by secessionists (May 16) and of Union troops (volunteers) being fired upon by a mob on their way to their station in the north part of St. Louis (May 12). Reports are to be found in OR, ser. 1, vol. 3, pp. 9–10.

27. See OR, ser. 1, vol. 53, p. 692; this letter may be found as document no. 3 in appendix 2.

28. See references to Governor Jackson's proclamation in notes 18 and 20 and OR, ser. 1, vol. 53, p. 696, in appendix 2, no. 4.

29. E. C. Cabell was aide-de-camp to General Price.

30. General Lyon had acted aggressively and shipped troops by steamboat to Jefferson City; they captured the capital city with no resistance. Lyon then moved farther west along the river, landed troops just east of Boonville, and easily dispersed a small Missouri State Guard contingent, forcing them to flee, ultimately to southwest Missouri.

31. Christensen et al., *Dictionary of Missouri Biography*, 16–19. David Rice Atchison (1807–1886) was a former U.S. senator from Missouri. He had been active in the State militia before the Civil War and carried the

title of major general from that activity. Atchison had a warm friendship with Jefferson Davis from their days in the U.S. Senate and was an ideal advocate with Davis for Missouri issues.

32. James M. Loughborough served as Missouri State Guard Fifth Division paymaster general. (The Fifth Division enrolled its companies from the Platte Purchase counties plus Clay County.)

33. Allardice, *More Generals in Gray*, 59. John B. Clark (1802–1885) should not be confused with his son, John B. Clark Jr. (1831–1903). The senior Clark was a pro-slavery Democrat, elected to the U.S. House of Representatives in 1857 and expelled in 1861. He was appointed brigadier general of the Third Division of the Missouri State Guard and fought in the battle of Wilson's Creek, where he was wounded. He was elected to the first Confederate Senate and the second Confederate House of Representatives.

34. Earl Van Dorn (1820–1863) was given command of the Army of the West (the Trans-Mississippi Army) to bring some order to the conflicts between Sterling Price and Ben McCulloch. He commanded (and lost) the battle of Pea Ridge and then was transferred back east of the Mississippi River and lost the battle of Corinth. He was assassinated in 1863, supposedly by a jealous husband.

35. Thomas L. Snead has been mentioned previously as fiercely loyal to Sterling Price, and he served as his chief of staff. Probably the best article on Snead is by Robert E. Miller, "Proud Confederate: Thomas Lowndes Snead of Missouri," *Missouri Historical Review* 79 (January 1985): 167–191.

36. Peterson et al., *Sterling Price's Lieutenants*; and Christensen et al., *Dictionary of Missouri Biography*. George Graham Vest (1830–1904) fought in the battle of Wilson's Creek and served as colonel and army judge advocate general in Price's army. He was then appointed as one of Missouri's commissioners to the Provisional Confederate Congress. He was then elected to the Confederate House of Representatives, where he served until January 1865, when Governor Reynolds appointed him to the Confederate Senate. He served there until the fall of the Confederacy. In 1879, he was elected to the U.S. Senate from Missouri,

where he served until his retirement in 1903. He died in August 1904 and was the last surviving member of the Confederate Senate.

37. William Mordecai Cooke served on the staff of Governor Jackson as colonel and aide-de-camp. In April 1861, he was sent to Richmond to seek assistance and armament from that state's government. In this, he was successful (see OR, ser. 1, vol. 2, p. 798, in appendix 2, no. 1). He later represented Missouri in the Confederate House of Representatives.

38. Edwin Price, son of Sterling Price, was elected brigadier general of the Third Division of the Missouri State Guard in December 1861. He was captured by the Federals in February 1862, paroled, and exchanged (for Brigadier General Benjamin Prentiss). When repatriated to his father's camp, he resigned his commission and returned to Missouri, taking an oath of loyalty. This subject is also treated later in this manuscript. See Bartels, *The Forgotten Men*, 296, and Peterson et al., *Sterling Price's Lieutenants*, 107, as well as the discussion in Castel, *General Sterling Price and the Civil War in the West*, 188–196. See also OR, ser. 2, vol. 4, pp. 642–643; 742, in appendix 2, nos. 8 and 9.

39. OR, ser. 2, vol. 7, pp. 228ff. Copperheads (antiwar Democrats) and other Southern sympathizers were said to be active in the Middle Western states in trying to separate these states from the Northeastern states. There were supposedly secret organizations plotting to overthrow various state governments. In Missouri, they were called OAK, the Order of American Knights.

40. "J. W. Tucker and the Missouri Army Argus/Jackson, Mississippi Argus," http://www.civilwarstlouis.com/History2/jwtucker.htm (accessed June 24, 2007); see also Castel, *General Sterling Price and the Civil War in the West*, 63–64, 133, 135. J. W. Tucker, sometimes called "Deacon" Tucker, was the publisher of the *Missouri Army Argus* and later the Jackson, Mississippi, *Argus* (or *Argus and Crisis*). This publication seemed to follow General Price and his army and was accused of being Price's house organ, although Price vehemently denied this.

41. Warner, *Generals in Gray*, 232. John Pemberton (1814–1881), West Point class of 1837, chose the Southern cause in 1861. He is best remem-

bered as commanding at Vicksburg, Mississippi, and surrendering this
key point on the Mississippi River to Ulysses S. Grant on July 4, 1863.

42. The general orders probably were "Special Orders, No. 82" alluded to
in the letter from Reynolds to Confederate Secretary of War James A.
Seddon, which is found in OR, ser. 1, vol. 22, pt. 2, p. 780, shown in
appendix 2, no. 10, plus notes following on pp. 781–783, shown in nos.
11–14.

43. Warner, *Generals in Gray*, 29. John Stevens Bowen (1830–1863) led the
First Missouri Infantry and fought at Columbus, Kentucky, at Shiloh,
Tennessee (where he was wounded and promoted to major general),
and in the Vicksburg campaign, where his unit contested Grant's progress at Port Gibson. He fought in the other battles leading to the siege,
contracted dysentery, and died only a few days after the surrender as a
paroled prisoner of war.

44. Warner, *Generals in Gray*, 266. Albert Rust (1818–1870), a politician
and former member of the U.S. House of Representatives, served as
colonel of the Third Arkansas Infantry, a regiment he had recruited. He
served in some Eastern campaigns and was appointed brigadier general in March 1862. In April 1863, after the battle of Corinth, he was
sent back west of the Mississippi River. After this point, he is best remembered for his dilatory and unsuccessful movements to trap General
Samuel R. Curtis, which resulted in the Confederate defeat at Cache
River in Arkansas.

45. See OR, ser. 1, vol. 22, pt. 2, p. 780–783, reproduced in appendix 2,
nos. 10–14.

46. Ibid.

47. Dr. Montrose A. Pallen, resident of the Fifth Ward, St. Louis, was listed
in the 1860 census as "Physician"; age twenty-four; birthplace, Mississippi; and wife, Ann, age twenty-one.

48. OR, ser. 1, vol. 41, pt. 2, p. 564, found in appendix 2, no. 27, reports
a speech made by "Brig. Gen. E. Price, of the Confederate States of
America, and fifth corporal of Moberley's militia," which complains
about the lack of Union protection against the marauding of William
"Bloody Bill" Anderson and others.

49. OR, ser. 1, vol. 53, p. 852; see appendix 2, no. 16. These letters place a great deal of trust in Governor Reynolds in terms of what Davis asks of General Smith and the governors.

50. Colonel John Polk does not appear in Peterson et al., *Sterling Price's Lieutenants*, or Bartels, *The Forgotten Men of the Missouri State Guard*. In the 1860 census for St. Louis, there is a John Polk, age forty, living at the Planters House Hotel, with no occupation listed. His wife, Eliza, age thirty, and two children, ages eight and three, are also listed. Reynolds later notes that he wished to visit Polk's family in Jackson, Mississippi. In the 1860 census for Hinds County, Mississippi (the county that Jackson is in), there are no John Polks listed; therefore, it is possible that Jackson represented a temporary home for his family, who had fled St. Louis.

51. Celsus Price was one of Sterling Price's children. According to the 1860 census, all the family lived in Chariton County, Missouri. Sterling Price, age fifty; his wife, Martha, age forty-nine; and his children, Celsus, age nineteen, Heber, age sixteen, Martha, age thirteen, Quintus, age eight, and Athol, age three, lived together. His oldest son, Edwin, age twenty-six, lived separately with his wife.

52. Information on General Stith could not be found. According to Peterson et al., *Sterling Price's Lieutenants*, 32, Governor Jackson's quartermaster general was Brigadier General James Harding.

53. François-Michel Le Tellier, Marquis de Louvois, (1639–1691) was credited with the reorganization of the French army and the instutition of improved quartermaster supply systems. Stanton is, of course, Union secretary of war Edwin Stanton.

54. Warner, *Generals in Gray*, 116. Martin Edwin Green (1815–1863) first saw action at the battle of Athens, Missouri, in August 1861. He fought at Lexington, Missouri, and at Pea Ridge (Elkhorn Tavern) and was commissioned brigadier general in July 1862. He participated in the siege of Vicksburg, where he was killed by a sharpshooter.

55. Warner, *Generals in Gray*, 57. Francis Marion Cockrell (1834–1915) rose through the ranks to colonel and fought at Carthage, Missouri, Wilson's Creek, and Pea Ridge. In July 1863, after the siege at Vicks-

burg where he commanded the Missouri Brigade, he was promoted to brigadier general. He fought in the Atlanta campaign and was severely wounded at Franklin, Tennessee, with General Hood. He was captured again at the surrender of Mobile, Alabama, in the spring of 1865. He was elected to the U.S. Senate in 1874 and served there for thirty years.

56. William Preston Johnston (1831–1899), the son of Albert Sidney Johnston, served as aide-de-camp to Jefferson Davis from April 1862 until the end of the war. He was captured along with the fleeing Davis in Georgia in May 1865. After the war, he became president of Louisiana State University (in Baton Rouge, serving 1880–1883) and then the first president of Tulane University (in New Orleans, serving 1883–1898).

57. Edmund Kirby Smith (1824–1893) became major general in October 1861, lieutenant general in October 1862, and full general in February 1864. He served in command of the Trans-Mississippi Department from February 1863 to the end of the war, surrendering his troops on May 26, 1865. See Warner, *Generals in Gray*, 279.

58. See OR, ser. 1, vol. 53, p. 871, in appendix 2, no. 17.

59. These letters are not found in the Official Records.

60. J. T. Thornton of Reynolds's staff was paymaster general of Missouri. See OR, ser. 1, vol. 22, pt. 2, p. 935, in appendix 2, nos. 19, 20.

61. These letters are not found in the Official Records.

62. Theophilus Hunter Holmes (1804–1880) became brigadier general in June 1861, major general in October 1861, and lieutenant general in October 1862. After combat in the Eastern theater, he was named to command the Trans-Mississippi Department in June 1862 and was replaced in this post by General E. Kirby Smith in March 1863. His command was then the District of Arkansas, reporting to General Smith. It is generally conceded that his ability to command at that level was extremely limited. Warner, *Generals in Gray*, p. 141.

63. Records were not found to further identify the members of the staff of General Price.

64. See OR, ser. 1, vol. 22, pt. 2, p. 935, to be found in appendix 2, nos. 19, 20.

65. An excellent treatment of the attack on Helena, Arkansas, can be found in Castel, *General Sterling Price and the Civil War in the West*, 140–152.

66. OR, ser. 1, vol. 22, pt. 2, p. 863, to be found in appendix 2, no. 18, seems to indicate that Price, not Holmes, was the proponent of the expedition to Helena.

67. James Fleming Fagan (1828–1893) fought (as colonel) at Shiloh and advanced to brigadier general in September 1862. He was promoted to major general in April 1864. His units generally fought under Sterling Price. Warner, *Generals in Gray*, p. 85.

68. OR, ser. 1, vol. 22, pt. 1, p. 408ff. (These are the battle of Helena reports.)

69. Dandridge McRae (1829–1899), as colonel, led Arkansas troops at Wilson's Creek and Pea Ridge and was promoted to brigadier general in November 1862. He fought under Price at Helena and Jenkins' Ferry, Arkansas, but resigned his commission in 1864.

70. General Price commended General McRae in his report (OR, ser. 1, vol. 22, pt. 1, p. 416), and McRae was cleared of the charges brought by General Holmes (ibid., p. 438). Warner, *Generals in Gray*, p. 206.

71. Ibid., pp. 423–427. (These are the battle of Helena reports.)

72. Ibid., pp. 436–437. (These are the battle of Helena reports.)

73. Ibid., pp. 413–417. (These are the battle of Helena reports.)

74. Ibid., p. 416. gives this name as "Maclean."

75. John A. Schnable, originally with the Missouri State Guard, was captain of a cavalry unit in the Seventh Division. During Price's raid into Missouri in 1864, he served as lieutenant colonel of "Schnable's Cavalry Battalion" in Jackman's brigade of Shelby's division.

76. A good account of the Little Rock campaign may be found in Castel, *General Sterling Price and the Civil War in the West*, 153–170.

77. OR, ser. 1, vol. 22, pt. 2, pp. 931ff, 1003ff. The Marshall conference of the governors of the Trans-Mississippi states was called by General E. Kirby Smith to consider a strategy after the fall of Vicksburg.

78. In spite of "optimistic" communications, General Price did inform General Smith of the coming onslaught by General Steele and did ask for reinforcements and make attempts to meet the threat. (See OR, ser.

1, vol. 22, pt. 2, pp. 941–943, which is found in appendix 2, no. 21.)

79. OR, ser. 1, vol. 22, pt. 1, pp. 474–478. Little Rock was occupied by the Union forces under General Steele on August 11, and he wrote his report on the campaign, titled "Little Rock, Ark., September 12, 1863."

80. "Arkansas Senators Johnson and Mitchell" were Robert Ward Johnson (1814–1879) and Charles Burton Mitchell (1815–1864). Johnson served in the U.S. House of Representatives and in the U.S. Senate, resigning in 1861. He served as a delegate to the provisional government of the Confederate States in 1862 and was elected and served in the Confederate Senate, 1862–1865. Mitchell practiced medicine in Washington, Arkansas, for twenty-five years until he was elected to the U.S. Senate, serving from March until July 1861, when he withdrew. He was then elected to the Confederate Senate, where he served until his death in September 1864. Augustus Hill Garland succeeded Mitchell and served until the end of the war.

81. Recognition of the Confederacy by France was a hope, unrealized, based on the expansion of the French empire into Mexico during the Civil War. The Confederacy felt that such a violation of the Monroe Doctrine, an action that would have led to strong U.S. reaction, was possible only because of the Civil War and that it was in the interests of France to support a division of the United States into two nations.

82. Waldo P. Johnson (1817–1885) had resided in Osceola, Missouri, and was elected to the U.S. Senate in 1861. He served from March 17, 1861, to January 10, 1862, when he was expelled from the U.S. Senate for disloyalty. Governor Reynolds appointed him to the Confederate Senate to replace Robert L.Y. Peyton, who died on September 3, 1863, of malaria contracted in Vicksburg during its defense.

83. See OR, ser. 1, vol. 53, p. 918, in appendix 2, no. 22.

84. For details of the battle of Jenkins' Ferry, see Castel, *General Sterling Price and the Civil War in the West*, 171–187.

85. James S. Rollins (1812–1888), originally of the Whig Party, was a major force in Missouri politics. He is considered the founder of the University of Missouri. ("father" is the term that usually is used). He was

elected to the U.S. House of Representatives as a constitutional Unionist in 1860, and though a slaveholder, disliked slavery and thought it
unnecessary in Missouri for the state to prosper. He voted in favor of
the Thirteenth Amendment in the House.

86. Thomas Price is listed in the 1860 census in Chariton County as age
thirty-one and a lawyer. While not part of the direct family of Sterling
Price, he most likely was related to him in some way.

87. The Reynolds manuscript cites "Johnson's Universal Cyclopedia article on Sterling Price."

88. Reynolds's letter of May 17, 1864, is not found in the Official Records,
but a "private letter" of that date is noted in OR, ser. 1, vol. 53, p. 998,
in appendix 2, no. 24.

89. This is not entirely true. In a letter to Reynolds, Price mentions the
three official letters sent by Reynolds (March 23, April 11, and June 2),
but makes no mention of the receipt of the private letter, nor of any
comment on its contents. See OR, ser. 1, vol. 53, p. 999, in appendix
2, no. 24.

90. Dr. Thomas D. Wooten is listed as colonel and medical director of
the Patriotic Army of Missouri (Missouri State Guard; Peterson et al.,
Sterling Price's Lieutenants, 35) and later as lieutenant colonel and Seventh Division surgeon general of the Missouri State Guard (ibid., 196),
with the notation "appointed Medical Director, I Division, Army of
the West, 28 March, 1862."

91. For correspondence on this matter after the 1864 Price expedition
to Missouri, see OR, ser. 1, vol. 41, pt. 4, p. 1123; and John Newman
Edwards, *Shelby and His Men—or—The War in the West* (Waverly, MO:
General Joseph Shelby Memorial Fund, 1995; reprint of 1867 edition),
pp. 467–474.

92. Warner, *Generals in Gray*, 299. Richard Taylor (1826–1879) was the son
of President Zachary Taylor. He became a sugar planter in Louisiana
and at the beginning of the war was appointed colonel of the Ninth
Louisiana Infantry. He served under Thomas J. "Stonewall" Jackson in
the Valley campaign and in the Seven Days battles near Richmond. He
was promoted to brigadier general in October 1861 and major general

in July 1862. He was named to command the District of West Louisiana in the summer of 1862. He is best known for his major victories over Nathaniel Banks in the Red River campaign (Mansfield and Pleasant Hill, Louisiana). After an argument with E. Kirby Smith, he was assigned to the Department of Alabama and Mississippi and promoted to lieutenant general in April 1864. The surrender of his troops was the last east of the Mississippi River.

93. Warner, *Generals in Gray*, 38. Simon Bolivar Buckner (1823–1914) was named brigadier general in the Confederate service in September 1861. He is remembered for being the general who surrendered Fort Donelson, Tennessee, in 1862 after both Generals Floyd and Pillow fled the fort before its capture. After exchange, he participated in Bragg's invasion of Kentucky, fought at Perryville, Kentucky, and directed a corps at Chickamauga, Georgia. He was transferred to the Trans–Mississippi theater in 1863 and then was appointed lieutenant general and chief of staff to General E. Kirby Smith in September 1864.

94. See OR, ser. 1, vol. 41, pt. 2, pp. 1011, 1020, in appendix 2, nos. 25, 26.

95. The conflict between Gen. Magruder and Governor Murrah of Texas was apparently over the enforcement of the conscription laws and conscription of Texas militia troops into the Confederate army.

Bibliography

Allardice, Bruce S. *More Generals in Gray*. Baton Rouge: Louisiana State University Press, 1995.

Bartels, Carolyn M. *The Forgotten Men: Missouri State Guard*. Shawnee Mission, KS: Two Trails Publishing, 1995.

Castel, Albert. *General Sterling Price and the Civil War in the West*. Baton Rouge: Louisiana State University Press, 1968.

Christensen, Lawrence O., William E. Foley, Gary R. Kremer, and Kenneth H. Winn, eds. *Dictionary of Missouri Biography*. Columbia: University of Missouri Press, 1999.

Downhour, James G. "Thomas C. Reynolds, Missouri's Forgotten Governor." Ph.D. diss., Southern Illinois University–Carbondale, 2002.

Kirkpatrick, Arthur Roy. "Missouri, the Twelfth Confederate State." Ph.D. diss., University of Missouri–Columbia, 1954.

———. "Missouri's Secessionist Government, 1861–1865." M.A. thesis, University of Missouri–Columbia, 1949.

Laws of the State of Missouri: Passed at the Called Session of the 21st General Assembly. Jefferson City, MO: J. P. Ament, Public Printer, 1861.

McElroy, John. *The Struggle for Missouri*. Washington, DC: National Tribune Co., 1909.

Miller, Robert E. "'One of the Ruling Class,' Thomas Caute Reynolds: Second Confederate Governor of Missouri." *Missouri Historical Review* 80, no. 4 (July 1986): 422–448.

————. "Proud Confederate: Thomas Lowndes Snead of Missouri." *Missouri Historical Review* 79, no. 2 (January 1985): 167–191.

Monaghan, Jay. *Civil War on the Western Border, 1854–1865*. Lincoln: University of Nebraska Press, 1955. Reprint, Lincoln: Bison Books, 1984.

Peterson, Richard C., James E. McGhee, Kip A. Lindberg, and Keith I. Daleen. *Sterling Price's Lieutenants: A Guide to the Officers and Organization of the Missouri State Guard*. Shawnee Mission, KS: Two Trails Publishing, 1995.

Rea, Ralph R. *Sterling Price, the Lee of the West*. Little Rock, AR: Pioneer Press, 1959.

Shalhope, Robert E. *Sterling Price: Portrait of a Southerner*. Columbia: University of Missouri Press, 1971.

Snead, Thomas L. *The Fight for Missouri*. New York: Charles Scribner's Sons, 1886. Reprint, Shawnee Mission, KS: Two Trails Publishing, 1997.

Tucker, J. W. "The Confederate Camp." *Missouri Army Argus*, December 12, 1861. Reprint, *Civil War St. Louis*, August 17, 2002. http://www.civilwarstlouis.com/History2/jwtucker.htm (accessed June 24, 2007).

United States War Department. *The War of the Rebellion: A Compilation of the Official Records of the Union and Confederate Armies*. Washington, DC: Government Printing Office, 1887.

Warner, Ezra J. *Generals in Blue*. Baton Rouge: Louisiana State University Press, 1964. Reprint, Baton Rouge: LSU Press, 1992.

————. *Generals in Gray*. Baton Rouge: Louisiana State University Press, 1959. Reprint, Baton Rouge: LSU Press, 1992.

Index

Page numbers in italics refer to illustrations.

A

American Knights of the State of Missouri, 162
Argus and Crisis newspaper, 48, 55

B

Belton, J. F., 99
Benton, Thomas H., 11, 14–17
Blair, Francis P., Jr., 12, 33
Blair, Francis P., Sr., 13
Blair, Montgomery, 13
Boonville, battle of, 37
Bowen, John, *72,* 72–74
Brown, B. Gratz, 13
Buckner, Simon Bolivar, 123

C

Cabell, E. C., 36, 39, 44–48, 51, 60, 77, 98, 106, 120, 134–135, 155, 264
Camp Jackson affair, 24–28
Clark, John B., Sr., 46
Clarke, John B., 43, 104–105, 112–114, 257

C

Cockrell, Francis M., 73, *144*
conditional Unionism, 7
"Copperhead" movement, 48

D

Davis, Jefferson, 7, 36, 39, 42, 52–53, 58, 240

F

Fagan, James, 85, 87–89, 92, 96, 111, 122, 135–137, 146, 148, 167–173, 176–177, 179–181, 184–187, 190–193, 200–201, 217–218, 220, 242, 245, 247–248, 270
fall of the Confederacy, 218
Frost, Daniel M., 96–97, *97*

G

Gamble, Hamilton R., 62–63, *63*
Green, Martin E., 73–74, *75*
Greene, Colton, 27

H

Harney, William S., 29, 31–33, 222
Harney-Price Agreement, 32–35, 221
Helena, battle of, 85–94
Holmes, Theophilus, 68, 81, 85,
    87–92, 95, 98, 108, 131

J

Jackson, Claiborne Fox, 7–8, 13,
    19–21, *20*, 23–33, 35, 37–41,
    43–44, 48, 55, 69, 70–71, 77, 81,
    91, 129, 219, 223, 226, 228–233,
    236, 239–240, 255, 260–264, 266,
    268, 272; death, 45
Johnson, Waldo P., 101, 105–108

L

Little Rock, battle of, 95–110
Lyon, Nathaniel, 7, 18, 27–29, 31, 33,
    36–38, 227–228

M

Mackey, T. J., 167–218
Marais des Cygnes affair, 146, 184,
    194, 208
Marmaduke, John S., 85, *121*,
    121–122, 126, 134–135, 139, 146,
    155, 170, 181, 200
McClellan, George B., 45, 139
McCulloch, Ben, 32, *41*, 264, 265
McRae, Dandridge, 88, 90

N

"North West Confederacy," 48, 54

O

Order of the American Knights of
    the State of Missouri, 162

P

Pemberton, John, 49, 56, 59, 68, 71,
    74, 236, 238
Peterson, Cyrus A., 10, 132
Peyton, R. L. Y., 23, 26, 49, 62, 100,
    105, 129
Pilot Knob, Missouri, 177, *178*
Polk, John W., 68, 77, 96
Price, Edwin W. , 47, 62–66, 108, 113,
    115, 117–119, 233, 235; capture,
    47; converts to Unionism, 47;
    oath of allegiance to U.S. govern-
    ment, 62–64
Price, Sterling, *12*; and *Argus and
    Crisis*, 48, 55; attack on Helena,
    85, 88, 241; background, 7–9;
    battle of Little Rock, 95; becomes
    Confederate major general, 41;
    considered for Senate, 100; "Cop-
    perhead" movement, 48; Court of
    Inquiry, 164–218; death, 8; desire
    to be major general of the Mis-
    souri State Guard, 51; disparaging
    remarks about Reynolds, 60, 69,
    77, 112; eagerness to command

an expedition to Missouri, 51, 55, 74, 124; 1857 senatorial election, 15–17; 1860 Democratic convention, 18–21; 1861 state convention, 24; end of war and exile in Mexico, 218; expedition into Missouri, 134, 167; failure at Iuka, 48, 98; governorship nomination, 14; Harney-Price Agreement, 32–35, 221; lax discipline in troops, 42, 48, 82, 136, 142; Mexican-American War, 11; "North West Confederacy" movement, 54; poor leadership, 83, 87, 125, 134; pronunciamento against Jefferson Davis, 52; reaction to Reynolds's description of Missouri expedition, 153; request for Confederate troops in St. Louis, 35; scheme to be named president of Confederacy, 46; siege of Richmond, 45; son converts to Unionism, 47; Special Order No. 82, 73, 235; takes command of Arkansas troops, 109; transfer to Arkansas, 56–59

R

Record of the Price Court of Inquiry, 164–218
Reynolds, Thomas Caute, 7, *9*; becomes governor of Missouri, 45; considers Price for Senate, 100, 249; describes Price's Missouri expedition, 134; disparaged by Price, 60, 69, 77, 112; end of war and exile in Mexico, 218; finds no evidence of Price's popularity, 78; plan for provisional government, 79; prefers Price to lead Missouri expedition, 124–131
Rollins, James S., 113–115

S

Seddon, J. A., 56–60, 64
Shelby, Joseph O., 8, *147*, 159–160, 169, 218
siege of Richmond, 45
Smith, E. Kirby, 68, 77, 87, 92–96, *93*, 99, 118, 123, 126, 218
Snead, Thomas L., 8, 38, 45, 54, 56, 74, 77, 79, 88, 126
Special Order No. 82, 58, 73, 235

T

Thompson, M. Jeff, *86*, 86–87, 158
Thornton, J. T., 77
Tucker, J. W., 48, 54–55

V

Van Dorn, Earl C., 44, 86, *128*
Vest, George G., 46, 104, 114–116, 257